The Reordering of British Politics

The Reordering of British Politics

Politics after Thatcher

DENNIS KAVANAGH

Oxford University Press
1997

Oxford University Press, Great Clarendon Street, Oxford OX2 6DP

Oxford New York

Athens Auckland Bangkok Bogota Bombay
Buenos Aires Calcutta Cape Town Dar es Salaam
Delhi Florence Hong Kong Istanbul Karachi
Kuala Lumpur Madras Madrid Melbourne
Mexico City Nairobi Paris Singapore
Taipei Tokyo Toronto Warsaw

and associated companies in
Berlin Ibadan

Oxford is a trade mark of Oxford University Press

Published in the United States
by Oxford University Press Inc., New York

British Library Cataloguing in Publication Data
Data available

Library of Congress Cataloging in Publication Data
Kavanagh, Dennis.
    The reordering of British politics: politics after Thatcher/
Dennis Kavanagh.
    Includes bibliographical references and index.
    1. Great Britain—Politics and government—1979–.
    2. Thatcher, Margaret—Influence. I. Title.
    DA589.7.K38 1997 320.941—dc21 97–15978
ISBN 0–19–878202–0
ISBN 0–19–878201–2 (Pbk)

Typeset by Hope Services (Abingdon) Ltd.
Printed in Great Britain
on acid-free paper by
Biddles Ltd.,
Guildford & King's Lynn

IN MEMORIAM

Peter Morris
1946–1997

Preface

This study is a follow-up to *Thatcherism and British Politics*, the second edition of which was published in 1989. That book analysed the forces making for the rise of the post-war consensus and its collapse in the late 1970s and 1980s. As Jim Bulpitt pointed out in a review in *Political Studies*, the main concern of the book was to explore the interplay between political ideas and practice in twentieth-century British politics and to show, in particular, how the collectivist policy formulas were being undermined in the 1970s. Thatcherism was both an architect and a beneficiary of this change, but it was only one aspect of the book. It was a study of how political agendas change.

So much has altered since the 1989 edition that a new book has had to be written. Changes include Mrs Thatcher's downfall, John Major's struggles to cope with her legacy and make his own mark, the crippling Conservative divisions over Europe, and the efforts of the Labour Party at first to oppose and then to emulate much of the Thatcher agenda. In the twenty-two years since 1975, the year of Mrs Thatcher's election to the leadership, Labour has had five leaders, the Conservative party two.

Three chapters from *Thatcherism and British Politics* remain (Chapters 2, 3, and 5), but they have been substantially rewritten. These chapters are largely historical and deal with the making of the post-war consensus, its breakdown, and the critique advanced by right-wing think-tanks and policy advocates. In the present volume, Chapter 1 deals with a number of the key issues raised by the Thatcher experience—changes in political ideology, the role of political parties and political leadership, and the impact of ideas on policy. New chapters discuss the Thatcher record and legacy (Chapter 6), the translation of ideas into policy (Chapter 7), Labour's response (Chapters 8 and 10), and the extent to which John Major has carried on the Thatcher legacy (Chapter 9). A Postscript has been added so that the book's argument can take account of the outcome of the 1997 General Election (Chapter 11).

The book is dedicated to the late Peter Morris, for a number of years my colleague and close friend in the Politics Department at Nottingham. Like many others, I was indebted to Peter for stimulating discussion and constructive criticism of drafts of previous editions. He died, alas, before I sent this version to the publisher.

D.K.

Liverpool
June 1997

Contents

List of Figure and Tables

Figure

Tables

Abbreviations

ASI	Adam Smith Institute
CBI	Confederation of British Industry
CPS	Centre for Policy Studies
CPRS	Central Policy Review Staff
EC	European Community
EEC	European Economic Community
ERM	Exchange Rate Mechanism
EU	European Union
HMO	health maintenance organization
IEA	Institute of Economic Affairs
ILEA	Inner London Education Authority
IMF	International Monetary Fund
IPPR	Institute for Public Policy Research
LAPAC	Life Amendment Political Action Committee
MTFS	medium-term financial strategy
NEC	National Executive Committee
NEDC	National Economic Development Council
NHS	National Health Service
NIC	National Incomes Commission
NUM	National Union of Miners
OECD	Organization for Economic Cooperation and Development
OMOV	one member, one vote
PESC	Public Expenditure Survey Committee
PLP	Parliamentary Labour Party
PSBR	public sector borrowing requirement
QMV	qualified majority voting
SAU	Social Affairs Unit
SEA	Single European Act
SMF	Social Market Foundation
TUC	Trades Union Congress

1 Perspectives on Thatcherism

Another book on the Thatcher years needs justification. Thatcherism, after all, has become one of the most studied topics in British politics, a staple of the publishing industry and higher education.

Now that we are in a post-Thatcher era and Mrs Thatcher and many of the key participants have had their say, the time is ripe for an assessment. What is the legacy? Has she so changed the political agenda that successor governments of whatever party have to operate in parameters laid down in the 1980s? Has New Labour accepted that agenda, just as Conservatives in the 1950s and 1960s accepted the achievements of the 1945–50 Labour Government? Did she define a style during her premiership that is now regarded as an ideal of prime ministerial leadership (Foley 1992)? How do political agendas change? The later chapters of this book try to answer these questions.

A second justification lies in the controversy surrounding the Thatcher record. It helped break the mould not just of post-war British politics but also of its study. Political parties, policy-making, local government, economic policy, the civil service, political leadership, interest groups, electoral behaviour, political ideology, and even the constitution have all required rethinking. It is hardly an exaggeration to say that the Thatcher experience has required a rewriting of the textbooks and raised key issues in economics, sociology, and political science. It is, therefore, not surprising that there are radically different—even opposed—assessments, even when there is agreement on the facts.

Leaders of many right-wing political parties in Western Europe and of anti-communist parties in Eastern Europe were impressed both by the Conservative Government's electoral successes in the 1980s and the apparent economic benefits of a regime of markets, monetarism, and authoritative government. The collapse of the Soviet Union, and with it the ideas of state ownership and central economic planning, only added to the appeal. Thatcherism became part of the international triumph of liberal democracy and the market economy celebrated in *The End of History* (Fukuyama 1992). By contrast, British critics (including a number of Conservatives) condemned the Thatcher economic record, particularly the costs of increased unemployment and the loss of manufacturing capacity; or claimed that it failed to cut public spending and taxes as a share of GDP; or asserted, finally, that the policies had little impact. The political left and a number of academics presented a separate indictment of economic failure: growing social division and exclusion, and authoritarian government.

Perhaps a more pressing reason for a new study is the mythology that has developed about the period, led largely by the boastful claims of politicians and part of the media. Mrs Thatcher's memoirs—and the associated newspaper serialization and television series—have been an attempt to 'manage' history. There is even a Thatcher Foundation, to promote her values as well as her place in history. There has been nothing like this in British politics before. No longer are political leaders content to wait for the verdict of history. They seek to be their own historians while they are still active. Increasingly, students of politics are competing with the instant histories in the form of memoirs, diaries, and commentaries of the participants themselves. Few of these memoirs, however, stand the test of time. Who today refers to the five volumes of Harold Macmillan's *Diaries*, or Harold Wilson's *The Labour Government*, the self-exculpatory thousand pages on his 1964–70 Labour Government? Politicians' memoirs have become the political and publishing equivalent of the 'benefit match' given to footballers or cricketers near the end of their playing careers (Gilmour 1994).

One must acknowledge the dangers of writing so close to events. The passage of time provides an opportunity to acquire a sense of perspective and an awareness of the longer-term consequences of events and decisions, and non-decisions, as well as access to more official and private papers. Significantly, most studies of the Thatcher record were written when she was still in office. Although some were hurriedly revised to report her fall from power, they could take account only of the immediate aftermath. But a need for caution does not excuse us from making an attempt to understand ourselves in our time, not least before myths become established. It needs restating that all history is a product of its own time. If observers refuse to record and analyse contemporary events, they leave the field free to the participants, who often have an axe to grind. No other social science abstains from analysis of its own period; one should not have to wait thirty years to write a first draft of history.

The Thatcher Experiment

There is no doubt that Mrs Thatcher will have a secure place in British history as the only post-war party leader to have lent her name to an 'ism', as the longest continuously serving Prime Minister this century and the only one to have won three successive general elections, and as shaper of the political agenda. She also overturned much of the post-war conventional political wisdom: that the Conservatives had to be led from the political centre if they were to win elections and govern effectively; that no government could win general elections at a time of mass unemployment; and that it was necessary for ministers to cooperate with the major economic interests to govern the country.

One has to recall the threatening context in which Mrs Thatcher became party leader in 1975 and Prime Minister in 1979. The rise of nationalism in Scotland, violence in Ulster, soaring inflation, trade-union power, declining support for the main parties, and weakness of government all suggested a system at breaking point. Whether it was a crisis of capitalism (as the left asserted) or a crisis of social democracy (as the right proclaimed), political scientists were forced to search for new models and a new vocabulary. 'Bankruptcy', 'Overload', 'Ungovernability', and 'Britain in Agony' were typical book titles and themes. Some expressed doubts that representative institutions could cope with inflationary pressures, sectional rivalries, and the determination and ability of particular groups to dislocate society. It was not just journalists and academics, such as Samuel

Brittan, Peter Jay, Anthony King, and Richard Rose, who wrote in this vein. To read the accounts of well-placed insiders in governments in the 1970s, such as Douglas Hurd (1979), Joel Barnett (1982), Edmund Dell (1991), and Lord Donoughue (1987), or to recall Mr Callaghan's remarks that, without a Labour government, there would be rioting in the streets, is to appreciate the crisis of confidence at the heart of government. President Ford, in a farewell interview in 1976, warned the American people: 'It would be tragic for this country if we went down the same path and ended up with the same problem that Great Britain has' (cited in Rose and Peters 1978: 16). Britain was an anti-model—'the future that does not work' (Tyrell 1977).

Today, however, talk of trade-union power, soaring inflation, and ungovernability has a dated air. People no longer discuss the weaknesses of the British state. In 1958 General de Gaulle emerged from the ruins of the Fourth French Republic and restored the authority of government. Mrs Thatcher herself and her admirers claimed that she did something similar for Britain (Thatcher 1993: 10). The Conservative Party, so long the party of government, appeared to be in decline, and Labour was the natural party of government. Labour won four out of five general elections between 1964 and 1974 (already, however, there were signs of its long-term electoral decline), and the Conservative defeats in the two 1974 general elections saw the party gain its lowest shares of the vote in the twentieth century. Labour's collectivist values and links with the trade unions were more suited to the prevailing political formulas of incomes policy and group politics. Edward Heath's government started in 1970 with a bias against government intervention in the economy and a determination to make the market economy work. It then switched direction dramatically in 1972, under pressure from rising unemployment and the failure of its existing policies. The party's traumatic general-election defeat in February 1974 served only to reinforce the view that it had lost its way.

After four successive Conservative general-election victories, that gloomy picture changed. In 1992, even against a background of economic recession and support for change after thirteen years in government, the party won a fourth election victory. The doom-laden analyses of the mid-1970s about the Conservative Party's future were now applied to Labour. Commentators speculated about the 'Japanization' of British politics, or the emergence of one-party (Conservative) government (A. King 1992).

How Agendas Change

Big shifts in the climate of political ideas occur rarely in Britain. The normal pattern of policy development is for change to be incremental; the lessons learned from shortcomings of existing policy produce marginal changes to the status quo.

There have perhaps been three occasions this century when there has been a significant agenda shift, in 1906, 1945, and 1979, years which produced the elections of Liberal, Labour, and Conservative governments respectively. The dates coincide with changes of government and are significant more as registering shifts in mood which were already under way. In each case a party long considered to be the minority displaced the normal party of government; the new government was backed by a large House of Commons majority and a change in the climate of opinion; the governments introduced far-reaching reforms which set the agenda for their successors. The first combined social liberalism with constitutional reforms, the second a mixed economy with the welfare opportunity for leaders to change the agenda. If successful, the new dominant party takes advantage of the mood for change, shapes the agenda, and over time influences the policies of opposition parties. This occurred with F. D. Roosevelt's New Deal in the USA after 1932, the Social Democrats' 'middle way' in Sweden in the 1930s and 1940s, the social-market approach of Christian Democracy in post-war West Germany, and Thatcherism in Britain after 1979.

The Consensus Debate

It has been broadly taken for granted that there was a good deal of continuity in government policy in many areas for the thirty years or so after 1945. At times this has been called a post-war consensus, or settlement. It is possible to quarrel with the use of the term 'consensus' on the grounds that it suggests unanimity and fails to do justice to the differences of values and emphasis between the parties, while others have complained that the term is used to describe too many different phenomena (A. Butler 1994). David Marquand (1988: 319) expresses his unhappiness about 'an imprecise term, denoting an unprecise and fluctuating reality' and acknowledges that what in retrospect has been called a consensus did not appear as such at the time. He does not, however, object to the thinking behind the term, for he acknowledges that party differences and government policy were settled 'within a framework of common commitments and common assumptions'.

The arrival of Mrs Thatcher in Downing Street in 1979 certainly consolidated the perception among commentators and politicians of a rupture, a turning point in public policy from the wide measure of agreement between the frontbenchers which had gone before. In other words, the perception that there had been a consensus became most apparent just as it was breaking down. A telling moment was the publication in 1975 of Paul Addison's *The Road to 1945*. Addison claimed that the consensus was not forged after 1945 but emerged largely during the last months of the wartime coalition government (also Anthony Seldon, 1981: 617). Ironically, the book was first published in the same year that Mrs Thatcher became Conservative Party leader and the Labour Government was abandoning Keynesianism and full-employment budgets.

It is possible to extract from academic debate and everyday discussion the following overlapping usages of the term consensus when applied to post-war politics. They include:

1. *ends*, i.e. widespread agreement between the leaders of the main parties about policy goals, demonstrated by continuity in government policy;
2. *style*, i.e. widespread agreement on policy goals and means reached after a process of deliberation, bargaining, and compromise;
3. agreement on what is *excluded* from the policy agenda, a *negative* consensus;

4. relative, historical, or cross-national, i.e. widespread *relative*
   agreement on policy in comparison with an earlier or later
   period or with other countries.

Samuel Beer, in his much-lauded *Modern British Politics*, clearly uses
consensus in the first sense. He claims that a collectivist politics, covering a mixed economy and a welfare state, prevailed in the post-war
era, that policy differences between the parties dealt with questions
of 'more' or 'less' and that such questions, in spite of the partisan
rhetoric, were 'marginal, statistical, quantitative' (1965: 242). Intense
electoral competition between two evenly matched political parties
for the support of producer and consumer groups also forced them
to converge. In a later study, Beer writes that 'A process of mutual
adjustment brought the parties closer together in what they said they
would do, and even more, in what they actually did in office (1982:
85). The Conservative Government elected in 1951 spurned the
opportunity to reverse Labour's measures and 'One of the most
remarkable features of the government was the extent that
Conservative policy followed on logically from Labour policy in the
previous six years' (Anthony Seldon 1981: 421). For Marquand, the
social-democratic consensus, based on Keynesian economic assumptions, was 'a set of commitments, assumptions, and expectations,
transcending party conflicts and shared by the great majority of the
country's political and economic leaders, which provided the framework within which policy decisions were made' (1988: 18).

Paul Addison's study of the legacy of the wartime Churchill
coalition illustrates both the first and the second usages. By 1945 the
coalition government had issued a series of White Papers and proposals covering employment, social security, health, and education,
an agenda that prepared the way for much of the Labour
Government's legislative programme.

Others (e.g. Middlemas 1979) use the term to refer to a style
of decision-making, involving a readiness by government to compromise, not push policy beyond its acceptability to the opposition party
or major interests, and consult with interested groups over policy.

Writers from the dissenting left and right are particularly
prone to view the consensus as a 'negative' one, in its agreement on

what to exclude. It also favours certain interests and directs attention to certain issues and procedures while neglecting others. Here is what social scientists now call 'a second face of power', one that shapes the political agenda. One has only to think of the negative reception given, until the mid-1970s, to many free-market ideas and, today, to the ideas of Labour's left wing. In economic management the dominance of Keynesian ideas until the mid-1970s resulted in there being only a perfunctory hearing for proponents of monetarism.

The fourth usage rests on the claim that the level of post-war agreement on policy between the parties was higher in comparison to other periods or to other states. In his study of the development of the British welfare state, Roderick Lowe refers to the post-war period as one involving a 'historically unusual degree of agreement' (1990: 156). Certainly compared to the party conflict immediately before 1914, the 1930s, or the 1980s there was much inter-party agreement on policy. Comparison with abroad reinforces the judgement. In the immediate post-war period, France and Italy had large Communist parties which, if not clearly opposed to the political system, differed fundamentally from the centre-right parties on economic, defence, and foreign-policy issues. In West Germany, Christian Democrats and Social Democrats were also bitterly opposed until the latter party abandoned its Marxist heritage in 1959 at the Bad Godesburg conference.

Some scholars question whether there was a consensus at all. Ben Pimlott (1988) suggests that it is a mirage, largely the product of retrospective wisdom. In the early 1980s both Conservative 'wets', beleaguered in their battle against Thatcherism, and Labour right-wingers, unhappy with the party's shift to the left, looked back nostalgically to their years of ascendancy in the 1950s and 1960s. Pimlott observes that in the 1950s electoral support for the Liberals was at its lowest and class-based voting was at its height—both of which he finds incompatible with consensus or centrist politics. Neither feature, however, carries much force in refuting the idea that there was a broad continuity in government policy. Indeed, the squeeze on the Liberals might be regarded as a symptom of the convergence of the two main parties around the middle ground. Another sceptic, Jeffrys

(1987), argues that the two main parties were far apart in the 1945 general election and it was only shock at the scale of electoral defeat that forced the Conservatives subsequently to accept the new agenda. The argument casts doubt on the assumption that there was an accommodation between the parties by 1945, but does not disprove the continuity in government between the parties during the 1950s and 1960s. Charles Webster (1990) similarly disputes the claim that the creation of the National Health Service (NHS) was the product of consensus. Again, however, such a claim does not refute other studies which are impressed by the amount of continuity in management of the NHS *after* the scheme came into operation in 1948 (e.g. Anthony Seldon 1981: 270; Klein 1983).

Consensus is not an ideal term because, although it is a firmly established concept, it is used in so many different ways. My main interest in using the term is to identify a set of policies or values which, to a large extent, were shared by all post-war governments until 1979. In referring to political consensus students have usually had in mind one or all of the following:

1. A high level of agreement across the political parties and governing élites about the substance of public policy. On many areas—defence, foreign affairs, Northern Ireland, and so on—this has clearly been the case for much of the time. The classic case of adaptation is the record of Conservative Governments between 1951 and 1964, which substantially accepted the 1945 Labour Government's initiatives in the fields of public ownership, full employment, welfare, NHS, and transition from Empire to Commonwealth.
2. A high level of agreement between the political parties and governing élites about the nature of the regime or about the rules of the political game. Institutional change in Britain has been incremental, and over the past sixty years there has been little popular support for proponents of comprehensive constitutional change. The political stability of the inter-war years was a sharp contrast to the breakdowns in Italy, Germany, Austria, Portugal and the extremism of the right or left which characterized policies on much of the Continent.

3. The political style by which policy differences are resolved—namely a process of compromise and bargaining and a search for policies which are acceptable to the major interests. Disagreements have rarely been pushed to breaking point and the legitimacy of the government rarely called into question. The British élites have managed to make timely concessions to new interests, though there were near misses in 1914 in Ulster and 1926 over the General Strike.

The term has long been a 'hooray' word, along with 'moderate', 'centrist', and 'reasonable' and contrasted with 'ideological' or 'extreme' or 'dogmatic'. Mrs Thatcher had the term firmly in her sights. In a prepared speech during the 1979 general election she compared herself to the Old Testament Prophets, who did not say 'Brothers I want a consensus', and she proclaimed the importance of conviction and principle in politics—as if these were incompatible with consensus. In 1981, in Australia, she replied to criticisms from Mr Heath that she was abandoning consensus politics: 'For me, consensus seems to be the process of abandoning all beliefs, principles, values and policies.' Some part of the explanation for her hostility was that she realized (correctly) that it was often code for criticism of her own political style and policies. Mrs Thatcher's Press Secretary, Sir Bernard Ingham, claimed that she would often ask 'What is this thing called consensus? Consensus is something you reach when you cannot agree' (Ingham 1991: 384). To her it protected interests, policies, and values, and was a style which she wanted to abandon. She also complained that too often it was an excuse for the appeasement of pressure groups and the avoidance of tough decisions, and assisted the country's decline.*

As a style of policy-making, consensus was already coming under criticism before Mrs Thatcher. The emphasis on consultation with interests, incremental change, and the demonstrated ability of important pressure groups to frustrate government initiatives

---

* In August 1978 David Butler and I interviewed Mrs Thatcher at some length, in connection with our study of the forthcoming general election. In the course of the interview we used the term consensus. She pounced on it in a mix of contempt and anger, saying that she could think of five or six meanings of the term. She offered various definitions and invited us to specify which meaning we had in mind.

amounted, some critics alleged, to pluralistic stagnation or political inertia. British government places a high premium on surface unity—witness the muzzling of potential Cabinet dissenters by the doctrine of collective responsibility or the emphasis on consultation and agreement in the top ranks of the civil service. Critics complained that unity and agreement were too often purchased at the cost of policy. It was a directionless consensus (Rose 1969).

There were two broad reactions to this perception of the power of groups and the limits they imposed on government. One was to call for a 'strong' political leadership, which would resist sectional interests. Both Mr Wilson and Mr Heath, for example, tried to tackle trade-union power by legislation and appeals to public opinion. The former retreated from the reforms proposed in *In Place of Strife* in 1969, when he found that he could not carry his Cabinet, in the face of TUC opposition; and the latter's resort to a general election in February 1974 to defend his statutory incomes policy against the strike by the miners failed. The alternative was to call for a coalition-monger, for a political leader skilled in power-sharing and conciliating different interests. This is what Wilson offered voters in 1974 in the so-called social contract with the unions, and Heath followed suit in the October 1974 election with his call for a coalition government. Later, I refer to these approaches as appealing, respectively, to the political leader as *mobilizer* and *conciliator*. Throughout her leadership there was little doubt which role Mrs Thatcher envisaged for herself and her government.

Studies

The literature on Thatcher is now immense. Only Churchill and Lloyd George, among British politicians, have seized the public imagination to the same degree, and both at times of national crises. Yet they were the subject of few biographies when they were still in office. In contrast, Mrs Thatcher had already been the subject of at least a dozen biographies by late 1988, and another dozen were available for the tenth anniversary of her premiership in May 1989. To date, James Callaghan and Sir Alec Douglas-Home have each had two biographers and Edward Heath three. Since her fall, she and over a dozen of her former Cabinet colleagues have published their memoirs. Publishers eagerly snapped up books on the lady and her works, and usually ensured that her name (and photograph) dominate the jacket. The attention to her personality as a means of understanding public policy is interesting in itself. Suetonius, in his *Life of the Caesars*, warned that such an approach was a symptom of a declining political order.

Much of the academic literature is interdisciplinary, drawing on history, sociology, economics, and political science. The studies concentrate largely on domestic politics, neglecting defence and foreign policies, perhaps because there was so little discontinuity in these areas, (Douglas 1989: 404) Much is also narrowly national; little interest is shown in what was happening in other countries. Yet doubts among policy-makers about state-owned enterprises, public-sector solutions, demand management, and Keynesian economics were growing in other states apart from Britain. New Right ideas about politics, society, and economy transcended national boundaries. In the 1980s governments of the right and left, the latter often reluctantly, were cutting marginal rates of income tax, borrowing, and regulations, squeezing public spending, and accepting rising unemployment as a cost of curbing inflation.

Much of the literature is also heavily partisan, especially that by Conservatives. Thatcherite sympathizers have usually been hostile towards the records of the previous Conservative governments, particularly of Harold Macmillan and Ted Heath. Conservatives who have written from a One Nation or 'wet' perspective, on the other hand, have regarded Mrs Thatcher as an unfortunate aberration in the party's history. What is welcome is that the growth of this literature has helped to reverse one of the major imbalances in the study of British politics—the greater concern with the Labour rather than the Conservative Party, even though the latter has been the usual party of government.

The studies differ according to whether they are primarily descriptive, explanatory (examining the electoral, ideological, or socio-economic forces that lay behind Thatcherism), or evaluative (assessing the impact). The positive case advanced by courtiers, who were largely associates of the leader, virtually all the former Cabinet memoirists (at least for the time that they were in office), many journalists, and some academics is that her governments smashed the post-war consensus and achieved many of their intended objectives. Much of the political left and a Conservative critic like Ian Gilmour also regard the Thatcher years as having had a significant impact on British politics, even though it is one that they deplore.

Some, on the other hand, question whether there was much impact at all. Writing while Mrs Thatcher was still in office, the journalist Peter Riddell (1989) argued that her governments fell far short of most of their central objectives. Academics, such as Richard Rose (1984) and David Marsh and Rod Rhodes (1992), who examine the outcomes rather than the intentions of legislation and policies are similarly sceptical.

Courtiers

This category includes books written by self-styled advisers and supporters. There is no shortage of claimants to have influenced policy, personalities, and public opinion. Many have sought a high profile and some have achieved it. The media have been interested in identifying backstairs influences on political leaders and many of the participants have enjoyed the spotlight. John Ranelagh has interviewed some of them for his *Thatcher's People* (1992), including Sir Keith Joseph and Enoch Powell. A picture emerges of a group of 'true believers', conscious of no longer being political outsiders and confident that their truth is winning through. Russell Lewis, George Gardiner, Patrick Cosgrave, and Jock Bruce Gardyne were all closely involved with Mrs Thatcher when she was opposition leader and in her first few years as Prime Minister. All had had reason to feel neglected by Ted Heath and they gave vent to their resentment. Sir Alan Walters, her economic adviser, wrote *Britain's Economic Renaissance: Margaret Thatcher's Reforms 1979–84* (1985), another insider account, one which might alternatively be entitled *How I Saved Britain*. He reinforced her scepticism of the Foreign Office and Treasury line on monetary union. The late Shirley Letwin's *The Anatomy of Thatcherism* (1992) received deserved acclaim. She is one of the few females to have written about Thatcherism and was a Director of the Centre for Policy Studies (CPS) as well as a member of other right-wing think-tanks. She stresses that Thatcherism was distinguished by the objective of the policies; it was about the development of what she calls 'vigorous virtues'—hard work, thrift, and self-reliance. In contrast to the usual emphasis of Thatcherism as economics, Letwin was more impressed with Thatcherism as a moral agenda in which government sought to do what was 'right' and to enable people to make as many decisions as possible for themselves.

Sympathy does not guarantee quality. Martin Holmes's *The First Thatcher Government 1979–83* (1985) is by a self-proclaimed Thatcherite, and is relentlessly hostile to anything to the left of the lady, particularly to 'wet' Tories. He had no doubt that even at that early date Mrs Thatcher had transformed her party and the political agenda. The book reads more as a contribution to Tory inner-party battles and gives contemporary history a bad name. An economist reviewing the book in the *Times Higher Educational Supplement* complained that it 'does justice to neither the Thatcher Government, nor the discipline of politics'. More significantly, these books are a crucial part of a revisionism of post-war British history, one which sees pre- and post-Thatcher Conservatism as a story of retreat and betrayal.

Political Journalists

Unlike most other academics, political scientists face competition from journalists in assessing contemporary political events. The journalists' contribution is a mark of both the new breed of journalist and the impact of Thatcher. Traditionally, few political journalists have written books. Yet the late Peter Jenkins wrote over 400 pages on *Mrs Thatcher's Revolution* (1987), placing the topic in the context of Britain's relative economic decline. Hugo Young's biography, *One of Us* (1989), is a major study running to over 600 pages. Young also places the rise of Thatcher in the context of the decline of consensus politics and the weakening of the political and cultural establishment. Both journalists, not surprisingly, are strong on *haute politique* and portraying political personalities. Readers of the *Independent* newspaper know that Jenkins's standpoint for much of the 1980s was that of the disenchanted centrist. He despaired of the Labour Party and came to be a reluctant admirer of Mrs Thatcher. He would doubtless have wished the Alliance to have broken the mould, but recognized that it was Mrs Thatcher who did so. She had presided over a 'Thatcher Revolution' and paved the way for a 'post-socialist era'. His broad sweep of political, economic, and social dynamics provides a good understanding of the forces behind Thatcherism.

Having parted from the Murdoch-owned *Sunday Times*, Hugo Young eventually replaced Peter Jenkins as the *Guardian*'s political commentator. Young is always a polished and independent commentator. He mourns the passing of the old One Nation Conservatism, and the excesses of both the left and right often suffer at his hand. Mrs Thatcher not only radicalized politics but politicized many areas in which party-political considerations had traditionally been only a minor element, if one at all. She asked 'Is he one of us?' in making a vast range of appointments. For Young, Oxford University's decision in January 1985 not to award its most famous daughter an honorary doctorate 'perfectly crystallised the cultural change that she wrought' (*Guardian*, 4 February 1985).

Academics

Social scientists have been more interested in explaining the sources and policy impact of Thatcherism and trying to draw conclusions about the British political process. The intellectual (largely Marxist-inspired) left quickly coined the term Thatcherism and regarded it as a hegemonic project, one which sought to reshape the institutions and practices which stood in the way of the success of the market economy. The project started with the economy, then moved on to tackle institutions of the old order like the trade unions, local government, and much of the public sector, and culminated in an attempt to reshape values and attitudes. This view credits Thatcherism with higher ambitions—a deliberate, coherent exercise at social engineering, as much as an assault on much of the post-war consensus. Among the first to argue this case was the theoretical journal of the Communist Party, *Marxism Today*, as well as the *New Left Review* and the *New Socialist*. The pioneers were Stuart Hall and Martin Jacques, with *The Politics of Thatcherism* (1983), a collection of essays originally published in *Marxism Today*. They coined the influential labels 'populist authoritarian' and 'free economy strong state', to describe Thatcherism. For Hall, the breakdown of so much of the old political economy, particularly Keynesianism, full employment, and the problems posed by the unions, gave an opportunity for the New Right. It could make a populist appeal against high income taxes, high household rates, welfare shirkers, and poor public services. But it was also hegemonic in seeking to make the Conservative Party dominant and in restructuring the role of the state so that successors would have to follow the path laid out.

They were followed by Andrew Gamble, *The Free Economy and the Strong State* (1988; 2nd edn., 1994), Bob Jessop and colleagues, *Thatcherism* (1988), and Stuart Hall again, *The Hard Road to Renewal* (1988). 'Thatcherism' is largely an invention of the academic left, and contending schools go their different ways. Gamble's study is a rich and finely balanced study of the broad forces which helped the rise of Thatcher—international recession, Britain's economic decline, the break-up of the post-war settlement, and the tensions within the Conservative Party. For Gamble, she redefined modern Conservatism by emphasizing a *strong state* and a *free economy*. Thatcherite Conservatism blends authoritarianism with economic liberalism, and, because of the determination with which she defends the two, it is a radical package. Thus the state is strong on defence (e.g. the Falklands, and an increased defence budget), national identity (a tougher stand on immigration and resisting demands for integration in the European Community (EC)), law and order (supporting identity cards for soccer crowds, and greater spending on the police), and internal security (treatment of terrorists). It is coupled with a support for authority figures (e.g. teachers, parents, and managers) when they defend traditional moral values. In March 1982 she promised the old virtues of discipline and self-restraint. She regularly voted for the restoration of capital punishment, even though she was in a minority in her Cabinet. Much of this is, of course, quite alien to nineteenth-century liberalism.

Jessop's *Thatcherism* covers the massive literature that had amassed on the subject by the time of writing, particularly on the political left, and provides an incisive analysis of the origins, nature, and significance of the subject, organized around various approaches. Jessop and his colleagues claim that Hall and Gamble attribute too much coherence to Thatcherism, credit it with too much success, and accept too readily that it has broken the old consensus. Instead, they see Thatcherism as a ragbag of policies serving different groups, and occasionally the consequences of frustration with earlier reforms rather than a well-worked-out strategy.

This literature of the left has many strengths, not least in its awareness of the role of the state and how Mrs Thatcher has used it. Paradoxically, an exercise in rolling back the state, encouraging the market, and promoting freedom has required an interventionist state to weaken the veto of interest groups and unions and bring market forces to bear on the delivery of local government on welfare and other public services. Quasi-corporatist bodies such as the National Economic Development Council (NEDC) and wages councils have either been abolished or had their remits severely reduced and privatization has 'recommodified' parts of the former state sector. Jessop *et al.* (1988: 26–8) are also persuasive in their critique of what they regard as conventional political science: 'Although as usual' studies of public opinion and measures of macro-economic indicators may suggest that not much has changed, the changes in policy-making and the role of the state and interests may not be amenable to such approaches.

The writers of the left regard Mrs Thatcher's combination of populism and authoritarianism as mould-breaking. Free-market economic policies were fused with 'tough' positions on law and order, patriotism, standards in schools, and industrial relations. The programme was populist, because it exploited dissatisfaction with unpopular features of the old consensus, and authoritarian, because of its centralizing tendencies. Here is Mrs Thatcher in 1986, speaking about her Conservatism. 'It is radical because when I took over we needed to be radical. It is populist because I would say many of the things I've said strike a chord in the hearts of ordinary people— why? Because their character is independent, because they don't like to be shoved around.' In early 1983 Hall and Jacques wrote that Thatcherism should be judged in terms of its success or failure 'in disorganising the labour movement and progressive forces, in shifting the terms of political debate, in reorganising the political terrain and in changing the balance of political forces in favour of capital and the right. In that sense, Thatcherism has already achieved a great deal' (1983: 13). The word Thatcherism was originally coined as a term of abuse by her critics—who identified it with unemployment, monetarism, cuts in services, racism, and cold-war rhetoric, and was then accepted with pride by Mrs Thatcher and her supporters. In 1958 the cartoonist, Vicky, ridiculed Harold Macmillan as 'Supermac'. The joke backfired on its creator, as Macmillan was widely seen as a successful leader.

Another view, one which concentrates on politics rather than ideas or culture, dismisses the distinctiveness or 'exceptionalism' of Thatcherism. Professor Jim Bulpitt (1986) has described the Thatcher premiership as a modern application of traditional Conservative statecraft, which he defines as 'the art of winning elections and achieving some necessary degree of governing competence'. During the 1970s both Conservative and Labour governments compromised their authority in seeking agreement with the trade unions. Thatcher's ministers returned to a Tory tradition in seeking a degree of autonomy for conducting such matters of 'high politics' as curbing inflation, cutting taxes, and controlling public spending. Hence the need to break the powers of trade unions, professions, and local government, which were barriers to implementing the strategy. This is a *political* explanation: policies were adopted to maintain political authority and win elections, not to shore up the interests of capital.

Marsh and Rhodes have also cast doubt on many of the ambitious claims made for the Thatcher record. They concentrate on policy outcomes, in a number of policy areas, and conclude that some objectives were not realized, some outcomes would have happened anyway or were shaped by other factors, and some policies have had unintended consequences. Their verdict is that 'The Thatcherite Revolution is more a product of rhetoric than of the reality of policy impact' (1992: 187). The record appears to be like that of most other British governments, one in which policy is often its own cause, the adjustment to or modification of an existing line, and largely shaped by circumstances outside the government's control. An assessment of the record of the Thatcher government's first term, *Implementing Government Initiatives* (Jackson 1985), is similarly deflating, and Richard Rose regards the economic record of Mrs Thatcher's governments, except for inflation, as being pretty similar to those of her predecessors. From the left, this view is shared by MacInness (1987) on the economy, but not by Edgell and Duke (1991), whose *A Measure of Thatcherism* acknowledges a number of political and social changes.

Perhaps the most withering critique of the Thatcher ideas and record in government has come from a dissident member of her first government, Sir Ian Gilmour. In two elegantly written and learned books he has mounted a formidable attack on its economic approach—*Britain can Work* (1983)—and on her record—*Dancing with Dogma* (1992).

To a large extent the New Right in the 1980s was an Anglo-American phenomenon. At no time in the post-war period have British and US domestic and foreign policies been so clearly aligned as they were under Thatcher and Reagan. Most of the comparative studies of Thatcherism have been Anglo-American. This is implicit in two works from 1987: Desmond King's *The New Right* and David Green's book of the same title. A work of Anglo-American cooperation and comparison, which explores the New Right ideas and how they were carried through in policy terms, is provided by Kenneth Hoover and Raymond Plant in *Conservative Capitalism in Britain and the United States* (1988). Not surprisingly, given the book's subtitle 'A Critical Appraisal', the authors provide a critique of the ideas and policies and suggest how the left might react. More damning of the Reagan and Thatcher records is Krieger's (1986) analysis of the policies as a response to a crisis of capitalism.

The edited collection by Grant Jordan and Nigel Ashford, *Public Policy and the Nature of the New Right* (1993), is particularly useful. A number of essays explore the New Right ideas in the two countries and the extent to which they have been reflected in various policy areas, including education, health, housing, local government, privatization and deregulation, and the economy. On the whole, the answer that emerges is that, in Britain, the ideas were not significant for policy but were a little more so in the USA.

The best of the literature appreciates, however implicitly, the interaction of circumstances, ideas, and politics. What is needed to take the study of Thatcherism further is the case-study approach, examining policy areas and how the three factors interact to produce particular policy choices. Marsh (1995) calls for a multi-dimensional, as opposed to a one-dimensional, approach. Once we move from broad political or social analyses, from which, he claims, much of the literature suffers, or from New Right ideology to the particular policies, then the impression of a grand design recedes. Events and politics—the calculations by politicians of what is possible, taking account of public opinion, administrative practicability, and the strength of likely opposition—are more important than ideology. Ideology is more of a tool, as Marsh expresses it. The trade-union reforms, for example, evolved piecemeal after 1979, and privatization gathered pace only after 1983, as political and electoral opportunities presented themselves. As leader of the party in opposition before 1979, Mrs Thatcher had to take account of the scepticism, even hostility, of many of her Shadow Cabinet to a number of her plans. Her memoirs describe her sense of frustration with the party's policies before 1979 and admit that, had Mr Callaghan called an election for the autumn of 1978, the Conservative manifesto would have differed in crucial respects from that of eight months later. That Thatcherism proved to be so dominant in the 1980s owes much to the discrediting of the corporatist and incomes-policy approach to tackle inflation, the weaknesses of the opposition forces, the gradual disarming of her critics in the party, and the opportunities that these in turn provided for a radical approach.

Thatcherism

There are problems in analysing Thatcherism, not least because we have to separate Margaret Thatcher's personal beliefs and goals from the policies of her administrations, and distinguish these from what is attributed to them by malicious opponents and fervent supporters. The term Thatcherism has been used in at least three different contexts. The first refers to Mrs Thatcher's no-nonsense style of leadership and her hostility to the premium placed on gaining agreement by compromise or 'partnership' with interests. She regarded politics as a suitable arena for the expression of personal beliefs and the purpose of government 'to do the right thing' (Letwin 1992: 30). A second usage refers to a set of policies designed to produce a strong state and a government able to resist the selfish claims of pressure groups. Particular emphasis was laid on law and order, traditional moral values, and a stable currency. This was coupled with the pursuit of a free economy (to be achieved by cutting state spending and taxes, reducing government intervention in the economy, curbing the powers of the trade unions, and privatization). The third use of the term is as part of an international reaction against high inflation, trade-union militancy, and unease about ungovernability in the mid-1970s. The economic recession and slow economic growth undermined popular support for tax-funded welfare in a number of states. The Thatcher Governments' policies of cuts in direct taxes, privatization, placing low inflation ahead of employment, squeezing public expenditure, and eliminating loss-making state enterprises had echoes in other Western states.

Such terms as 'Thatcherism', 'monetarism', and the 'New Right' are also often interchanged as if they are the same thing. The term 'New Right' covers various social and economic doctrines and policies and political personalities. As we see in Chapter 4, in economics it is identified with Austrian economics, monetarism, public choice, and supply-side economics. It also consists, uneasily, of *libertarians*, who believe in the free market and considerable personal choice in such matters as abortion, drugs, and the wearing of seat belts, and *authoritarians*, who take a dim view of such permissiveness and support a strong role for authority-only figures. For the present, we need to note that a monetarist believes that excessive increases in the supply of money (that is, above the increase in production in the economy) cause inflation, a case of too much money chasing too few goods. In political rhetoric, however, the term monetarist was often used to refer not to an approach to economic analysis but as a pejorative label to attach to a right-wing Conservative who dismissed Keynesian economics and uncritically supported the free market and monetarism, regardless of the costs in unemployment. But there are varieties of monetarism, and monetarism is analytically quite separate from, and not necessarily linked with, a market economy, high unemployment, lower public spending, balanced budgets, and so on. It is also important to separate those libertarians who favour a reduction in the role of the state in both social and economic areas from right-wing authoritarians who are concerned with the restoration of the authority of the state, family, and other social institutions, and hostile to many aspects of 'permissiveness'.

No British Prime Minister has stated so forcefully or so frequently his or her fundamental beliefs about morality, life, economics, education, the scope of the public and private spheres, or indeed about virtually any subject. More representative of the approach of British political leaders was Harold Macmillan's plea that, 'If people want a sense of purpose, they should get it from their archbishop . . . not from their politicians.' What made her a novel Conservative was that she was a crusader about changing attitudes and restructuring society and economy—social engineering. Traditional Conservatives would shudder at such an enterprise—such a task is for sociologists or eugenicists. In an interview with Michael Charlton on BBC Radio Three, she replied to the charge that, because she was radical, urgent and populist, she was not Conservative: 'It [her Conservatism] is radical because at the time when I took over we needed to be radical' (17 December 1985). In an *Observer* 1979 interview she said: 'I felt, and the Conservatives who elected me presumably felt, that the next leader of the party must clearly stand up against the direction in which the country had been moving under both previous governments. . . . At the time of the leadership contest which began in November 1974 we were coming to a stage when there really wasn't a party which was clearly standing for the limitation of government'.

A determinant of the leader's political style is his or her political beliefs. Few doubt that Mrs Thatcher had a coherent set of political ideas and that these guided her behaviour. She often related them to her early experiences rather than to abstract theory, occasionally invoking early memories of her father, life in the corner shop in Grantham, the need to balance the weekly household budget, her schooldays, and even her headmistress. Hugo Young reminds us that she did not spring from the working class but from the petty bourgeoisie, the ranks of the self-employed and shopkeepers who were to vote overwhelmingly for her in the 1980s. Her father owned two shops and, as a Grantham alderman and Mayor, was a considerable local political figure. She grew up politically aware, for 'politics infused the atmosphere in which she was reared'. From her secure family background came the values of self-reliance, hard work, thrift, the family, and a belief in just deserts and not looking to the 'nanny state'.

In her memoirs *The Path to Power* (1995: 30), Mrs Thatcher recalls being influenced as a student by reading Herbert Agar's *A Time for Greatness* (1943), which attacked the West's moral weakness for allowing the rise of Hitler. Winston Churchill's strong leadership during the war allowed the British people to give of their best. These notions were subsequently reinforced by her reading of some of the economic writings of Milton Friedman, particularly on incomes policies and his advocacy of monetary control and the free market, and the philosophical works of Friedrich von Hayek.

As opposition leader (1975–9) she also turned for intellectual support to Sir Keith Joseph and the free-market suggestions of think-tanks such as the Institute of Economic Affairs (IEA) and Centre for Policy Studies (CPS). But she was not simply a borrower of ideas. A remarkable early statement of her beliefs was contained in a speech she gave to the Conservative Political Centre in 1968. In it, she argued that British government had become too interventionist and should not decide the level of increases of wages and salaries. Conservatives should aim to reduce the range of government decision-making and restore greater individual choice. 'What we need now is a far greater degree of personal responsibility and decision, far more independence from the government, and a comparable reduction in the role of government.' In the same speech she said: 'There are dangers in consensus; it could be an attempt to satisfy people holding no particular views about anything. It seems more important to have a philosophy and policy which, because they are good, appeal to a sufficient majority.' These beliefs came out in her party conference speeches and, more explicitly, in interviews. To a lesser extent, inevitably, they were reflected in the actions of her government.

One always has to take care in analysing the rhetoric of politicians, whose speeches are made on different occasions for different purposes and different audiences. The analyst of Mrs Thatcher's speeches and interviews, however, does not need to be so careful. She was what she says she is. A content analysis of her speeches in the 1979 general-election campaign revealed an emphasis on two themes. The negative one was 'socialism'; the positive one was 'freedom' or 'a free society' or 'freedom under the law' (Pinto-Duschinsky 1981). Use of the bully-pulpit to lecture and to elevate the nation was regarded by Mrs Thatcher as an important duty of political leadership.

The main elements in her belief system can be stated in terms of certain propositions:

1. The government has a limited capacity to do lasting good, but a great capacity to do harm.
2. State action should never weaken the sense of right and wrong.
3. The state should be strong enough to perform its 'primary' tasks of ensuring adequate defence and law and order.
4. People should solve their own problems (or help their families and neighbours solve theirs), rather than turn to the government.
5. Increasing public expenditure, without economic growth, involves more borrowing and/or taxation and less freedom for people to spend their money as they wish.
6. The market is the best means of promoting economic growth and free choice and of safeguarding personal liberty.
7. More expenditure on one service usually means less on another, unless one resorts to extra borrowing, taxation, or inflation. Each service is paid for by 'hard-pressed' taxpayers, many of whom may be poorer than the beneficiaries of particular programmes.
8. Government intervention may be counter-productive in terms of

slowing down society's ability to adapt in a changing world; 'correct' policies (in terms of the above) are more useful than expressions of sympathy for the weak, the unemployed, and the sick.

Many of Mrs Thatcher's admirers and detractors describe her as an intellectual. This is not so and to have been one would not have helped her to be a successful politician. Whilst she has passionately held principles and instincts, she agrees with Edmund Burke and Michael Oakeshott in rejecting abstract thinking as a guide to political conduct. Although she is systematic in her thinking about politics and derives her stances from principles, it is stretching things to say that she is the child of Hayek and Friedman. They may have given some substance and intellectual respectability to her beliefs and instincts, but most of these derive from her own experience and her ideas of what is common sense. Her beliefs in limited government, widespread ownership as a safeguard for liberty, the need for government to concentrate on its basic tasks, the connection between personal morality and freedom of choice, and the values of careful household budgeting and deferred gratification, all derive from her own experience. In this way she responded to what was once a 'hidden agenda' of Conservatism—the populist authoritarianism of the activists rather than the leadership. In many respects her case was greatly assisted by the events of the 1979 Winter of Discontent—the activity of the Labour Government, the failure of incomes policies, the weakness of union leaders, and the irresponsibility of local officials in some public-sector unions. These events followed years of slow economic growth and relative economic decline. Here was proof that the consensus not only undermined state authority but was economically debilitating.

Thatcherism was a matter of both style and policies. The political style—emanating from Mrs Thatcher herself—vigorously challenged many established beliefs and interests, boldly expressed personal and often right-wing views, and did not compromise on many deeply held political principles. As a set of policies it rested on four main principles.

First, there was the determination to reduce the rate of growth in money supply so that inflation would be squeezed out of the system. This involved the abandonment of formal incomes policies and 'deals' between government, employers, and trade unions as part of an attack on inflation. If the two sides of industry settled for a rate of increase in wages higher than the growth in productivity, they ran the risk of losing markets and pricing themselves out of jobs.

A second was the reduction in the size of the public sector and the encouragement of a free-market-oriented economy. This involved setting tight financial targets for the nationalized industries and, eventually, the privatization (or sale to the market) of state-owned industries and services, removing 'stifling' regulations on business, and encouraging the sale of council houses. The government would not bail out or subsidize loss-making industries indefinitely. Lower public spending would facilitate tax cuts and these in turn would encourage economic growth and the creation of new businesses.

The third was for the government to free the labour market and encourage responsible trade-union practices through reforms (pre-strike ballots, periodic and secret ballot elections of union leaders, restrictions on secondary picketing, and removal of some immunities which unions had long enjoyed under common law). Control of the money supply had to work in tandem with the creation of a more effective free-market economy. The above measures would, it was promised, eventually create the enterprise society and economy. According to one of the most articulate exponents of 'the New Conservatism', Nigel Lawson: 'Our chosen course does represent a distinct and self-conscious break from the predominantly social democratic assumptions which have hitherto underlain policy in post-war Britain' (1980: 7).

A final policy goal linked all three of the above: the restoration of the authority of government. This involved both strengthening the nation's military defence and forces of law and order and resisting damaging claims of interest groups. There would be significant increases in resources for the armed forces and police. Interest groups would be curbed by limiting the responsibilities of government, for example, for full employment, and by the firm control of public spending. In all, the four themes married the values of a strong state and a free economy (Gamble 1994).

The ideas, particularly those about relations between individuals and the state, amounted to a forceful assault on the Butskellite consensus which, it was claimed, had failed to address the major problems of the country and had even added to them. It had led people to have expectations of the state (for example, the 'welfare-state mentality') which could not be satisfied, for, in principle, there is no limit to the money that might be spent on services, just as there is no limit to the demand which could be made for them. But many of the services were inadequate anyway, and only the virtual state monopoly of such services as health care and education prevented people from voting with their feet. Critics also claimed that the state was seen less as an enforcer of rules and more as a provider of benefits, an agency which cushioned people from the sometimes harsh—but ultimately beneficial—disciplines of work and the market. But, if the state intervened to alleviate the cost of adversity, then how could people learn from their mistakes? How might one evoke what Keynes once called 'the ancient vein of Puritanism'?

What followed from this analysis of past errors was the need to reduce the role of the government *vis-à-vis* society and economy. The government would not, could not, provide full employment in a free society or subsidize market 'failures'. It would control the money supply, to produce 'honest money' and maintain law and order. In the spirit of John Locke, government would no longer provide 'positive' goods but a 'negative' one—namely, the sense of security upon which the attainment of all other, privately chosen goods depends. In the new society there would be a high degree of personal liberty (income tax reduced, liberty under the law, more scope for private enterprise, more choice for members of trade unions, consumers of the education and health services, and so on). Government would be authoritative, doing what it could and should do—for example, curbing inflation and maintaining law and order. It would not, however, be a permissive society; the counterpart of a strong if limited government is that parents, teachers, managers, and other authority figures are also respected. In many ways this was an old liberal view of the state, but it was also radical in that the analysis goes to the root of problems. In contrast to the old consensus language, it sharpened rather than blurred distinctions between state, society, and individual.

The Thatcher experience is an interesting case study of the interplay of political ideas and practice in late-twentieth century Britain. It provides a unique vantage point for studying ideology, personality, political parties, and policy-making. The next two chapters explore these themes in the context of the rise of the consensus after 1945 and its breakdown in the 1970s. The Conservative Party, originally the loser from the collapse of Keynesianism, turned outside for a credible and politically persuasive explanation of what had gone wrong. The rise of Thatcher in the Conservative Party is analysed in Chapter 4. Chapters 5 and 7 deal with the work of the think-tanks and intellectuals of the right. To have an impact ideas need clients, preferably clients with political clout, and Mrs Thatcher was such a figure. The record and legacy of her government are assessed in Chapter 6.

The second half of the book deals with the consequences. Chapter 7 points to the lessons from the 1980s about the conditions in which new ideas can enter the heads of politicians. The period between Thatcher's election as party leader in 1975 and departure in 1990 were dismal for Labour. In government (1974–9), it struggled to cope with the collapse of so many signposts, particularly of Keynesianism. In opposition, the party quarrelled bitterly over its record in government and rejected outright Conservative attempts to forge a new political settlement on the ruins of the old. Chapter 8 deals with this period and Chapter 10 covers Labour's post-1992 acceptance of much of the new agenda. The impact of John Major's Conservative leadership on the Thatcher legacy is assessed in Chapter 9.

2 The Making of Consensus Politics

By the early 1950s it was already possible to refer to a post-war consensus across much of the political agenda. The return of the Conservatives to government in 1951 did not produce much discontinuity from the outgoing Labour Government. In foreign affairs there developed a widespread agreement across the parties about Britain's role as a nuclear power, membership of NATO, and granting colonies their independence. Until 1961 there was a front-bench agreement that Britain should stand aside from the European Economic Community (EEC), although from 1967 onwards there was broad if fluctuating support for British entry. The invasion of Suez in 1956 excited bitter divisions between the Labour and Conservative parties. Labour was also divided over nuclear weapons and membership of the EC in the early 1970s. But the continuity in policy between governments was impressive. In spite of Conservative rhetoric about Britain's role as a world military power and Labour's about Britain's role as a moral leader, the political leaders acceded to the country's loss of status.

The post-war package of policies on the domestic front is familiar: full employment as a goal of economic policy; acceptance of the trade unions, whose bargaining position was strengthened by increased membership and full employment; public ownership of basic and monopoly utility and industries; state provision of social welfare, requiring in turn high levels of public expenditure and taxation; and an active role for government via a large public sector and regulation of the market. These policies form the vocabulary, as it were, of modern capitalism and social democracy and are discussed below.

The different elements in this domestic policy package were in many ways interconnected. Universal welfare provision depended in part on the achievement of full employment so that the welfare system would not be overloaded. Ironically, both Beveridge and Keynes originally envisaged a level of unemployment well in excess of that which was to be the norm over the following thirty years. The ideas of Keynes legitimized a large public sector, active government, and welfare expenditure. As Hugh Heclo remarks: 'Spending for social purposes could serve economic purposes of increased production, investment, and stable fiscal policy. Social policy was not only good economics, but the economic and social spheres of public policy were integrally related with each other' (1984: 391). The trade unions favoured welfare, full employment, and public ownership. Keynesian techniques of economic management also enhanced the role of the experts—economists, the professions, and social engineers. Economic management and the welfare state gave them an opportunity to exercise influence on a larger scale than hitherto.

The experience of total war between 1940 and 1945 altered popular and élite perceptions of many established policies and ways of carrying them out. With national survival at stake, shortcomings in economy and society had to be tackled urgently—usually by state action. The war experience showed that Keynesian economics 'worked' and that the state could tackle social problems more effectively then the market. Policy-making in the two great wars differed from that in peacetime. The latter usually involved preparation or 'softening up' public opinion for a new line of policy, bargaining with interests, proceeding through the legislative cycle in Parliament, and then allowing time for administrators and the public to adjust to the new policy. But during the war, 'it was as though there was a major acceleration in the entire historical process' (Beloff 1984: 23).

The Impact of War

An immediate effect of the Second World War—as of the First World War—was to enhance the power of organized labour. This was recognized and then furthered by the appointment of Ernest Bevin, General Secretary of the Transport and General Workers' Union, as Minister of Labour with a seat in the Cabinet in 1940. Trade leaders were drawn into the work of government and came to share many of the wartime government's assumptions about the national interest. Many of these industry-wide committees continued to operate after 1945.

Another change in response to war was the notion of an implied social contract between government and people for the creation of a better post-war Britain. According to Titmuss's (1950) official history-of-the-war volume on social policy, public opinion became more egalitarian and collectivist under the impact of war and the experience of evacuation, and this increased pressure on the government to create something like the welfare state. This interpretation may be exaggerated. Many Conservatives were fearful of the financial consequences of a hasty acceptance of the Beveridge proposals, and there is little evidence that ministers and civil servants were convinced of the role of welfare in promoting social solidarity or economic efficiency. It took a backbench revolt in February 1942 to force the government to accept the Beveridge package. Yet the notion of an implicit contract in which there would be 'better times' in return for the sacrifice endured in war was widely believed.

Particularly important in reflecting the convergence between the parties was the work of the Cabinet Committee on Reconstruction, established in 1943 and containing heavyweight ministers from the main parties. This body reached broad agreement in many areas, covering a national health service, regional policy, full employment, social insurance, and housing, but not the future nationalization of basic industries. The Coalition Government produced the 1944 *Employment* White Paper (Cmnd. 6527), passed the Education Act in 1944 and the Family Allowances Act in 1945, and made progress on other aspects of the Beveridge proposals and social insurance. It also issued reports on the future of the Bank of England, and of the coal, gas, and electricity industries. There is some justification for Addison stating that 'the new consensus fell, like a branch of ripe plums into the lap of Mr Attlee' (1994: 14). The war and its boost for ideas of state-ownership, planning, welfare, and public spending was a good example of how an outstanding event can alter the views of policy-makers, particularly their perceptions of what is politically and administratively possible. Keith Middlemas notes that 'slowly but inevitably the state came to be seen as something vaster and more beneficent than the political parties' (1979: 272). For most of the inter-war years state spending rarely exceeded 25 per cent of GNP; after 1945 it never fell below 36.5 per cent. Public opinion, under the impact of war, adjusted to higher levels of taxation and state spending (Peacock and Wiseman 1961).

Full Employment

We turn now to a discussion of the main features of the domestic policy consensus. Conscious pursuit of full employment as a goal of government economic policy was first stated authoritatively in the 1944 White Paper, which accepted 'as one of the primary aims and responsibilities the maintenance of a high and stable level of employment after the war'. That commitment was hedged with many qualifications and acknowledged the importance of pursuing prudent fiscal policies. The goal was, however, gradually accepted by all parties (the Conservatives still had reservations in 1945) and was also important for maintaining the insurance basis of the welfare state. By 1950 the Conservative manifesto stated: 'We regard the achievement of full employment as the first aim of a Conservative Government.' A key moment was in 1958, when Harold Macmillan acquiesced in the resignation of his Treasury ministers rather than agree to their demands for an extra £50 million in spending cuts. Between 1948 and 1970 the annual average level of unemployment never exceeded 3 per cent, compared with the norm of 10 per cent during the inter-war years. Perhaps no other economic change presented such a contrast between pre- and post-war Britain.

The central figure in this story of full employment is John Maynard Keynes. Keynes was a polymath, gifted in philosophy, economics, finance, and the arts (Skidelsky 1983, 1992). Although he never held elective office, he always seemed to be hovering near the centre of political affairs between 1919 and his death in 1946. He exercised influence through his writings, membership of government and Liberal Party committees, and access to ministers and Treasury officials. Until 1940 he was like a one-man opposition to the financial and economic establishment of the day. His attacks on the economic provisions of the Versailles Peace Treaty and Churchill's decision to restore Britain to the gold standard at $4.80 in 1925, as well as his co-authorship of the Liberal Yellow Book Proposals in 1928, were all notable publishing *coups*. He took an instrumental view of the political parties, which he used 'as vehicles for his ideas' and abandoned when he judged that they had served their purpose (Moggridge 1976: 38). He was, says Moggridge, a 'demi-semi-official'.

Keynesian techniques of economic management reconciled the limitations of the free-market economy with political freedom. The great choice of the inter-war years appeared to be state planning (and coercion) versus freedom (and uncertainty), both in the political and the economic realms. Keynes reconciled the two, by showing politicians how to curb the risks and uncertainties associated with the market. As a tool of economic management, Keynesianism could lend itself to both Labour and Conservative interpretations. The economic depression showed that the market economy was not working as theorists had surmised. Classical theories of supply and demand held that these would balance to provide full employment, a theory aptly summed up in Say's Law that supply creates its own demand. Unemployment occurred, therefore, because wages were too high. In his *General Theory*, Keynes argued that there was no necessary link between savings, investment, and consumption. Government had a role in stabilizing economic activity, and should set its levels of expenditure, interest rates, and investment with the goal of achieving an appropriate level of aggregate demand. If demand was deficient and the national income and employment fell below otherwise possible levels, the Treasury should budget for a deficit and encourage state and private spending *via* a mix of tax cuts, public works, and reduced interest rates. If demand was too high, then the government should budget for a surplus by reversing these measures.

It is a matter of debate whether Keynesianism was responsible for the full employment which lasted until the mid-1970s (Skidelsky 1977). The situation was probably due more to favourable international conditions, particularly the long investment 'boom' from which many Western countries benefited. British governments had in fact usually been deflationary in fiscal policy and had run an average surplus on the current account of some 3 per cent of national income each year (Matthews 1968). And the well-known 'stop–go' cycles of economic management were influenced less by pursuing the goal of full employment than by concern to protect the value of sterling and the balance of payments. Because of the Bretton Woods system of fixed exchange rates against the dollar, a priority of government economic policy was to maintain the parity of the currency. Foreign pressures on the value of sterling provided an incentive to pursue 'prudent' financial policies and practise monetary discipline (Brittan 1971: 93).

A Mixed Economy

Between 1945 and 1951 the coal, rail transport, civil aviation, iron and steel, road passenger and freight transport, electricity, and gas industries were taken into public ownership. To some extent, this continued the process of rationalization or 'cartelization' of the depressed industries in the 1930s and the wartime regime of planning, control, and consultation. The idea of the public management of undertakings had already been established before the war in such public corporations as the Port of London Authority, the British Broadcasting Corporation, the Central Electricity Generating Board, and the London Passenger Transport Board. Most nationalization measures after 1945 involved the state taking over and reorganizing industries, and providing investment. Labour usually justified its measures on pragmatic rather than ideological grounds. Its *Public Ownership: The Next Step* (1948) laid down five conditions which would make an industry suitable for nationalization: inefficiency (for example, poor management or low investment), bad industrial relations, monopoly position, need for large capital investment, and being a major supplier of raw materials. The industries were established as statutory monopolies, run as public corporations, and instructed to 'break even' taking one year with another, rather than make profits. There was, however, little that was distinctively socialist about the programme.

The party became less ambitious about public ownership. The 1955 manifesto promised merely to renationalize iron and steel and road haulage and take over sections of chemicals and machine tools. In the 1959 manifesto the renationalization proposals were retained, largely for historical and sentimental reasons, together with an assurance (or threat) that 'We have no other plans for further nationalisation. But where an industry is shown . . . to be failing the nation we reserve the right to take all or any part of it into public ownership if this is necessary.'

Conservatives had not originally welcomed the nationalization programme after 1945. But, back in government in 1951, the party accepted all the measures, except for iron and steel, which was denationalized in 1953 (later renationalized by Labour in 1967). Most of the electorate seemed to have accepted the other measures. Although the Conservative Party was committed to private enterprise, it had never been anti-statist. According to Quintin Hogg (later Lord Hailsham): 'Modern Conservatism inherits the traditions of Toryism which are favourable to the activity and authority of the state' (1947: 294). In the same vein, Anthony Eden claimed in 1947: 'We are not the party of unbridled, brutal capitalism . . . we are not the political children of the laissez-faire school' (Beer 1965: 271).

By 1974 the above industries were still in public ownership, notwithstanding Conservative reservations. In 1971 the Heath Government, having earlier announced that it would not rescue 'lame ducks' or troubled firms, saved Rolls-Royce and the Upper Clyde Shipyard firm from imminent bankruptcy by taking them into public ownership. The party's authoritative *Campaign Guide 1974* accepted the status quo on the mixed economy and dismissed the prospect of denationalization: 'Conservatives much prefer private enterprise to run a high proportion of the economy but it is simply not feasible to sell off all the nationalized industries regardless of price or consequences. In many instances, the industries are natural monopolies and must remain subject to public control.' The 1974 Labour Government also rescued 'lame ducks', taking a share of the ailing Chrysler car company, and 95 per cent of Leyland car company, then transferring its holdings to a newly formed National Enterprise Board. It also took into public ownership the aerospace and shipbuilding industries, both of which were already receiving substantial state aid.

Active Government

Keynes obviously provided an important justification for an active role for government in economic management. The greater role of government as employer and distributor of benefits also seemed to be a useful tool for mobilizing popular consent. Countries which had highly socialized patterns of consumption and distribution and a large social wage (or state-provided benefits) had fewer strikes and industrial disputes than those countries which ranked low on these features (Hibbs 1978). Processing issues through the political area rather than the free market went with greater industrial harmony, at least in the 1950s and 1960s.

Governments also gradually came to assume a commitment to promote economic growth. In 1954 the Chancellor of the Exchequer, R. A. Butler, pledged the Conservative Government to doubling the standard of living in the following twenty-five years. In spite of some scepticism at the time, the pledge was fulfilled. In the early 1960s governments adopted economic planning, established targets for growth, consulted with the two sides of industry, and even, in 1965, drew up a National Plan for the economy. Andrew Shonfield's classic work *Modern Capitalism* (1965) could take for granted the continuation of steady economic growth, full employment, and the provision of comprehensive social welfare in Western states. From the 1959 general election onwards political parties competed on their ability to make the economy grow faster and then distribute the fiscal dividend of economic growth. Economic growth would both provide social welfare and protect the take-home pay of workers. At the same time, public spending steadily grew on the assumption of future economic growth. The trouble was that, even when the economy failed to grow by the anticipated amount, public spending was rarely cut back in proportion. The result was that by 1975 public spending, as then measured, amounted to nearly 60 per cent of GNP. In the twenty years after 1953 state spending was increasingly devoted to welfare goods and services, such as pensions, education, and health. In the same period spending on traditional 'core' activities, such as defence and law and order, actually fell as a proportion of total state expenditure (Rose 1985: 395).

The first serious post-war attempt to break with the syndrome of interventionist government was during the first two years (1970–2) of Mr Heath's administration. The government speedily abolished Labour's Prices and Incomes Board and the Land Commission, wound up the Industrial Reorganization Corporation, repealed the Industrial Expansion Act, and phased out the Regional Employment Premium. It announced tax cuts in its first Budget and cut back the rate of increase in public spending. By 1973, however, not only had the spending cuts been reversed, but the government had poured public funds into ailing firms and imposed statutory limits on wage increases. Its 1972 Industry Act acquired such extensive powers of intervention that Tony Benn, as Labour's Industry Minister in 1974–5, extended state control over manufacturing firms, without passing any new enabling legislation.

Welfare

Under the impact of war there was a greater acceptance among policy-makers that modern citizenship encompassed a range of social as well as political rights. The Beveridge 1942 review of social security, *Social Insurance and Allied Services* (Cmnd. 6404), had a great impact on many MPs and the public. Beveridge proposed a scheme to combat 'Want, Disease, Ignorance, Squalor, and Idleness' by the consolidation of existing separate schemes for pensions, unemployment, and sickness benefits into a universal national insurance scheme. Instead of a means test, flat-rate benefits would be paid as of right in return for flat-rate contributions. There would also be a 'safety-net' of means-tested national assistance benefits for those not covered by social insurance. The author envisaged that social security should be part of a comprehensive plan for welfare and be supported by a national health service and full employment. In the first two years of the 1945–50 Labour Government, family allowances had already been made available from general taxation, a National Insurance Act (1947) provided flat-rate benefits for those insured, covering unemployment, sickness retirement, and widowhood, and a National Assistance Act (1947) covered those who did not have a complete contributions record. The NHS was established to provide free medical services at the point of entry for all.

These measures built on what had gone before. By 1939 Britain already had a relatively advanced system of welfare provision and the idea of a national health service had been trailed earlier in the Dawson Report (1920), a Royal Commission on National Health Insurance (1926), and the Coalition Government's 1944 White Paper on the health service. Only the passage of legislation establishing the NHS in 1946 encountered serious Conservative opposition.

Conservative governments largely accepted the main features of the welfare state, which acquired an ideological life of its own, incorporating ideas of fairness, community, and collectivism. The report, however, retained an important strand of individualism, which was subsequently seized on by Conservatives. Beveridge wrote: 'The Welfare State should not stifle incentive, opportunity, responsibility, in establishing a national minimum. It should leave room and encouragement for voluntary action by each individual to provide more than the minimum for himself and his family' (1942: 6–7). Some Conservatives, however, looked more favourably on the idea of selectivity, or the concentration of aid on those in real need, as opposed to universality. The idea received a bad press, because it evoked memories of the hated, pre-war means tests. The growth in spending had to be curbed to make way for lower taxes. Welfare expenditure was also increasing rapidly in other Western states during these years, partly as a response to economic growth. Interestingly, the highest spenders were Denmark, Norway, and Sweden, which had predominantly socialist governments, as well as the highest living standards in Western Europe. Flora and Heidenheimer (1984) argue that the original stimulus for establishing many welfare measures was largely defensive, as non-socialist political leaders adopted these measures in part to ward off pressure for more fundamental economic and political reform from working-class parties and movements.

Hardly anywhere did the working-class movement initiate or enthusiastically support the early social insurance principles (Heclo 1984). The policies usually originated from policy experts and middlemen (such as the Webbs, Beveridge, or Titmuss) who believed they knew what was good for the working class. Over time, however, the welfare constituency expanded beyond the poor to include much of the middle class.

Welfare was also linked to broader economic policy. The connection was clearly seen in the social contract drawn up in 1973 between the TUC and the Labour Party in which the former promised to exercise restraint in wage negotiations in return for a social wage, of food subsidies, controls on prices and rents, and increased pensions. Yet many observers and trade-union leaders were aware that rising welfare spending, in so far as it came out of higher taxation, also stimulated pressure for wage increases.

Conciliation of the Trade Unions

The trade unions soon turned away from their brief flirtation with direct action in 1921 and 1926. They regarded Labour as 'their' party and wanted a Labour government because this was a way of ensuring favourable industrial-relations legislation and economic policies. At party conferences in the 1930s and again in the 1950s the major trade unions acted as a hammer of the left in support of the leadership. Yet there were always tensions between the unions and the party. Some Labour leaders, in a desire to demonstrate their 'fitness' to govern, calculated that they had to appeal beyond the unions and indeed at times stand up to them. At the same time, the Trades Union Congress had to be prepared to work with governments of both parties, if it was to represent its members. By tradition, the party was run according to a separation of spheres between the two wings of the movement; the trade-union leaders left political matters largely to the parliamentarians and in return expected to be given a free hand on wage bargaining and industrial relations.

Both Keynes and Beveridge had been worried about the potential inflationary effects of free collective bargaining in a situation of near full employment. The corollary of a full employment policy was that the unions would exercise moderation in wage matters, which Keynes described as an essentially political problem. The 1944 White Paper (para 49, 18) stated: 'If . . . we are to operate with success a policy for maintaining a high and stable level of employment, it will be essential that employers and workers should exercise moderation in wage matters.' In so far as incomes restraint was ruled out for the first two post-war decades, we can say that the consensus, represented by the ideas of Beveridge and Keynes, was a selective one.

The Labour Government operated a voluntary policy with some success from 1948 until 1950. Succeeding Conservative governments relied on exhortations, warnings, and occasionally restraint in the public sector as an example to the workforce as a whole. The combination of steadily improving living standards during the 1950s and a deliberate policy of conciliation of the unions by the Ministry of Labour helped to avoid any major confrontation between government and the unions. In 1961, however, Selwyn Lloyd's 'pay pause' adopted an incomes policy as an answer to wage-induced inflation. Macmillan wanted to couple a search for ways of stimulating faster growth and economic planning with lower wages settlements. To this end he set up the National Economic Development Council (NEDC) for the former and a National Incomes Commission (NIC) for the latter. The unions would have nothing to do with the NIC and it was soon wound up.

The agreement on the role of the unions was an uneasy one. Successive Labour and Conservative governments felt pressures to intervene because of the inflationary consequences of free collective bargaining and the damage caused by unofficial strikes. The first Wilson Government was elected in 1964 on a platform of economic modernization which included an ending of restrictive practices. But restraint on incomes soon emerged at the forefront of policy to deal with inflation and support sterling. In 1966 the government established a National Board for Prices and Incomes, to which proposed wage increases were to be referred and which had the power to impose a three-month standstill. This was soon followed by a phase of statutory controls on prices and incomes which lasted until 1968.

Potentially more significant was the appointment in 1965 of a Royal Commission to inquire into the unions' and employers' organizations. To the government's disappointment its report in 1968 was largely non-interventionist in its recommendations to curb the increasing number of unofficial strikes. Notwithstanding the report, the government produced its own proposals in 1969. It wanted to wind down the incomes policy but take some steps which would impress the money markets. The proposals included a twenty-eight-day cooling-off period before strikes took place, pre-strike ballots, and penal sanctions against unfair industrial practices. As a sweetener there was also a series of measures favourable to workers and unions. The proposals were abandoned in the face of widespread opposition among unions, Labour MPs, and the Cabinet. In 1970 the new Conservative Government produced its own Industrial Relations Act, to regulate collective bargaining, moved to a statutory incomes policy in 1972. Interestingly, Labour had tried to legislate in the sphere of industrial relations as a replacement for incomes policy; the Conservative Government reversed the order of the two approaches. The Industrial Relations Act was consciously designed as an alternative to incomes policy, and the U-turn in 1972 to incomes policy was closely connected to the non-operation of the Act.

The Wilson and Heath governments rejected the voluntarist approach of the Royal Commission and believed that the law not only had a role to play but was indispensable in reforming industrial relations. Paradoxically, the failure of the Wilson Government's initiative and the ineffectiveness and political and industrial costs of the Heath lesiglation appeared only to confirm the validity of the voluntarist case. Successive governments came to view trade unions as a major barrier to their policies for arresting the country's relative economic decline and attacking inflation. From 1964 senior figures in both main parties came to regard the trade-union question as central in British politics. Incomes policies were variously statutory or non-statutory, compulsory or voluntary, and were often linked with bargaining about social and economic policy. They were also accompanied by an array of commissions and boards to provide guidance on particular claims and settlements.

Although the policies produced a temporary slow-down in inflation, in every case where there was a target set for the average level of pay, the out-turn, as measured by increased basic hourly wages, exceeded the target, and by the second or third year the policy had collapsed (Brittan and Lilley 1977). As in 1950, it was usually caused by a failure of trade-union leaders to carry their members. Incomes policies usually ended in grief and damaged relations between government and union leaders and between the latter and their members. The lack of central authority within the TUC or even within many unions made it difficult for the movement to cooperate with government in a long-term policy. The resort to an incomes policy was invariably justified by an alleged economic crisis—high inflation or the weakness of sterling. In no case did a party in government promise in advance of its election that it would have such a policy.

Every post-war Labour Government has operated an incomes policy. Usually it was dressed up as an instrument of redistribution and economic planning, while free collective bargaining was criticized as a format which rewarded the strong and penalized the weak. Some might see irony in the explicit abandonment of market principles in the field of incomes alone, given the absence of shared agreement over differentials and other issues. Governments were prepared to consult and bargain, notably over the social contract in 1974–5, and in 1977 a Labour Chancellor of the Exchequer traded tax reductions in his Budget for moderation in wage settlements. Under the social contract, the high point of the new group politics, the trade-union movement gained much favourable legislation from the Labour Government and was in regular and close touch with it.

In the 1950s and 1960s only a few ministers or officials accepted a monetary explanation of inflation. And, if they did, they usually regarded the cost—in the form of higher unemployment following from a monetary squeeze—as politically and electorally unacceptable. In 1958 the resigning Conservative Chancellor of the Exchequer and his junior ministers also wanted a tighter control on money supply (Brittan 1971: 212). The resort to incomes policy rather than money supply as an answer to inflation stemmed from the intellectual climate.

The British opinion-forming classes—civil servants, politicians, commentators and academics—had largely stopped thinking in terms of the market mechanism. They felt much more at home with politically determined 'strategies'. Consequently the market was readily assumed to have 'failed' even when it was working, and when inflation did worsen this was always attributed to the inherent weaknesses of collective bargaining rather than to prior monetary excess.   (Brittan and Lilley 1977: 198)

Expertise

There was general optimism that many of the widely shared goals in social policy could be achieved and a belief that the relevant knowledge for social engineering was available. After all, if the government had managed to achieve full employment, then why could it not produce similar improvements in education, housing, poverty, regional policy, and other fields? David Donnison (1982) has itemized the key features of this outlook: state provision of the social wage combined with progressive taxation could reduce inequalities of income; economic growth could be assumed and would provide the resources for a relatively painless shift towards a more equal society; governments (usually Labour), aided by the public-service professions, would take initiatives, the Conservatives would largely acquiesce (compare Sir Keith Joseph and the 'ratchet'), and 'middle England' would approve. In education, for example, academic studies pointed to a great waste of talent which could profit from the ending of selection at age 11 and the expansion of further and higher education. The belief fuelled an expansion of higher education, the raising of the school leaving age, and the shift to comprehensive secondary education. By the 1970s the commitment to greater equality in race and gender was expressed in the establishment of such bodies as the Race Relations Commission, the Equal Opportunities Commission, and the Royal Commission on the Distribution of Income and Wealth (1974–9).

Another strand of the belief in expertise was the vogue for managerialism, incomes policies, and economic planning. The Public Expenditure Survey Committee (PESC) system was introduced in 1961 and planned totals of public spending for five years ahead. The

NEDC worked to an economic growth target of 4 per cent per annum. The 1964 Labour Government established a Department of Economic Affairs which could argue for economic expansion against the Treasury. In 1965 it drew up a national plan which proposed policies for government intervention in industry, training, and manpower, with the objective of achieving a growth rate of 25 per cent between 1965 and 1970.

In July 1966, however, faced with a major sterling crisis, the government took severe deflationary measures and aborted the much-trumpeted economic plan. The activist political leadership in both parties at the time had little sympathy for relying on the price mechanism. For Harold Wilson, 'If resources were to flow to where they were most needed—to exports and industrial investment—they had to be pushed there by "direct intervention", by physical controls or official and unofficial arm-twisting. What was needed, if British industry was to be modernised and to compete in the world, were improvements in management, industrial training, new techniques and their embodiment in new investment' (Stewart 1977: 28). The shift to economic planning gave a greater role to experts and the bureaucrats and also encouraged calls for continuity between the political parties. Trevor Smith has noted (1979: 88): 'Indeed, as was so often stated in the great debate (about planning), the role of consensus was to depoliticise those areas of policy (mainly economic and industrial) where, it was believed, a free-ranging application of appropriate skills would be the most effective means of achieving prosperity.'

The mood was also reflected in the institutional reformism of both Mr Heath and Mr Wilson between 1964 and 1976. Local government was restructured, a new system of parliamentary select committees established, the Central Policy Review Staff (CPRS) (1970) and a Policy Unit (1974) for the Prime Minister were created, and attempts were made to reform the trade unions, introduce devolution for Scotland and Wales, and reform the House of Lords. The last three failed, and of the others only the Policy Unit survived.

No doubt the reformers hoped that institutional change would be a catalyst for other changes. But institutional change, largely because it is easier to achieve than economic growth or substantive policy changes, may easily be a form of displacement activity.

Party Politics

One has to guard against viewing the first half of the post-war period as politically 'normal'. In the inter-war years, the rise of Labour, the creation of a much larger electorate, and the rise of new issues led to a great deal of electoral instability. The Lloyd George wartime coalition in 1916 was both a cause and a consequence of the Liberal split. The coalition broke up in 1922 and was replaced by a Conservative Government which was shorn of many of its leading figures. This was followed by a short-lived minority Labour Government in 1924, a Conservative Government (1924–9), another minority Labour Government (1929–31), and then a coalition or largely Conservative Government for the rest of the decade. In 1940 Winston Churchill formed a genuine coalition government.

But after 1945 two major parties alternated in office and the lines of the new, post-war settlement became clear. Between 1918 and 1945 the country had moved from a predominantly Conservative–Liberal party system to a Conservative–Labour one. The instability in the inter-war years in the parties' electoral fortunes and the volatility in voting behaviour could be seen in retrospect as symptoms of the realignment process. In the 1945, 1950, and 1951 general elections, class alignment reached its peak, and many voters saw major differences between the political parties (Butler and Stokes 1969). For the decade or so after 1945 there was a great stability in party support, as reflected in opinion polls, by-elections, and stability in the opinion polls during general elections. The stability broke down in the late 1950s and has never been restored. The 1980s, with the rise of the Liberal and Social Democratic parties, were particularly unstable.

Gallup surveys during each election found a steady increase, until 1964, in the proportion of voters regarding the political parties as 'much of a muchness' and agreeing that it did not make a great deal of difference which party won the general election (see Table 2.1). David Robertson's (1976) analysis of the major themes in the

TABLE 2.1. *Voters' perceptions of differences or similarities between the parties, 1951–1979 (%)*

	1951	1955	1959	1964	1966	1970	Feb. 1974	Oct. 1974	1979
Are important differences	71	74	66	59	55	54	57	54	54
Much of a muchness	20	20	29	32	37	41	38	41	41
Don't know	9	6	5	9	8	5	5	5	5

Source: Gallup.

Conservative and Labour election manifestos from 1924 to 1966 found that the two parties had converged towards the centre by the mid-1960s. By 1964 the distance between them on major economic issues was only one-fifth that of 1931, when the parties were at their extremes (Fig. 2.1). This development appeared to confirm Anthony Downs's (1957) claim that, on a left–right spectrum, there is a posi-

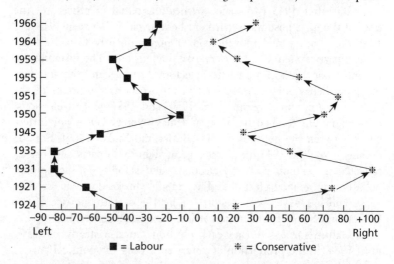

Fig. 2.1. The greater agreement between parties on economic issues, 1924–1966
Source: Adapted from Robertson (1968: 98)

tion at which parties can maximize their votes. This is not necessarily at the mid-point of the spectrum, for voters may bunch at any point on it. But, where two parties are evenly matched in a largely consensual electorate, they will converge in the middle in their policies to win the decisive votes of the floating voters.

Apart from the survey evidence of consensus and the formal theory of convergence, some commentators also argued that a large measure of consensus and policy continuity between the parties was desirable. In view of the interventionist nature of modern government and its role in promoting far-reaching social and economic objectives, a good deal of continuity and predictability was desirable. Parties and elections, in other words, should not make too much of a difference.

It is worth noting, however, that whether a party was in government or opposition was important in influencing whether it moved in an adversary (left, or more state control and nationalization, for Labour; right, or free market, for Conservative) or a consensus direction (Rose 1984). For the ten general elections from 1924 to 1966, Robertson's analysis showed that Labour moved to the left (compared to the previous election) five times—in 1929, 1931, 1951, 1955, and 1959—and it was in opposition on all of these occasions except 1951. We would almost certainly add the manifestos of February 1974 and 1983 to the list of occasions when Labour also moved to the left when it was in opposition. Of Labour's four moves to the centre, two were when it was in opposition (1945 and 1964) and two when it was in office (1950 and 1966). We would probably add the manifestos of 1970 and 1979 as occasions when it moved to the right and was in office.

There is a similar pattern of opposition status inducing the Conservative Party to move away from the centre. Of its five moves to the right—in 1929, 1931, 1950, 1951, and 1966—three occurred when it was in opposition. We could add the 1979 election to this list. The five moves which the Conservative Party made to the centre were in 1935, 1945, 1955, 1959, and 1964—each of which occurred while it was in office.

The policy convergence also had consequences for internal politics in the two main parties. Although these are discussed more fully later, it is worth noting some of the important outcomes. In the Conservative Party, defenders of active government and welfare became dominant and the neo-liberal wing was effectively routed by the late 1940s. The Conservative manifestos in 1950 and 1951 called for a halt to further nationalization rather than a reversal (except for the cases of iron and steel and road haulage) and a repudiation of 'political theory' (i.e. market economics) as a guide to economic policy. The party would live with most of the nationalization measures of the 1945 Labour Government. Similarly, full employment was accepted as a major objective of economic policy. In 1956 Prime Minister Eden wrote to Harold Macmillan, then Chancellor of the Exchequer, about his concern over rising prices and wages. In considering ways to cope with the pressure of trade unions for higher wages, he dismissed as 'politically not tolerable' the use of unemployment to weaken their bargaining power (Beer 1965: 360). Macmillan had been a rather isolated Conservative prophet of what he called the middle way in the 1930s—neither socialist nor capitalist. In 1958 as Prime Minister he was able to look back on how much of his early thinking was now accepted.

The Labour Party leadership took a more pragmatic attitude towards public ownership, explicitly so under Hugh Gaitskell, covertly under Harold Wilson. In many large firms, ownership was divorced from managerial control; managers in large firms had reservations about the free market, distrusting its unregulated competition and unpredictability, and distinctions between public and private enterprise increasingly became blurred. For many in the Labour leadership, socialism appeared increasingly to be based more on demand management and the promotion of economic efficiency than on state ownership and economic planning.

In both parties, there was a pragmatic acceptance rather than a principled agreement of the policies of the mixed economy and welfare state and there were dissenters in both parties. Conservatives could remain critical about the extent and methods of economic planning and controls as practised by Labour, and indeed the Conservative Party did not turn to economic planning until 1961. Similarly, within the Labour Party there was always a large minority that pushed for wider policies of public ownership. One should not overstress the uniqueness of the British experience in this respect. In many other Western states so-called 'catch-all', voter-orientated, political parties sought support from most sections of the electorate. At elections they relied increasingly on public-relations techniques and played down distinctive sectional and ideological appeals. For the general election in 1959 the Conservatives hired an advertising agency to market their campaign. In 1960 Harold Macmillan had written to a party official: 'Who are the middle classes? What do they want? How can we give it to them?' After the 1959 election defeat the Labour leader, Hugh Gaitskell, also realized that the process of social change among the working class meant that Labour would have to update its policies and image. By 1964 Labour had turned to private opinion polling to inform it about the public mood and help it to present its policies.

Conclusion

Much of the agreement on broad policy goals and methods existed at the élite level. 'Reasonableness' came from on high. Although opinion leaders in the mass media, front-bench politicians, senior civil servants, and many pressure group leaders supported the above policies, they did not necessarily reflect popular attitudes. Surveys showed no great support for some of the 'core policies' in the consensus—public ownership, universal welfare benefits, ending capital punishment, some practices of trade unions, and at times British membership of the EC (by contrast, Atlanticism was favoured at élite and popular level); and, perhaps above all, the belief that all British subjects (some 700 million) should have unrestricted entry to Britain. The importance of Enoch Powell's speech about immigration in 1968 (see p. 73) was that a senior figure broke with the high-minded consensus and, for a brief period, was the most popular politician in the land. Powell used mass fears to attack élite attitudes—the classic populist strategy—and in so doing showed how the consensus could be undermined. He blazed a trail for Mrs Thatcher.

There is no gainsaying that the first thirty post-war years of consensus politics coincided with both a steady slide in Britain's international standing and its relative economic decline. The politics of consensus was to be seen as the politics of decline. Equally, one has to acknowledge that in every post-war year until 1973 (except 1958) the economy grew and that the period saw a significant improvement in living standards and social welfare. The consensus coincided with some economic success, even though Britain's economic performance was failing to match that of most other Western states. Defenders of the consensus may also object that the country's relative economic decline dates back for over a century and clearly pre-dates the era of consensus politics.

Some other countries—notably Sweden, Austria, and Norway—pursued consensual social-democratic policies and had successful economic records. Governments in these states bargained policies on welfare and the labour market in return for moderation in wage settlements from trade unions and other producer groups. These 'tripartite' arrangements worked well enough in the 1950s and 1960s in such states as West Germany, Sweden, Norway, Austria, and the Netherlands, all of which had low levels of inflation and unemployment. These countries usually had centralized trade-union confederations which were able to bargain authoritatively for their members, and (except for West Germany) a strong social democratic presence in government. There was an emphasis on seeking consensus, providing for continuity of policy, working through an array of councils, commissions, and so on, and separating as far as possible economic management from partisan considerations. In Britain, as noted, the incomes-policy approach was followed episodically but usually collapsed after two or three years.

Claims about the demise of ideology between the parties and the convergence across many industrial Western states not surprisingly prompted the question, 'Does Politics Matter?' According to one observer, 'This ideological agreement, which might best be described as "conservative socialism", has become *the* ideology of major parties in the developing states of Europe and America' (Lipset 1964: 244–5). Broadly similar policy packages were emerging in a number of Western European states in the same period. The growth of scientific thought and expertise, exemplified in Keynesian economics, appeared to weaken the appeal and relevance of ideologies of left and right. Affluence softened social and class polarization and narrowed policy differences between the parties. The government's role of public spending and state employment grew. Between 1950 and 1980 the latter more than doubled as a share of the workforce in Italy and Sweden (Rose 1985). The government's 'take' from citizens in direct and indirect taxes amounted to over a third of GDP, and the provision of welfare moved in similar directions in Western states, despite their different histories, party systems, and forms of government.

It is possible to argue that the dissatisfaction so widely expressed in the 1960s and onwards signalled a break in the consensus. The attacks on many prevailing assumptions in industry, trade unions, civil service, and Parliament were coupled with appeals for modernization in industry, the professions, Whitehall, education trade unions, and so on. In fact, the 'What's wrong with Britain?' school of Royal Commissions, government inquiries, and literature was in many ways an attempt to shore up the old consensus. The outlines of the post-war settlement, which was largely accepted among the political élite, civil service, economic interests, and mass media, were rarely called into question. The proposed remedies for the most part were institutional change, better management, and a more technocratic style of leadership.

3 Breakdown

For a quarter of a century or so after 1945 the policies outlined in Chapter 2 were widely accepted by the élites and dominant groups in the main political parties. This broad policy agreement coexisted with a much-praised political system, stable government, a largely supportive electorate, two political parties evenly matched in electoral support, and low levels of inflation and unemployment. But, in comparison with Britain's competitors, this was no golden economic age. Economic growth was slow, sterling was often under pressure, and there were regular balance-of-payments crises, two forced devaluations in 1949 and 1967, and a falling share of world trade in manufacturing. There were, of course, minorities in both the Labour and Conservative parties who always dissented from the policies. In the face of a gathering economic recession, which followed the sharp increase in Arab oil prices in 1973–4, slowdown of economic growth, and clear repudiation of each party in government in the February 1974 and 1979 elections, these critics found greater support. As the decade wore on, the left grew in strength in the Labour Party and the free-market right gained ground within and around the Conservative Party. In the course of the 1970s unemployment doubled in OECD countries but trebled in Britain, and British inflation rose twice as fast as the average in OECD countries. Neither party could credibly claim that it was successful in government, or popular among the electorate. We now turn to the consequence for the post-war policies examined in Chapter 2.

Full Employment

There was no doubt about the success of economic policy in delivering very high levels of employment. Compared to the inter-war years, when the unemployment figure rarely fell below 10 per cent, it rarely exceeded 2.5 per cent in the thirty years after 1945. The famous 'Phillips curve', of Professor W. A. Phillips (1958), demonstrated a relationship between rates of inflation and unemployment; for the 1950s an increase in the pressure of demand was associated with a rapid rise in prices and a fall in unemployment. One could therefore trade off price stability against economic expansion and levels of unemployment, and politicians could choose between differing amounts of inflation and unemployment. By the end of the 1960s, however, it was clear that the British economy could have increasing levels of both; the term 'stagflation' referred to the combination of low growth with rising unemployment and inflation. Moreover, it was taking larger injections of demand to reduce unemployment at each stage of the economic cycle; at each stage the relationships between levels of unemployment and inflation were deteriorating (see Table 3.1). Reflation by increased government spending not only caused inflation to accelerate but eventually left unemployment higher at the next downturn in the cycle. Keynesian economics faced something of an intellectual crisis.

Defenders of Keynes have made various claims on his behalf. Some have tried to rescue him from vote-seeking politicians, and his most recent biographer has argued that post-war British politicians were overloading the economy, by expanding public spending too fast (Skidelsky 1992). In an era of full employment and economic growth, one might expect budget surpluses—to offset inflation—as often as budget deficits. In fact, most Western states practised 'one-eyed Keynesianism', budgeting for deficits. In the UK, for example,

TABLE 3.1. *The worsening economic performance, 1951–1979*

Government	Date	Average annual increase in prices (%)	Average number unemployed, of UK adults, seasonally adjusted
Conservative	1951–64	3.5	330,000
Labour	1964–70	4.5	500,000
Conservative	1970–4	9.0	750,000
Labour	1974–9	15.0	1,250,000

deficits were registered in eighteen of the twenty-five years between 1951 and 1975 (Rose and Peters 1978).

Others have claimed that Keynes's ideas have been misused and that, had he lived, he would have taken account of significant changes, particularly the collapse in 1973 of the Bretton Woods system, which had fixed the values of currencies in relation to the US dollar, and the growing power of trade unions. Sir Keith Joseph and Mrs Thatcher tried to distinguish Keynes from the post-Keynesians, or those economists and politicians who added their own gloss to his ideas, and claimed that he also believed in sound finance. Selective interpretation is surely the fate of most theories which are vulgarized when used in the real world by politicians and also by policy-makers. Keynes was not indifferent to inflation, money supply, or the problems which collectivism and active government might pose for individual liberty. Sir Keith Joseph claimed that 'what was said and done in his (Keynes) name has been quite different', and that 'from what Keynes wrote it seems likely that he would have disowned most of the allegedly Keynesian remedies made in his name and which have caused so much harm' (1975: 11).

A side effect of injecting monetary demand at a rate above the rate of productivity growth was higher inflation, which governments, in turn, tried to control by resorting to incomes policy and deflation. In 1972 and 1973 the Heath Government, still committed to full employment, expanded money supply and reflated the economy when faced by rising unemployment figures. This was accompanied by a statutory incomes policy to curb inflation. Heath still accepted the full-employment commitment. Frightened by soaring inflation (reaching an annual rate of 26 per cent in July 1975), the Labour Government changed course. Denis Healey's March 1975 Budget abandoned the full-employment goal. With unemployment exceeding one million, the Budget would have been expected to reduce taxes and/or increase public spending. Instead, Healey did the opposite, a historic breach with one of the main planks of the post-war consensus. In a speech to his party conference in 1976, the Labour leader, Mr Callaghan, boldly proclaimed the new thinking about political economy: 'We used to think that you could just spend your way out of recession and increase employment only by cutting taxes

and boosting government expenditure . . . it only worked by injecting bigger doses of inflation into the economy followed by a higher
level of unemployment at the next step . . . The option (of spending yourself out of a recession) no longer exists.'

This began something of an intellectual revolution in economic
policy. By the end of 1976, after the International Monetary Fund
(IMF) rescue package of sterling, there was a new economic regime
of pay policy, cutting income taxes and public spending, reducing
the public-sector borrowing requirement, fixing cash limits for much
central and local government spending, and setting targets for M3
money supply. Unemployment doubled over the lifetime of the
1974–9 Labour Government to 1.2 million or 6.2 per cent. The idea
of a government spending its way out of recession had already been
abandoned before the arrival of Mrs Thatcher in office.

The growing importance of economic management increased
the influence of economists on governments. But the old Keynesian
dominance was no longer unquestioned. By 1975 it was possible to
distinguish various voices among the economics profession about the
best mix of policies to achieve the objectives of high employment,
stable prices, and a satisfactory balance of payments. The neo-
Keynesians of the National Institute of Economic Research wanted
to curb inflation by an incomes policy while still pursuing economic
growth. A second group, commonly identified with the Department
of Applied Economics at Cambridge University, argued that, because
Britain's manufacturing was uncompetitive, the home market needed
to be protected by import controls and, if necessary, an incomes policy, in order to suppress inflationary tendencies when demand was
boosted. The group's support for import controls achieved some
influence among Labour's left wing and was incorporated in its alternative socialist strategy. Finally, there was a growing school of monetarists, who argued that the key to curbing inflation was a reduction
in the money supply. Unlike income policies, which required cooperation from employers and unions, this was a task for government,
which had to be resolute enough not to print more money when
unemployment was rising. If wage bargainers pushed for inflationary
wage increases (i.e. at a level above that of output), this would result
in an increase in unit costs, a decline in competitiveness, a loss of

markets, and the destruction of jobs. People should be educated in these 'facts' of economic life; they would then change their behaviour and bargain responsibly. Yet the Keynesian idea was still dominant in the economics profession and monetarism attracted few followers (see p. 145).

Trade Unions

The position of the trade unions also changed. By 1970 the Labour Government had rejected the two features of what has been called 'compulsory collectivism'—that is, incomes policy to control inflation, and legal regulation of the unions to curb strikes, particularly unofficial ones. The new Heath Government in 1970 opted for reform of the unions, in part as an alternative to incomes policy, although by the end of its period of office it had reversed the emphasis. The failure of its Industrial Relations Act of 1971, coupled with the damage it did to industrial relations (the number of working days lost in 1972 due to strikes reached 23 million, and was the highest figure since 1926) and the harm done to the government's relations with the unions, led many to conclude that such a measure was doomed to failure. After the Conservative defeat in the 1974 elections, reforming (or limiting) the legal privileges of trade unions and imposing statutory incomes policies seemed to have been taken off the political agenda. Gaining the consent of the unions seemed to be the key to social and political stability in Britain, and Labour won two general elections in 1974 largely on the claim that it could get on with the unions.

British governments tried various approaches to curb inflation in the 1960s and 1970s—a mix of voluntary and statutory incomes policies, legal regulation of industrial relations, a social contract approach, and, finally in 1975, the abandonment of a commitment to full employment. Under both Labour and Conservative governments, policy oscillated between burden-sharing, social and political partnership, persuasion, and coercion—all to sustain full employment. Most incomes policies lasted for two to three years before breaking down in the face of workers' reaction against rigidities, compressed differentials, and growing disparities in incomes between public- and private-sector workers.

The so-called Winter of Discontent was a rash of strikes, often unofficial and largely in the public sector, against the Callaghan Government's attempt to impose a 5 per cent norm for wages and salaries. In December 1978 the Ford Motor Company eventually settled a strike at the cost of a 15 per cent wage rise and a similar figure settled a strike of BBC technicians. In the New Year there was an outburst of strikes and militant picketing by lorry drivers, ambulance drivers, oil-tanker drivers, and local-government manual workers which resulted in the closure of schools, disruption of hospitals, and in one well-publicized case a refusal to bury the dead. Ministers and union leaders seemed powerless to act. All this was graphically reported by the mass media, the unions reached new heights of unpopularity, and Labour's claim to have a 'special relationship' with the unions was destroyed.

One route to redistribution is via social policy and welfare expenditure—the Beveridge package. Another is via free collective bargaining—the trade-union approach. The Labour movement in Britain was reluctant to acknowledge the tension between these two approaches and the experience of the 1974–9 Labour Government undermined the belief that the unions would or could trade off wage claims for an increased social wage. In various ways the Winter of Discontent in 1979 may have spelt the bankruptcy in Britain of a political tradition and style of government. Governments had been wary of the alternative anti-inflation policy (stricter control of money supply), which achieved wage restraint through weakening the unions. They feared that the consequent higher unemployment which would follow a monetary squeeze would be politically unacceptable. By 1979, however, the new Conservative Government's strategy for beating inflation did not include a policy for wages and rested on the control of the money supply.

Welfare

The role and performance of the welfare state was attacked from both right and left flanks. There were differences among Conservative critics, but all professed concern about the mounting costs of the cradle-to-grave provision implied in the Beveridge proposals; the latter were not designed to cope with large numbers of unemployed and elderly and the growing number of family breakdowns. The system failed to concentrate resources on the most needy. They therefore favoured more selectivity in the distribution of welfare resources and encouraging people to take out private insurance to relieve the burden on the state. Correlli Barnett (1986) complained that, after 1945, Britain mistakenly invested scarce resources in housing and welfare, to build a new Jerusalem, instead of in industry and training. Selectivists also believed that restraint in spending was necessary to make room for tax cuts. Other critics who objected to the state playing such a large role in welfare favoured a greater private provision of services. Advocates of the free market, led by the Institute of Economic Affairs, urged that users of state services should be charged the full cost, that a reverse income tax should be introduced to help the poor, and that the state should confine itself to providing essential public goods. Giving people vouchers and cash would allow them to choose their own schools and medical treatment. The critics were, variously, cost-cutters, selectivists, moralists, and privatizers. Most also complained that the welfare state weakened the work ethic, undermined traditional forms of self-help through the community, charity, and friendly societies, and lessened the recipient's sense of personal reliance and responsibility.

From the other flank, Professor Richard Titmuss and his colleagues (Professors Townsend and Abel Smith) claimed that large-scale poverty still existed and was proof of the failure of welfare policies. They defined poverty in relative terms, raising the poverty line when living standards increased. Their 'rediscovery' of deprivation was joined to critical assessments of the 1964–70 and 1974–9 Labour governments' records in welfare and promoting equality (Bosanquet and Townsend 1980). The failure to eliminate poverty led the editors to doubt the ability of parliamentary socialism to produce 'radical structural change' in society, to claim 'that democratic socialism did not fail in the 1960s, it was not tried', and to conclude that 'the fundamental question left unanswered by Labour's rule is whether democratic socialism can be effective' (ibid.: 10–11, 229).

Marxist and neo-Marxist writers claimed that the slowdown of economic growth was producing a new 'contradiction' in advanced capitalist societies. High levels of welfare spending were necessary to gain popular support, but, increasingly, this was achieved at the cost of squeezing the profits of industry. Hence the 'contradiction', or fiscal crisis, of the capitalist state, arising from the conflicting needs to maintain political support and provide for capital accumulation (O'Connor 1973). This view, interestingly, joined with right-wing claims that welfare was being placed ahead of economic growth and that high taxes and egalitarianism were inimical to creating a prosperous economy.

Critics on the left also pointed to the failure of many existing policies to produce a more radical redistribution of life opportunities. Research could show that programmes of public expenditure did not always promote equality, that the middle class did well because of their ability to work the system, and that they benefited from the mix of expenditure and tax relief on such services as housing, higher education, and rail (Hills 1991). For example, the top fifth of income earners received nearly three times as much public expenditure in education per household as the poorest fifth.

We do not have good evidence about popular attitudes to the welfare state pre-1979, but an EC study conducted in member countries in 1976 showed the British to be rather tough-minded, in comparison to people in other countries. For example, 36 per cent of the British sample thought that the government was not doing enough for the poor, compared to an average of 54 per cent in other EC states, and a similar figure thought that people in Britain were living in real poverty compared to an EC average of 47 per cent. British respondents were more likely to attribute poverty in their country to personal failings of the poor rather than to structural reasons like unemployment, which other Europeans mentioned. It may be that low economic growth in the 1970s, far from promoting solidarity or radicalizing people, actually dented altruism—a crucial motive for supporting the welfare state and redistribution. Altruism was found more frequently among the affluent, the middle class, and the better educated (Alt 1979).

The advance of the welfare state has depended greatly upon

economic growth, perhaps more than upon political ideology (Flora and Heidenheimer 1984). Yet socialists as diverse as Karl Marx, Ramsay MacDonald, Anthony Crosland, and Harold Wilson (at least before 1964) all assumed that the problem of production was about to be solved. Crosland's *The Future of Socialism* (1956) envisaged a period in the near future when this might indeed be the case. Then, he wrote, he might be prepared to stop worrying about hard work and economic matters and even relax into greater leisure and more cultural pursuits. As a Cabinet minister he later recognized the indispensability of economic growth for the realization of his goals. A Labour government, like any other, depended on a thriving mixed economy to provide a surplus for welfare. Yet the party's commitment to socialism placed it in the position of seeming to fatten the golden goose of capitalism only to kill it off eventually. In the short term, the necessity to pursue politics which would encourage business and finance confidence depressed Labour's more ardent followers. The party's dilemma was whether to make capitalism work and deny its socialist ideology, or try to undermine capitalism and face turmoil in the financial markets in the short term. The latter strategy might help to achieve socialism, but it certainly made it difficult to deliver prosperity and win elections.

In the 1970s the onset of economic recession and the effects on employment and inflation meant that complaints about the rising costs of welfare were heard more frequently throughout Western Europe. Sir Keith Joseph regularly attacked the 'false gods' of egalitarianism, envy, and a swollen and non-productive public sector. Western government did not try to dismantle the welfare state in response to these pressures, but slowed down the rise in public spending, were reluctant to introduce new programmes, sought greater value for money, and trimmed existing programmes (Heclo 1984). Surveys suggested that there was a willingness to reduce expectations and that levels of life satisfaction remained high in spite of economic disappointments. The growth of welfare after 1945 had coincided with an expansion of personal liberty and opportunity for many. Given the contribution of welfare to the stability of regimes, it was perhaps ironic that some right-wing Conservatives should attack such an admirable conservative institution.

A Mixed Economy

Although a large publicly owned industrial sector seemed to be 'natural', the status quo had few positive supporters. Labour's left wing was more convinced than ever of the failings of British capitalism and more interested in establishing a powerful state-holding company which would take over profitable and strategically important firms. In opposition, Conservatives were determined to cut back public spending and squeeze the public sector borrowing requirement (PSBR), although they had not yet come round to privatization. They were determined to reduce the Treasury's role in financing nationalized industry investment and impose tough rates of return. If the rates were not achieved, then the industries would have to sell off assets, raise prices, or abandon uneconomic activities.

Cautious Conservatives were mindful of their defeat in the election of February 1974 and how their government's pay policy had led to confrontation with a powerful union in the nationalized coal industry. The party still had no effective policy for the nationalized industries. Free collective bargaining and incomes policy were both difficult to operate where there were powerful unions, centralized wage bargaining, and monopoly key services. The leaked findings of a Conservative Party report in 1978 noted that in the cases of strikes in key services the government would have to give in. Privatization was only a minor theme of the 1979 general election; the Conservative Party manifesto proposed selling off shares in the National Enterprise Board and the National Freight corporation, and returning the recently nationalized aerospace and shipbuilding industries to the private sector (Swann 1993: 138–9). Privatization emerged as economic concerns over public spending and continued losses in some nationalized industries led Conservative ministers to seek a new approach.

Active Government

The spectre of 'big government' and the need to reduce it loomed large in the rhetoric of right-wing politicians in the 1970s. The growth of government can be measured along many indicators—taxation, public spending, programmes, state ownership of industry, public sector, employment, and so on—and one should carefully distinguish between them. Some part of the right-wing attack on 'big government', bureaucracy, and high levels of taxation (a regular theme of successive Conservative election manifestos when the party was in opposition) was also a reaction to the economic recession and the problems which slow economic growth posed for funding government programmes. In a slow growth economy like Britain's pressures for increases in public spending collided with pressures from workers to protect take-home pay. In the thirty years' period 1951–1980 the UK economy grew by an average of 2.5 per cent annually, public spending by an average of 4.6 per cent, but take-home pay by only 1.7 per cent (Rose 1985: 220). There is some evidence that the 'wage-capping' effect was resented by well-organized groups of workers and led to industrial disruption (Wilkinson and Turner 1975). Comparative research also suggested that the political-protest or tax-backlash movements were strongest in countries where direct or more visible taxes increased the most (Wilensky 1976).

There was a predictable reaction to the failures of government. Commentators and politicians urged people to lower their expectations, particularly over economic benefits, and the public mood did change. If there was a strong correlation between changes in unemployment levels and the government's popularity until the early 1970s, this has virtually disappeared since. Steep increases in unemployment since 1974 have not been fatal for a government's popularity. There was a tendency for people to blame other factors than the government—for example, trade unions, world recession, rising oil prices, and personal failings—as a cause of high inflation and high unemployment in 1970s. According to James Alt's (1979: 236) analysis of survey evidence:

In a large measure, then, the story of the mid-1970s is the story of a politics of declining expectations. People attached a great deal of importance to economic problems, people saw clearly the developments that were taking place, and people expected developments in advance and thus were able to discount the impact of the worst of them. However, in unprecedented numbers, people also ceased to expect the election of their party to make them better off, largely because they also ceased to expect it to be able to do very much about what they identified as the principal economic problems of the time. The result of this—as well as perhaps some of the other factors discussed above—was not a politics of protest, but a politics of quiet disillusion, a politics in which lack of involvement or indifference to organised party politics was the most important feature.

There was also a new modesty about the possibility of social engineering. This was something separate from the traditional Conservative respect for the status quo and the Burkean view of the complexity and inter-dependence of society, the wisdom inherent in existing institutions and practices, and the scepticism about amenability of social conduct to political manipulation. Rather, the new modesty claimed to have been born out of experience and disappointment with the promises and interventions of government. The reorganization of secondary education, local government, and the health service, economic planning, or building high-rise council flats rarely produced more satisfactory outcomes for those using the services.

In the USA there was a similar disillusionment with the various Great Society Programs to improve educational standards, combat poverty, and promote greater equality of opportunity. There was a turning away from 'inputism', or the belief that complex social problems may be amenable to the investment of yet more resources. In the USA the famous Coleman Report (Coleman 1966) and the work of Jencks (1973), for example, appeared to demonstrate that differences in the level of resources and educational facilities had little or no, and sometimes even an adverse, relationship to student achievements. Other factors, such as the commitment of teachers, the quality of the head teacher, or the cultural capital of the family, seemed to be more important. Schooling also had limited effect as a tool of redistribution, according to Jencks, because of deeply entrenched and broader social and economic inequalities and the importance of the family. In Britain, even Labour policy-makers had doubts. Crosland (1975) was impressed by the work of Jencks, the head of the Number 10 Policy Unit regarded the National Union of Teachers' indifference to children as a major part of the problems in schools (Donoughue 1987: 110), and others complained that increases in public funding were too often swallowed up in higher pay for producers, not in improved services (J. Barnett 1982).

One can readily see how much of this research fuelled fiscal and social conservatism in many countries. Interestingly, the monitoring role of social science was being used to refute the problem solving claims of the various professions. Sceptics were quick to point out that the increased public expenditure and employment in services like health and education did not accompany evidence of improved performance. They warned that voters had been encouraged to expect too much from politicians, who in turn believed that, if the 'right' politics were adopted, then a wide range of economic and social problems could be solved. John Vaizey's *Breach of Promise* (1983: 5), a study of influential makers of the post-war consensus, commented that they were 'the first generation of Englishmen to believe that the solution to social and even political dilemmas lay in political action . . . the belated achievement of the Fabians.' As governments expanded their responsibilities, sometimes regardless of their ability to carry them out, so failure to satisfy the demands risked undermining popular confidence in them and the system. Samuel Brittan (1975) argued that there were 'contradictions' in democracy, arising from the tendency of competing politicians and groups to raise unfulfillable economic expectations among voters. More generally, government was seen to suffer from organized social complexity. Achievement of its policies required the cooperation of many other actors and the more it depended on these the more easily things could go wrong. The difficulty for government was that the range of problems for which it accepted responsibility grew but its capacity to deal with them did not. It was also possible to criticize these trends as a crisis of social democracy—a regime of active government, high public spending and taxation, and voters looking instrumentally towards the government for benefits. Britain was becoming harder to govern. Some of this gloomy analysis was a questionable extrapolation of current trends, some of it pertained to democracy in general, rather than just Britain, and survey evidence was at best ambiguous concerning many of the claims about popular attitudes.

It was easy to conclude from this thinking that the government's role should be reduced. Indeed, an academic suggested that political scientists could help with problems of political overload by suggesting ways in which the government could do less (A. King 1975). The 1979 Conservative manifesto echoed this concern: 'Attempting to do too much, politicians have failed to do those things which should be done. This has damaged the country and the authority of government. We must concentrate on what should be priorities for any government.'

Much concern centred on the growth of public expenditure. Under the PESC system the expenditure figures for departments were adjusted to allow for inflation, so that money values were expressed in constant prices. But the upsurge of inflation in the 1970s played havoc with the system. There was a loss of control of public spending between 1973 and 1976, as final outturns far exceeded those predicted, and increased from 51 per cent to 59 per cent of GDP, at factor cost (as public spending was then measured). The most important cause was the assumption that spending commitments could be financed out of predicted rates of economic growth, which were rarely achieved. In fact, much of the growth took the form of transfer payments of cash as pensions and various welfare benefits, which simply passed through the state's hands.

A more critical view of public spending was encouraged by the work of Bacon and Eltis, *Britain's Economic Problems: Too Few Producers* (1976), which described a shift in resources and employment from marketed to non-marketed goods and services. By 'market' they meant goods and services which are sold for a price, and by 'non-market' goods and services provided by the government out of general revenue (such as state education, defence, and the NHS). They argued that this shift reduced the opportunities for investment, employment, and growth in the market sector and at the same time encouraged inflation. The distinction is not quite one between 'unproductive' public and 'productive' private sectors, but is near enough. Employment and spending had increased in the social services, health, education, and administration, while it had actually fallen slightly in the productive market sector. It was easy to conclude from this analysis that the growth of the public sector was: (1) 'crowding out' investment and employment from the market sector, and (2) 'parasitical' on the market sector.

The thesis has been criticized on a number of grounds, not least for its inadequate appreciation of the productive impact of public services (for example, the role of the welfare state in improving morale and creating a healthy and educated workforce); not acknowledging that many public-sector goods are marketed; and overlooking the fact that many of the new non-market workers were part-time and female, for whom the alternative was probably unemployment. The actual growth in employment in the public sector was rather modest, from 23.5 per cent to 26 per cent of the total workforce between 1964 and 1974, was not out of line with what was happening in other Western states, and reflected in part the growth in numbers of old age pensioners and school-age children. The thesis could hardly be a sufficient explanation of Britain's decline, in view of the fact that similar trends were observed in other Western states. But the analysis was influential because it fed into concerns and it appeared to explain so many unrelated economic problems. As two critics noted: 'the work published by Bacon and Eltis in the late 1970s was exactly right for the political climate of the time' (Hadjimatheou and Skouras 1979: 392).

The Conservatives found the analysis attractive for ideological reasons, given their negative view of the growth of the public sector and public spending. In her famous 'Let the Children Grow Tall' speech in September 1975 Mrs Thatcher drew attention to the coincidence of the steady growth in public-sector employment and the contraction of the overall working population: 'So one must not overload it (the private sector). Every man switched away from industry and into Government will reduce the productive sector and increase the burden on it at the same time.' Labour ministers were also coming round to this view. They were aware of workers' resistance to higher taxes to pay for the social wage under the social contract and wanted to contain the rise in such spending and leave more in take-home pay. The Public Expenditure White Paper in 1976 (Cmnd. 6393) complained about the growing public-sector borrowing requirement. It noted that in the three years 1974–6 public spending had grown by 20 per cent in volume, and from 51 to 60 per cent as a proportion of GDP, but that output had risen by less than 2 per cent. It continued: 'As recovery proceeds we must progressively reduce the deficit. . . . more resources . . . will be needed for exports and investment.'

Conclusion

As the policy formulas broke down, the key political actors—the dominant groups in the Conservative and Labour parties, senior civil servants, and pressure groups—also lost support and, in some cases, self-confidence. In the 1974 and 1979 general elections the main parties sunk to new post-war lows of electoral support. Labour's dominant right wing and the Conservative 'One Nation', or progressive, wing were both discredited. Disillusioned Labourites, particularly among the trade unions and much of the public sector, and disappointed Conservatives, particularly supporters of the free market, campaigned for change. The election as party leader of Michael Foot for Labour and Margaret Thatcher for the Conservatives meant that in the early 1980s parties had their most left- and right-wing leaders respectively since 1945.

Just as the policies outlined in Chapter 2 were interconnected, so their decline had repercussions across the political agenda. Dissatisfaction with the performance of much of the public sector led to a new interest in markets, the urgency of tackling inflation meant that full employment was no longer a priority for policy-makers, the rising costs and low economic growth raised hard questions about universal welfare provision, and the shortcomings of the voluntarist approach in industrial relations encouraged a renewed interest in the use of law. On the political left and right the rallying cry was 'there must be a better way'.

4 Thatcher and the Conservative Party

Mrs Thatcher's rise to party and national leadership was in large part a response to a crisis within the Conservative Party as well as a breakdown of what was loosely termed the Keynesian settlement in post-war politics. This chapter examines the rise of Mrs Thatcher in the context of changes within the Conservative Party.

It is worth reminding ourselves of the dominance of the Conservative Party in Britain this century. Between 1931 and 1964 it lost office only twice (1945 and 1964), and both followed prolonged periods of Conservative government. By 1974, however, the sense that it was the natural party of government had been severely shaken, not least amongst Conservatives themselves. Labour had emerged victorious in four out of the five general elections held between 1964 and 1974 and had been in office for all but three and a half of the fourteen and a half years from October 1964 to May 1979. Surveys confirmed that the Conservative Party was increasingly regarded as out of touch and had little appeal to the young voters. The political agenda placed the party at a disadvantage. The trend to interventionist and collectivist policies, combined with the enhanced bargaining and political power of the trade unions, appeared more in tune with Labour than Conservative ideas. When Mrs Thatcher challenged Ted Heath for the leadership in February 1975, the party was in a state of trauma.

Conservatism and the Conservative Party

There is a remarkable consistency of view among writers on the character of British Conservatism. The party lacks a doctrine or settled principles—indeed, before Mrs Thatcher, many Conservatives took pride from this. There is a long list of policies and principles—

protection in the nineteenth century, union with Ireland, preserving the Empire, powers of the House of Lords, free enterprise, free collective bargaining, and so on—which the party has been pledged to uphold and has subsequently abandoned. Freedom from ideology, attachment to the importance of gaining and retaining office, and responsiveness to 'circumstances' have made it the adaptable party. It has been suspicious of intellectuals and some took pride in it being the 'stupid party'. Conservatives, however, draw freely on the writings and behaviour of Burke, Hume, Coleridge, Disraeli, and Salisbury. Conservatism is said to have its own logic and to be closely related to political practice, to be an 'attitude', a 'habit of mind', or even a 'way of life'. It includes respect for the traditions of society, rule of law, private property, and individual liberty. It has also been, at least until the mid-1970s, fairly sympathetic to the policy status quo. The party has been prepared to introduce reforms, but preferably gradually and cautiously, and to accept or consolidate what its opponents wrought when in office.

Mrs Thatcher's leadership and her impact occasioned intense debate about the character of British Conservatism and even whether she is a Conservative. The exercise is doomed, for there is no essence of Conservatism. There has traditionally been an interplay between two wings in the party which cannot be reduced to simple contrasts between 'dry' and 'wet', 'left' and 'right', or 'consolidator' and 'radical' (Greenleaf 1983). The dominant Tory strand regards society as an organic unity, denies the value or possibility of planned societal change, and stresses the government's responsibility for managing the economy and providing welfare. Edmund Burke is often quoted as the authoritative exponent of such an outlook. His *Reflections on the French Revolution* was a vehement defence of the status quo and, more importantly for modern Conservatives, established a model of the correct political order and appropriate political behaviour. Such a Conservative respects tradition—'the general bank and capital of nations and of ages'—makes change gradually, only when necessary, and is sure to bring about improvement, and is suspicious of abstract speculative reasoning. Burke also stressed the value of attachment to groups—the 'little platoons'—which were the first principle (the germ as it were) of public affection. His most celebrated recent disciple, Michael Oakeshott, claimed that the task of the politician was not to shape society but, more modestly, to pursue 'intimations'. Politics was a matter of keeping the ship afloat on a bottomless and boundless sea, rather than steering for a harbour.

The second and competing strand is that of classical liberalism, nowadays sometimes termed neo-liberalism. In this the individual is the key unit; society and the economy have their own mechanisms and by and large should be allowed to proceed unhindered by government. Government has a limited, if important, role covering such essential tasks as preserving law and order, maintaining a stable currency, and providing a strong defence, and should allow individuals to work out their own destinies. A hero of the liberal wing, Hayek, found much of the Tory philosophy objectionable and denied that he was a Conservative because they do not reverse changes, for they 'cannot offer an alternative to the direction in which we are moving'. Another hero, Milton Friedman, described himself as a Liberal and Mrs Thatcher as a 'nineteenth-century Liberal' (*Observer*, 26 September 1982).

Both themes have been influential in shaping Conservative practice. If the Tory tradition has produced paternalist legislation, social reform and Disraelian One-Nation rhetoric, the liberal tradition has preached the virtues of competition, private enterprise, personal freedom, and reducing the role of the state. Both elements have figures in Conservative practice in government at any one time.

Most Conservatives have taken pride in the fact that, unlike Socialists, they are not ideological. They agree on the virtue of holding office—indeed possessing office has been seen as proof of political wisdom. Being in government for two-thirds of the twentieth century has made it easy for Conservatives to identify the national interest with that of their party. Moreover, lengthy spells in office impose constraints on ideology. Ideas are tested and modified (often destroyed) when set against the criteria of political acceptability and administrative practicality presented by pressure groups, civil servants, and public opinion—what a senior civil servant has called 'ongoing reality'. Conservatism becomes what Conservative governments do. It is an instrumental politics producing what has been called a *situational* Conservatism, in which the party does what is necessary to preserve existing institutions and the social order. The search for office has, in any case, presented fewer problems of principle for Conservatives than for their rivals. They were the dominant group in coalitions under Lloyd George in 1915, Ramsay MacDonald in 1931, and Churchill in 1940. In October 1974 Mr Heath campaigned on a national-unity platform, claiming that, if elected, he could form a government of all the talents.

If Conservatism is what Conservatives do, then this gives the leadership great scope at any one time to shape it. Mrs Thatcher's decisive leadership was clearly in line with Tory traditions of authoritative government. Her rhetoric of duty, authority, discipline, and order echoed traditional Tory themes. But in many other respects she marked a change from the outlook of the party leaders from Baldwin in 1922 down to Heath. Many critics and sympathizers agree that the party's record over time, apart from Heath's neo-liberal period in office (1970–2), has been one of Tory men and collectivist, or even social democratic, measures. Distrust of the free market was reflected in such policies as the protectionism for industry and agriculture in the 1930s, regional policy in the 1950s, economic planning and incomes policies in the 1960s, backbench hostility to the abolition of resale price maintenance in 1963, and, finally, the statutory controls on prices and incomes and government intervention in industry in the 1970s. Many of the speeches of Neville Chamberlain, Sir Anthony Eden, Harold Macmillan, and R. A. Butler defended the positive role of the government. Party leaders have often held back from promoting 'Big C Conservatism' (the phrase is Jim Prior's). The party had to avoid ideology to be 'moderate' and 'balanced' and govern from the 'centre' (Gilmour 1978). In 1925 Stanley Baldwin, when faced with a private member's bill to abolish the trade unions' political levy (which provided funds for the Labour party), eloquently disarmed his union-bashing backbenchers. Although he accepted the merits of the bill and knew it could be passed, he urged its rejection in the higher interests of promoting social cohesion: 'We are not going to push our political advantage home.'

R. A. Butler and Harold Macmillan quickly came to terms with the work of the 1945 Labour Government. In 1946 Butler called for 'an acceptance of redistributive taxation and the repudiation of *laissez-faire* economics in favour of a system in which the state acted as a trustee for the interests of the community' (R. Butler 1971: 133–4). As Prime Minister in 1951 Winston Churchill thought the nation needed a rest 'if only to allow for Socialist legislation to reach its full fruition', and his Conservative successors became identified with the polities of the post-war consensus. Adjustment and adaptation were recurring themes of Conservative statecraft (Ramsden 1995).

The 1950s were a golden age for the party, in electoral terms at least. It won three successive general elections, in 1951, 1955, and 1959, on each occasion with increased majorities. It accepted virtually all of Labour's 1945–50 programme of nationalization, the NHS, the welfare state, and conciliation of the trade unions. After 1951 Conservative ministers, particularly Macmillan, grew increasingly concerned over the stop–go economic policy and the evidence that Britain was falling behind her European neighbours economically. As part of the great reappraisal of policy in 1961 the UK applied to enter the EEC and moved towards indicative economic planning and incomes policy in a search of greater growth.

Powellism

Not all Conservatives agreed with this approach. Enoch Powell attempted to restate a more free-market version of Conservatism in the 1960s. Powell had been a junior minister in the Treasury until he resigned in 1958, along with Peter Thorneycroft, the Chancellor, over the Macmillan Cabinet's refusal to accept the total public-spending cuts recommended by the Treasury. He entered the Cabinet as Minister for Health in 1961 but then refused to serve under Sir Alec Douglas-Home in 1963. With the party in opposition from 1964, he expounded a free-market, *laissez-faire* approach to the economy. His criticisms of incomes policy, economic planning, regional policy and high levels of public spending, and advocacy of flexible exchange rates and the importance of controlling the money supply, were aimed not only at the Labour Government but also at previous Conservative governments.

Enoch Powell is perhaps the only post-war British politician of whom it is possible to write a serious study of his or her political thought. He has always been concerned to derive his position on issues from fundamentals and addressed such topics as the purpose of political activity, the relationships between the individual, the community, and the state, and the nature of freedom (Schoen 1977; Shepherd 1996). He dismissed economic planning on the practical and ethical grounds that it was impossible to predict economic behaviour with sufficient accuracy, and, anyway, enforcing such a plan was incompatible with a free society. The free market is, according to Powell, essential for a free society, for distributing power as widely as possible; it is 'the subtlest and most efficient system mankind has yet devised for setting effort and resources to their best economic use' (cited in Wood 1965: 15). He also advocated targeting social benefits to the most needy.

Many of these views were expressed in bold, even startling language; when he spoke, politicians and commentators took note. Prices and incomes policy was dismissed as 'A nonsense, a silly nonsense, a transparent nonsense. What is more and worse, it is dangerous nonsense.' As a junior minister in 1958 he was already explaining inflation in terms of the rapid growth of government spending and the money supply. These sentiments gained a better hearing and influenced some of the policies adopted by the party in opposition after 1966. But Powell, the spokesman for the market economy, was soon overtaken by Powell the British nationalist, the opponent of immigration and of UK membership of the EC. His famous 'rivers-of-blood' speech about the dangers of coloured immigration in 1968 made him for a time a formidable rival to the party leader, Edward Heath.

Mr Heath dismissed Powell from the Shadow Cabinet after the 1968 speech, and the latter became a regular critic of the 1970 Heath Government, particularly for its statutory prices and incomes policy and membership of the EC. Powell resigned his seat when Parliament was dissolved in January 1974 but was re-elected the following October as an Ulster Unionist. Ironically, as a growing number of Conservatives (not least Margaret Thatcher and Sir Keith Joseph) came round to accepting many of his economic ideas, Powell had already broken with the party. Both Thatcher and Joseph (Ramsden 1996: 184) subsequentaly paid tribute to his path-breaking role.

Powell occasionally claimed to be no more than an echo of pop-ular feelings on issues such as immigration and the EC; the people were deprived, he asserted, of a choice because of the front-bench agreement on these issues. He also claimed, first on immigration and then on the issue of Ulster's relationship to Ireland, that a minor-ity—in the civil service and in the media—were manipulating the majority. The minority so controlled the means of communication 'that the majority are reduced to a condition in which they finally mistrust their senses and their own reason and surrender their will to the manipulator' (cited in Wood 1970: 108).

Impact of Heath

There is still a good deal of controversy, not to say bitterness, about the record of the Heath Government between 1970 and 1974. At the outset, the policies appeared to mark a clear break with his Conservative predecessors. Reducing state intervention in the econ-omy, cutting public expenditure and direct taxation, adopting greater selectivity in welfare, and creating a legal framework for industrial relations were all seen as breaches with the post-war approach. A number of commentators regarded them as a neo-liberal challenge to the post-war collectivist consensus (Campbell 1993). Joining the EC also marked a break with the Atlantic–Commonwealth outlook that had previously been so strong in the leaderships of both parties.

Within two years, however, the Heath Government had per-formed two spectacular U-turns, adopting an elaborate statutory prices and incomes policy and assuming power to intervene in indus-try—both policies were clear breaks with the manifesto on which the party had been elected in 1970. The result was a big increase in pub-lic spending and public borrowing, growth of state power at the cost of the free market undermined by changing international conditions, abandonment of the Bretton Woods system of fixed exchange rates, and the economic power of Arab oil producers. Apologists claim that these policies were pragmatic responses to rising unemployment and inflation, illustrations of Conservative adaptability and concern to achieve social order. What few realized at the time was that the post-war settlement of full employment and social partnership between government and the major interests was coming to an end. Middlemas describes the Heath Government as 'the last legal signatory of the 1944 pact' (1990: 390).

Views of the Heath record have been important in colouring assessments of Mrs Thatcher. It was during the Heath administration that the Conservatives lost, temporarily at least, their reputation as the party of competent government. The bitter industrial conflicts, resulting in 1970, 1971, and 1972 in the highest number of days lost in strikes since the 1926 General Strike, gathering inflation, the three-day week, and crisis general-election calls because of the miners' strike, all suggested a government under siege. By seeking so eagerly the cooperation of the Trades Union Congress (TUC) for an incomes policy, ministers were in danger, according to Tory critics, of compromising the authority of government. When the government fell in 1974, it was presiding over record post-war levels of public ownership, government intervention in the economy, public spending as a share of GDP, inflation, and the most far-reaching peacetime statutory controls on prices and incomes (Kavanagh 1996).

Both Heath and Thatcher were 'tough-minded' rather than 'tender minded', were impatient with the status quo and favoured a more radical free-market approach to the economy. Although many of the initial policies in 1970 anticipated those of the Conservative Party in 1979, there were also important differences between the two leaders. Mrs Thatcher justified many of the policies on the grounds that they promoted economic freedom, as well as prosperity. For Heath they were instrumental in assisting economic growth, in getting the country 'moving'. Mrs Thatcher also had a more deep-rooted dislike of an economically interventionist state—though not, of course, of the state as such (Chapter 1). Heath was a technocrat who thought that appropriate measures of government intervention could actually encourage individual enterprise to flourish. Mrs Thatcher objected to the level of taxation, whereas he was more concerned to change the balance between direct and indirect taxes. Mrs

Thatcher was not much interested in changing political institutions, whereas Heath believed strongly in institutional and structural reform as a way of improving performance (witness his creation in 1970 of the CPRS and super-departments in Whitehall).

Mrs Thatcher was clearly different. Although she had admirers and some Conservative free-marketeers viewed her as a potential spokeswoman for their cause, her election as party leader in February 1975 was hardly the expression of an ideological upsurge in the party. There was a vacuum in terms of both candidates (because none of the obvious contenders would stand against Heath on the first ballot) and policies. It was Sir Keith Joseph's speeches in late 1974, which called for a major shift of direction in economic policy, and then his support for Mrs Thatcher, which lent an ideological tinge to her challenge. Ironically, Sir Keith and she had been big spenders in the Heath Government at Health and Education respectively. But it needs emphasizing that the Thatcherite ideology came later, in spite of a school of Conservative historians and commentators who argue otherwise. Apart from a handful of MPs (Enoch Powell, John Biffen, Jock Bruce-Gardyne, and Sir Keith) and a few academics and commentators, there was little support for monetarism. Indeed, Mrs Thatcher may have won the leadership in spite of what her ideas were taken to be. Many voted for her largely because they wanted a change from Heath, under whom they thought they could not win another election, and some were critical of the policy reversals. They were joined by disappointed place-seekers—those who had not received honours they thought they deserved and those who had not received expected courtesies. Heath was niggardly with honours and many backbenchers felt that his manner of dealing with them bordered on rudeness.

Over time Mrs Thatcher increasingly distanced herself from previous Conservative governments. At first she was willing to express some sympathy for Heath's problems in government. However, as he attacked her policies, and 'wet' Cabinet ministers in her first government resisted the economic policies, so she counter-attacked. Her supporters were even more outspoken in dismissing him. For a brief time she bestowed her approval on the Macmillan Government (1957–63) and on the government of 'Winston'

(1951–5). But she knew that what she was doing was different from her predecessors. She regarded the problems which she faced— namely, high spending, high taxes, inflation, trade-union power, over-regulated industry, and an anti-enterprise culture—as the product of previous post-war governments, both Labour and Conservative. Their policies had helped bring about national decline.

There is an almost sociological explanation for her early rejection of consensus Conservatism. As early as 1975 she complained in a speech in New York that the 'bourgeois guilt' of her predecessors had prevented them from adopting the necessary tough measure. Haunted by the poverty and mass unemployment of the 1930s, and appreciative of the sacrifices which people made during the war, such leaders had allowed their upper-class 'guilt' to encourage them to debase the currency, appease trade-union power, expand state welfare, and avoid hard decisions. Consensus produced weak leadership and the lowest common denominator in policy. Unlike Eden, Macmillan, Butler, and even Heath (as well as Whitelaw, Carrington, Soames, Pym, Gilmour, and Prior in her 1979 Cabinet), she had no such guilt. The spirit of 1945 seemed not to have penetrated the corner shop in Grantham.

The social aspect may be significant. The Conservative Party in the twentieth century has been part of the British Establishment. Britain's dominant social, cultural, and economic institutions were tied, via personal links, social and educational background, and shared assumptions, to the party. The national press, the BBC, Oxbridge, the House of Lords, the senior civil service, the judiciary, and the Church of England have shared the Conservative disposition for much of the century. And leaders of the party were often drawn from this background. As has been well documented by Guttsman (1963), Blondel (1992), and others, Conservative front-benchers were usually drawn from the upper middle class and had been educated at prestigious public schools and universities.

As a Conservative leader, Mrs Thatcher—daughter of a grocer, a Methodist, a local grammar-school girl, a chemist, a first-generation member of a profession—was, if not quite an upstart, at least distinctive. She and Heath represented a more meritocratic strand. Previous leaders (Churchill, Eden, Macmillan, Home) were usually socialized among the élite for a long period before becoming leaders. Even Heath, for all his modest family origins, had been a member of the leadership for a decade before he became leader in 1965 in the party's first competitive election, and had been Chief Whip at the time of Macmillan's emergence as Prime Minister in 1957. He might well have 'emerged' as leader under the old consultative procedures. Mrs Thatcher's Cabinet experience was limited to the relatively minor department of Education. She had not been part of the inner circle before 1975, and was not indebted to it. She owed her election to her courage in standing (more fancied contenders refused to challenge Heath) and a backbench rejection of Heath (she had very little front-bench support). She was an intruder.

As leader of the party in opposition, Mrs Thatcher was cautious. Her senior colleagues had served under Mr Heath and most showed no signs of repenting of their role in his government. They included Whitelaw, Carrington, Hailsham, Prior, Maudling, and Gilmour. The only obvious supporters of her views were Sir Keith, John Biffen, and Airey Neave. The official party strategy statement, *The Right Approach* (1976), was moderate and gained the support of Mr Heath. Rather than campaigning to repeal Labour measures, some senior Conservatives turned to constitutional reform as a means of protecting Conservative values and curbing the 'dictatorship' exercised by a government elected on only 38 per cent of the vote. Lord Hailsham argued for a written constitution, and a number of MPs, including Sir Ian Gilmour, Chris Patten, and William Waldegrave, supported proportional representation and a Bill of Rights. Mrs Thatcher, however, showed no interest in either, and experience of the Lib.–Lab. pact in 1977, when the Liberals had stepped in to provide Labour with a majority in the Commons, confirmed her fears.

Mrs Thatcher's fierce denunciations of high taxation, trade-union power, inflation, and defence of freedom of choice made her a radical figure. She dismissed woolly talk of consensus politics. Much of the wisdom that allegedly inheres in many of the established institutions and practices were part of what she had regarded as the 'flabby' consensus that had dragged the country down. She did not approach the senior civil service, local government, universities, the BBC, the Church of England, the legal and medical professions, and public corporations with the reverence—or at least respect—with which Burke recommended that we regard established institutions and traditions. In the past these institutions had been supported by Conservatives because they provided checks on the power of the state and independent sources of decision-making. Centralized government was identified with Socialism. But under Mrs Thatcher these institutions, particularly the cultural bloc of universities, churches, and the BBC, came to be regarded as bastions of the left liberalism which she had vanquished in the party political arena.

The Impact of Sir Keith Joseph

The most eloquent critic of the consensus and advocate of what became Thatcherism was Sir Keith Joseph. His break with the Conservatism of Heath was significant, because he had been a prominent member of that government and had presided over a big increase in expenditure at the Department of Health and Social Security. He tried to disarm critics of his change of mind by his willing admission that he had learned from his mistakes and now invited others to join him. He created the Centre for Policy Studies (CPS) in 1974 to support his thinking. His speeches attracted funds for the new body and those who were disillusioned with the Heath record. His speech in Preston on 4 September 1974, on the eve of the second 1974 general election, came as a bombshell to the party and the public. It followed his failure in extensive Shadow Cabinet discussions to persuade colleagues to change course in fighting inflation and the refusal of Mr Heath to make him Shadow Chancellor of the Exchequer. The speech repudiated the role of incomes policy (on which the Conservative Party had fought the previous general election and which it still officially supported) and criticized increasing demand to offset unemployment. It also called for more stringent control of the money supply and claimed that, unless this was done, there was no effective way of controlling inflation. Colleagues complained that it was easy to read the speech as 'Joseph calls for more unemployment to reduce inflation'. In a series of subsequent speeches Sir Keith spelt out the case for a social-market economy and monetarism. But monetarism was not enough: there was a need also to cut public spending and the size of the public sector, and to introduce supply-side reforms. In his Preston speech, he said: 'The monetarist thesis has been caricatured as implying that if we get the flow of money spending right, everything will be right. That is not—repeat not—my belief. What I believe is that if we get the money supply wrong—too high or too low—nothing else will come right.'

Sir Keith's views gained added significance when Mrs Thatcher as leader gave him responsibility for supervising the party's research and policy development. In his speeches during 1974 and 1975 one finds the nearest statement to a 'New Right' credo, or what became Thatcherism. Government was granted a role primarily to create and uphold a framework of law and essential services which would permit people to make the maximum number of decisions for themselves. He claimed that not all unemployment is involuntary and that the official unemployment statistics actually exaggerated the number of those genuinely seeking work. The workshy, the unemployable, those engaged in the black economy but registered as out of work, and those in transition between jobs had to be distinguished from those genuinely seeking employment. The trouble was, Sir Keith insisted, that so often government based its management of demand on the 'unadjusted' unemployment figures. Although Keynes was often invoked in defence of these policies, Joesph said that Keynes had been less concerned about expanding demand *per se* than about getting a better distribution between demand and supply. Boosting demand was no answer to fictional and other sorts of unemployment, which were not due to deficient demand; it provided only temporary palliative and led to increased inflation. The reliance of governments on wage and price controls did not control inflation but did distort the natural working of a market economy.

Sir Keith also attacked the so-called 'middle way' of collectivism, which had resulted in extensive state regulation, high taxation, high levels of public spending, borrowing and subsidies, and Keynesian demand-management. An excess of socialism (usually equated with the pursuit of more equality, nationalization, and state intervention) was draining the productive, wealth-creating private sector. He urged a return to a policy of 'continence and smaller deficits'. The middle way had been pursued because politicians believed that most voters favoured it and that it provided for policy continuity and consensus. But, according to Sir Keith, the middle ground was an illusion and not a mid-point between Labour and Conservative positions. Often a Conservative government, in the interests of policy stability, accepted Labour policies which it had earlier opposed (for example, public ownership, high levels of public spending, or mandatory comprehensive education). As Labour moved to new left ground, however, so the mid-point moved with it, the so-called ratchet effect. Joseph urged his party to find the common ground, one supported by most voters, which was, he was convinced, nearer to Conservative than to Labour. His party had too often compromised too much with socialism and misread the electoral mood.

During these years Sir Keith Joseph was clearly hungry for ideas, eagerly studying economics textbooks and other works, and picking the brains of academics, think-tanks, and commentators. The ideas were not original to him but borrowed from Samuel Brittan, Alan Walters, Friedman, Peter Jay, Alfred Sherman, and others. He was a popularist. He explained his new thinking to the journalist William Keegan: 'I understood from the Alan Walters and Peter Bauers of this world that deficit financing and borrowing are one of the main causes of our troubles' (Keegan 1984: 46). This was wedded to the enthusiasm of the convert of the born-again Conservative. In a remarkable statement, he claimed that he became a Conservative only in 1974: 'But it was only in April 1974 that I was converted to Conservatism. I had thought that I was a Conservative, but I now see that I was not really one at all' (Joseph 1975: 4).

The acceptability of the Conservative policies was considerably eased by factors outside the party's control. There was some reaction, not least among Labour ministers, to the steep increases in taxation and the public spending between 1974 and 1976. Concern mounted over inflation, which exceeded 25 per cent on an annual basis in June 1975, and over the growth of public spending. In 1975 Mr Healey no longer budgeted for full employment, a major breach with the post-war consensus. Another influence was the sudden collapse of sterling in 1976—at one point it fell as low as £1 being worth $1.52—and then the IMF rescue package. From late 1976 a set of new policy instruments was imposed, including tighter controls on public spending. Mr Callaghan reacted to the concern over educational standards by launching a 'debate' on the issue. In voicing concern about the family and mooting the feasibility of appointing a minister for the family he was trying to steal some Conservative clothes.

Had Mr Callaghan called a general election, as he was expected to in autumn 1978, Labour's prospects would have been immeasurably better than was to be the case in 1979. Mrs Thatcher had not yet convinced the Shadow Cabinet of the feasibility of incomes policies or the need for radical trade-union reform. She was not satisfied with the draft party manifesto for an October 1978 manifesto (Thatcher 1995: 421, 435). Subsequent events helped the Conservative Party and her.

Conservatives were divided over the devolution proposals for Scotland and Wales, just as Labour was. A majority in the party was opposed to the government's proposals, but, when the referendums failed to carry the proposals by a sufficient majority in March 1979, devolution died as an issue. The Conservatives were also in a difficult position over the government's incomes policy, which was widely credited with reducing the rate of inflation during 1977 and 1978. But during the Winter of Discontent the government's 5 per cent target for increase in incomes clearly collapsed and Labour's claims that it alone could work with the unions and that a Conservative government would produce confrontation were shown to be hollow. Amid the unruly picketing and well-publicized suffering of the public during January and February 1979, many union members were contemptuous of agreements and spurned the instructions of their leaders and the exhortations of Labour ministers.

The Conservative manifesto of 1979 listed its proposals under five main headings. These were:

1. the control of inflation and trade-union power;
2. the restoration of incentives;

3. upholding Parliament and the rule of law;
4. supporting family life by a more efficient provision of welfare services;
5. strengthening defence.

The main proposals for controlling inflation included the strict control of the money supply and a reduction of both the government borrowing requirement and of the state's share of national income. A Conservative government would also try to sell off the recently nationalized aerospace, shipbuilding, and National Freight operations. On trade unions the party proposed three changes 'which must be made at once'. First, it would amend the law to limit the right of secondary picketing. Secondly, it would provide compensation for workers who had lost their jobs as a result of closed shop and also allow a right of appeal to the courts against exclusion or expulsion from any union. Finally, public money would be provided to finance postal votes of union elections and pre-strike ballots, and unions would be required to contribute to the support of strikers. On taxation, the party promised to cut both the top rate of income tax to the European average of 60 per cent and the bottom rate of tax in order to take the low paid out of the tax net. There would, in addition, be a switch from direct to indirect taxation.

The 1979 Election

The outcome of the 1979 general election was clearly a repudiation of Labour, another stage in the long-term decline of the party. The Conservatives won a decisive victory against a Labour government, which never recovered fully from the damage to its authority and popularity inflicted by the winter's industrial disruption. The Conservatives had a majority of seventy seats over Labour and one of forty-three seats over all the other parties combined. Commentators at the time saw the election as a turning-point. Given Labour's impressive electoral recovery during 1978, it was possible to argue that 1979 had seen a short-term swing towards the Conservative Party, largely as a reaction against the Winter of Discontent. Labour was still marginally ahead of the Conservative

Party when voters were asked to identify with a political party, and the Conservatives were not decisively preferred as the best party to handle issues of prices, unemployment, and trade unions. They were, however, clearly favoured by vote switchers on issues such as taxation and law and order. There was also a big swing to the Conservatives among trade unionists and the skilled working class, who were particularly attracted by the proposals to reduce taxation. Between 1964 and 1979 public opinion shifted to the ideological right and there was a growing correspondence between the views of Conservative supporters and official party policy. The opposite was the case for the Labour Party.

The Conservatives had won the election, in spite of being led by a right-of-centre leader. Few commentators or colleagues thought that she would prove to be as radical in government as she promised. Expressing the view that the area of choice was limited, the Conservative commentator Peregrine Worsthorne wrote in the *Sunday Telegraph* on 29 April 1979: 'Whatever happens in the election is not going to make much difference. There will be neither revolution nor counter-revolution . . .', and any change will be measured 'in inches not miles'. Sceptics could also note how preceding administrations had been overcome by obstacles and economic failures. But they might also have noted how Macmillan and Heath had each as Prime Minister managed to get the party to accept some remarkable leader-initiated switches of policy.

5 The Consensus Attacked

In much political-science literature there is a divorce between studies of concepts and theories and studies of processes and policy-making. In Britain in the 1970s, however, this was less true as political ideas were often explicitly connected to policy. Much established thinking about policy, on the party front benches and in Whitehall, was confronted from two wings. Supporters of economic liberalism argued for a reduced role for government and greater scope for markets, and had specific policy proposals to achieve these goals. The left called for a greater role for the state over the economy and more social and economic equality. The former won the argument. This chapter examines the free-market ideas, the role of the opinion-formers and think-tanks, and how the ideas were spread. First, however, we discuss how ideas shape policies.

Political Ideas and Practice

Keynes's well-known claim that practical men are often the slaves of some defunct economist is often quoted by proponents of the primacy of ideas. In contrast, Karl Marx regarded ideas and values as part of the superstructure, which in turn derived from economic interests; the dominant ideas of any epoch were, for Marx, the ideas of the ruling class. At the turn of the century a number of élitists such as Pareto, Michels, and Mosca, as well as a burgeoning school of psychologists, also argued that ideas and beliefs were often covers or rationalizations for interests. No doubt it is an oversimplification to see ideas and circumstances, or even ideas and interests, as always distinct and opposed. John Stuart Mill was correct when he wrote that ideas must conspire with circumstances if they are to be successful; the latter include the availability of administrative capacity, economic resources, political support, and a widespread sense that other ideas have been tried and failed or, for various reasons, have not been found to be politically or administratively practicable. Interests do shape ideas, and ideologies mobilize support, legitimize demands, undermine opponents, promote solidarity, and so on. But ideas may also promote interests or be only tenuously connected to them.

Many analyses of the emergence of new policies, although emphasizing the interaction of circumstances and ideas, have accorded priority to the former. Paul Smith's study of the social reforms of Disraeli's government between 1874 and 1880, for example, downgraded the importance of the young Disraeli's ideas. Smith (1967: 12) saw the reforms as the outcome of *ad hoc* and piecemeal decisions, 'an array of personal, departmental and technical considerations'. A more celebrated case of the alleged influence of ideas on legislation was that of the late-nineteenth-century Fabians, in particular the Webbs. The Webbs promoted their ideas by permeating the established Conservative and Liberal parties, and it was only when this approach failed that they turned to the infant Labour Party. Like latter-day think-tanks, they emphasized the importance of supporting their ideas with empirical research, demonstrating their feasibility, and then persuading politicians. They were action-oriented, campaigning and producing pamphlets on the main issue of the day. Yet an authoritative history of the Fabian Society has found that other forces were, on balance, more important as an influence on Liberal and Labour policies (McBriar 1962). A major study of the international diffusion of Keynesian ideas points to his influence on the conceptional apparatus of the economic discipline, but to the unevenness of the impact of his specific proposals. It concludes: 'One of the most striking findings of this study is the degree to which Keynes's ideas about demand management were resisted or ignored in many nations' (P. Hall 1989: 367). Memoirs of retired politicians and decision-makers usually downplay the impact of ideologies in comparison to the importance of events and pressures to take decisions to meet deadlines.

Sources

By repute, British politicians and civil servants are pragmatists, more interested in the practical than the theoretical aspects of policy, in

ideas which can be turned into 'doable' policies. If they were intellectuals, they would probably not be in politics. If Marxism has not
been strong in the Labour Party neither has 'theory' been significant
in the Conservative Party. But politicians are also interested in ideas
which suggest an attractive line of policy or which justify policies
they are associated with. They live in a public realm and need suggestions for policies, as well as themes and phrases to explain and
justify courses of action to an audience, be it colleagues, the media,
interest groups, or public opinion. As a rule, politicians often come
to the ideas second- or third-hand and may turn to groups or individuals who play a role as 'brokers' or mediators between the worlds
of ideas and political practice. According to Anthony King (1992:
43–4), they are 'typically pickers-up of other people's ideas', from
conversations, magazines, newspapers, broadcasts, seminars, and visits abroad.

Certain features of British public life help the diffusion of new
ideas among policy-makers. One is the small number of relevant
influential people—about 100 politicians and a similar number of
officials who are regularly in contact with ministers. This rather
small and pretty homogeneous group operates in a closely knit world
of inter-locking networks and institutions, centred in London SW1.
Politicians, according to Willson, 'are not—cannot be—reflective
moulders of ideas; they are the recipients, the collators, the compro-
misers among a mass of persuasive influences and persistent people.
They do not—and have not time to—think' (1969: 367). The small
size of the policy community means that an idea can make rapid
progress once it has entered.

Ideas come in different forms. They may be political and social
theories (for example, about social justice, equality, or political
order), or a political ideology (for example, about socialism, liberalism, or fascism). A second usage is as a climate of opinion. For
A. V. Dicey (1905), legislation in nineteenth-century Britain was
influenced at first by individualist, then by collectivist, ideas about
the role of the state (what he calls 'legislative opinion'). A third usage
is of ideas as rationalizations of behaviour. Indeed, some would argue
that much political behaviour is based on interests, with ideas often
being little more than rationalizations. In the memorable words of a

Labour Cabinet minister, 'Socialism is what a Labour government does.' Finally, ideas may be reflected in proposals for specific policies—the sale of council houses to tenants, school vouchers, a minimum wage, or pre-strike ballots.

Policy suggestions come from various sources—pressure groups, the parties' annual conferences, researchers, senior civil servants, policy-brokers, and experts from research bodies, universities, and other learned groups. One should not, however, exaggerate the amount of innovation that takes place within the formal policy process. A majority of former Cabinet ministers interviewed by Bruce Headey in the 1970s saw themselves as legitimators of an existing policy rather than as innovators. Much policy-making is rather routine, concerned with carrying out existing policies and making marginal adjustments according to changing circumstances—for example, establishing a new level of welfare benefit, altering the range of beneficiaries, changing the criteria of eligibility, and so on. Headey added: 'A principal reason for this state of affairs is that there are few sources of well informed advice outside Whitehall to which they can turn' (1974: 187). There is an opportunity, therefore, for innovative recommendations which are (*a*) politically acceptable and (*b*) administratively practicable.

Some observers argue that political parties in opposition are poorly prepared for office and that they spend too much time reacting to what the government of the day is actually doing. The research departments of the parties are not well staffed or financed and in recent years have concentrated more on campaign communications than preparing policies. Opposition leaders usually have little or no contact with senior civil servants or interest groups and may often lack an awareness of the administrative practicability of the particular policies that they are developing. But this freedom also gives them the opportunity to be radical.

Senior civil servants are confidential advisers to ministers and have a special responsibility for presenting policy options and advising on them. Although they are their own experts on many subjects, even they turn to leaders of relevant interest groups to seek advice about likely reactions to a policy and its implementation. It has often been noted that British administrators are not encouraged to be inno-

vative and indeed may act as a brake on radical change. A consequence of being permanent and anonymous is that the official has
probably had little to gain or to lose from commitment to particular
policies. Outsiders have been brought into the service, notably during wartime, and on a modest scale in departments as ministerial
advisers since 1964.

An important source of new thinking is from policy-brokers
who operate in the margins between politics and academe.
Individuals such as Beveridge or Rowntree were able to point to
weaknesses in existing policy and pave the way for reforms. Banting
describes these as 'middle men who are drawing upon a broader
stream of research theory and opinion developing in the academic
and professional communities' (1979: 5) In an echo of Finer's model
(see p. 142), today's cycle of politico–academic influence often starts
with the findings of scholarly research being reported to fellow
experts via journal and conference papers; the ideas gradually find
their way to a wider audience through the quality magazines and
newspapers and then they percolate through Parliament and the civil
service. Such work is important in promoting an awareness of a
problem, defining key issues, and specifying policy alternatives. A
well-known example of research changing the perceptions of policy-
makers in the areas of poverty and inequality was that of the so-
called 'Titmuss School' at the London School of Economics. The
research of Professor Richard Titmuss and colleagues such as
Michael Young, Peter Townsend, and Brian Abel-Smith demonstrated the failures of many existing welfare programmes to eradicate
poverty and argued that more radical egalitarian measures were
required. Banting notes: 'Their research was explicitly political: its
aim was to reshape policy-makers' interpretations of their environment' (1975: 70). Many new programmes followed in the 1960s and
1970s, including the educational priority areas, urban programmes,
housing action areas, and community action programmes. Similarly,
much research in education in the 1950s and 1960s cast doubt on the
notion that there was a fixed pool of ability which could profit from
academic secondary education. This in turn paved the way for the
adoption of comprehensive secondary education.

Not all academic disciplines are equally useful to the policy-maker (Rose 1976). To be useful a discipline requires at least (*a*) a scholarly consensus on its findings—although this very agreement may foreclose policy opinions—and (*b*) a set of politically and administratively feasible instruments or methods for transforming the knowledge into 'doable' policies. Economics has been one subject area on which policy-makers have drawn, since it has been assumed (although this is contestable) to possess the above features. Theologians, philosophers, or sociologists, *qua* practitioners of their subjects, have not been in high demand.

New Right

That free-market ideas gained a more sympathetic hearing among Conservatives in the 1970s was in part born of a reaction to the Heath Government's U-turns towards interventionist economic policies in 1972, to the obvious failure of those policies, and to two election defeats in 1974. The ideas were nourished largely outside the official Conservative Party machine (in large part because of its continuing Butskellite outlook) and the Conservative Research Department and reinforced by the failures (economic and electoral) of the subsequent Labour governments under Wilson and Callaghan. The result was that, according to a historian of the Conservative Party, Mrs Thatcher's task in 1979 was greatly assisted by 'the backing of an intellectual revolution; something which Mr Heath did not have' (Blake 1985: 310).

Two of the seminal thinkers in this revival of so-called New Right ideas, and who influenced Sir Keith Joseph, were Friedrich von Hayek and Milton Friedman. In his essay on 'Intellectuals and Socialism' (1949), Hayek had stressed the importance of ideas and of the role of authors, academics, journalists, and teachers in shaping the climate of opinion. He could point to the Webbs, Booth, Rowntree, Tawney, Burt, Keynes, Bowlby, and Titmuss, all of whom had combined empirical research with a commitment to influence debates on policy. To an increasing extent their latter-day equivalents are found in universities, research institutes, mass media, and think-tanks. The New Right think-tanks and lobbies sought to change the prevailing climate of opinion in Britain, in particular to overturn the dominant collectivist ideas and promote more market-orientated policies. They include such groups as the Institute of Economic Affairs (IEA), the Centre for Policy Studies (CPS), the Adam Smith Institute (ASI), the Social Affairs Unit (SAU), and the Social Market Foundation (SMF). Many of the groups turned to their counterparts in the USA for ideas and tactics. The IEA, for example, promoted the monetarist and free-market ideas of Friedman, the writings of Hayek, and the public-choice approach of the Virginia School of economists. Proposals for internal markets in health and vouchers in education, concern about an emerging 'under class', and debate about a culture of dependency were all largely imported from the US policy influentials. There is no major British writer—no equivalent of Keynes—who has emerged to inspire this New Right thinking. British figures are prominent in any Conservative pantheon, but not in this more policy-orientated, New Right collection.

Proposing a radical break with the status quo in many policy areas was a most un-Conservative stance. But because the party was in search of new policies and with Mrs Thatcher and Sir Keith Joseph in key positions in the party and willing to look outside the Research Department, the groups were assured of a more sympathetic hearing than hitherto. The publications of the think-tanks, and speeches of politicians such as Margaret Thatcher and Sir Keith Joseph, popularized (in the sense of simplifying and introducing to a wider or non-specialist audience) the ideas of people such as Hayek and Friedman. Accordingly, we start our examination of New Right ideas with these two seminal figures.

Hayek

Hayek's distinguished work across so many disciplines—economics, philosophy, and political theory—stamps him as a genuine polymath. Recognition of his talents as an economist was reflected in the award of a Nobel Prize for Economics in 1974. Yet he has so far been more influential in the world of affairs than academe, partly because his warnings appear to have been largely vindicated by the failures in the 1970s of Keynesian policies and central economic planning.

There is a remarkable continuity in his work dating back to his early training in Austrian economics (which emphasized the need for competition and choice because of the limits of our knowledge). He achieved some fame and notoriety with his critique of collectivism and planning in his *Road to Serfdom* (1944). Many of these ideas were developed later in *The Constitution of Liberty* (1960) and the three volumes of *Law, Legislation and Liberty* (1973, 1976, 1979). He was also a founder of the Mont Pelerin Society in 1947, an international forum for neo-liberal intellectuals which still meets regularly. It has included many luminaries of the New Right, including James Buchanan and Gordon Tulloch, as well as the Chicago economists Friedman and George Stigler.

Hayek's work can be organized around four main themes, all of which have been emphasized by the New Right. The first, most fully explicated in *The Road to Serfdom*, is that *central planning is mistaken*. He objects to a central plan rather than modest planning, arguing that it is both politically dangerous and economically inefficient. In practice, centralized economic planning by government reduces individual and group liberties, upsets the balance between political institutions (by giving too much power to the executive), weakens the role of Parliament, and undermines the rule of law by granting so much discretion to authorities. It invariably leads also to pressures for yet more controls as the 'logic' of intervention feeds on itself. It suppresses competition and leaves control in the hands of what are usually monopolies. Planners seek more control and predictability, whereas progress comes from experiments and voluntarism; the virtue of the market is that, by harnessing this knowledge, it increases the opportunities for creativity and innovation. These themes were pursued in Hayek's later writings, although his more specific targets were government controls of prices and incomes and policies of redistribution and welfare.

A second theme in Hayek's work concerns the *complexity of society*. He claims that there is a spontaneous natural order, which is the outcome not of a plan or of design but of human behaviour. Traditional institutions and patterns of behaviour have evolved into rules of conduct and a coherence emerges from these interactions. In *The Constitution of Liberty* Hayek writes like a classic conservative of the need for submission to undesigned rules and conventions, whose significance and importance we largely do not understand: he adds that, because we cannot know about more than a tiny part of society, we should be wary of intervening or trying to alter these relationships. This view is part of his scepticism about social engineering and awareness of the limits of social science, particularly the study of economics. He dismisses the belief that state intervention can improve a situation as a 'fatal conceit'.

A third theme in Hayek's work is the importance attached to *markets and prices for the allocation of resources* and registering preferences. The spontaneous interaction of buyers and sellers is more efficient than the activity of planners. He attacks trade unions, which in Britain had managed to force an increase in money supply above the growth of production, and so add to inflation. The structures and practices of trade unions prevent the efficient making of the labour market and slow down the response of the levels of wages and employment to changing market conditions.

Finally, the role of government is given an important but limited place in setting *the framework for social and economic activity and upholding the rule of law.* By the latter, Hayek means the existence of general rules which prohibit arbitrary behaviour. The government's task is not to promote social justice (which he regards as a vague, even arbitrary idea) nor to compensate for the working of the market. He is also critical of majoritarian democracy; too often this is a perversion of constitutionalism, as when a course of action is justified only on the grounds that it is backed by a majority: the point is that the amount of popular support is irrelevant if the action is arbitrary. He praises such principles as the separation of powers and the supremacy of the constitution and argues for prior political and constitutional reforms to ensure the smooth working of the market economy and the rule of law.

Hayek is often coupled, misleadingly, with Friedman as an intellectual godfather of New Right economics. Although both are from the classical-liberal tradition, there are important differences between the work of the two men. Hayek claimed that he was not a

Conservative—who, he believes, distrusts the market, presides over the status quo (even when it is collectivist) and may be authoritarian. Conservatism may succeed by its resistance to current tendencies in slowing down undesirable development, but, since it does not indicate another direction, it cannot prevent their continuance. It is easy to see how Hayek has been regarded as an arch-opponent of socialism and Keynesian ideas, even though *Serfdom* was written against 'the socialists in all parties'. But that book also attracted controversy because it challenged the belief, prevalent among parties of the moderate right and left, in a so-called middle way which combined freedom and planning. For Hayek there should be no compromise between what he termed the commercial and the military types of society.

Mrs Thatcher frequently cited the influence on her of Hayek in conversations and in interviews. An ex-member of the Conservative Research Department recounts a visit that she paid in the summer of 1975, shortly after she became leader. A 'moderate' Conservative was reading a paper but, 'before he had finished . . . the new party leader reached into her brief case and took out a book. It was Hayek's. "And this is the title of the book *The Constitution of Liberty.*" Interrupting she held the book for all of us to see. "This", she said sternly, "is what we believe," and banged Hayek down on the table' (Ranelagh 1991: p. ix).

Friedman

The American economist Milton Friedman has been the most prominent Anglo-American spokesman for monetarism, the market economy, and the counter-attack on Keynesian economics. Though never far from controversy, his academic reputation has been reflected in the award of a Nobel Prize (in 1977) and his election as president of the American Economic Association. Like Keynes, he is a skilled publicist. He had a regular column in the American *Newsweek* magazine and his best-selling *Free to Choose* (co-authored with his wife, Rose) was made into a television series in Britain and the USA.

Friedman has emphasized the importance of the supply of money in causing inflation. Put simply, monetarists claim that, if an increase in the money supply outstrips the growth of GDP, then it will produce inflation. In *A Monetary History of the United States*, he claimed that the main cause of the Great Depression was the rapid decline in the money supply (Friedman and Schwartz 1969). He also believes that there exists an underlying long-term equilibrium between supply and demand, where there are appropriate changes in money supply and exchange rates; there is, therefore, a natural wage level at which people will find work—the natural rate of unemployment. Trade unions may distort this level and push for higher wages but only at the cost of pricing workers out of jobs. In Britain, his natural-rate argument had much less influence on policy than monetary targets.

In principle, monetarist ideas are politically neutral between the left and right; after all, Denis Healey, the Labour Chancellor of the Exchequer, introduced monetary targets in 1976. But, because monetarists talk of a natural level of unemployment and admit that a short-term consequence of slowing down the rate of monetary growth may be an increase in numbers unemployed, they were attacked by the political left and the trade unions, and have been associated with neo-conservatism. Moreover, Friedman has also been an energetic proponent of the market economy. But a monetarist, believing in the monetary causes of inflation, may or may not support the market economy, oppose the trade unions, high taxes, and public spending, be a Thatcherite, and so forth.

Friedman expressed strong views on social as well as economic questions. He promoted such ideas as the negative income tax, by which the poor receive cash directly rather than 'free' services from the state, and education vouchers which people may use to purchase education in schools of their own choice. In his *Capitalism and Freedom* (1962) and later in *Free to Choose* (1980) he placed monetarist ideas firmly in a free-market context. The books present standard New Right themes—the inefficiency of government and the failure of many of its programmes, the benefits of lower taxes, and the need to denationalize and deregulate state industries and services and abolish rent controls, minimum wages, regional and industrial subsidies, and employment legislation. These are all seen as barriers to the efficient working of a market economy. The government's role should be limited to providing law and order, defence, and providing essential services which some groups—children, for example—are unable to provide for themselves. He also claims that there is a causal connection between capitalism and personal freedom, for markets disperse power and decisions whereas the political process concentrates them. Freedom for the individual consists in making choices and an absence of coercion by others. Capitalism, or the voluntary interaction between buyers and sellers of goods and services, permits this economic freedom which, in turn, is essential for political freedom. Not surprisingly, he has also advocated political reforms to limit the range of government, including constitutional limits on levels of taxes and public spending and amendments to require a balanced budget and fixed levels of monetary growth.

The Institute of Economic Affairs

The IEA was founded in 1955 as a 'research and educational trust' to study the role of markets and pricing in allocating resources and registering preferences. Its creation has been credited to Antony Fisher, a businessman, who was persuaded by Hayek that a research body would be the most effective way of countering the tendencies leading to 'serfdom'. It was run by Arthur Seldon and Ralph Harris. The starting point of much of the IEA's work is that the climate of opinion colours the thinking of politicians. Rather than capture a political party or politician, it believed that the case for the free market would be enhanced more effectively by shaping opinion in the educational and academic world. 'They [politicians] are puppets on a string, in the way they respond to fashions', was how the IEA's former Deputy Director, John Wood, expressed it in an interview.

During its forty years the IEA has published over 500 papers and in 1980 started its own monthly journal, *Economic Affairs*. It aims its pamphlets, seminars, and the lunches in its Westminster offices at opinion-formers. Although it often echoes Keynes's claims about the influence of ideas, the principal goal of its publications has been to combat much of Keynes's influence on economic thinking. By 1979 the IEA was firmly established as the intellectual home of free markets, economic liberalism, and monetarism in Britain, and came into its own as the ideas of Keynes, Beveridge, and the Fabians were in retreat. It has also been a prototype for other free-market think-tanks. It published a number of Hayek's essays, including *Agenda for a Free Society* (1961), a symposium on *The Constitution of Liberty* (1960), *A Tiger by the Tail* (1972) on the trade unions, *Full Employment at any Price* (1975), and *Denationalization of Money* (1976). By publishing Hayek's work in the 1970s, the IEA played an important part in reviving interest in his work. The ideas of Friedman needed less institutional publicity because of his own skills in this area, but it published his 1970 Wincott lecture on *The Counter-Revolution in Monetary Theory* (1970), which spread the monetarist case, as well as his *Unemployment versus Inflation* (1975).

The IEA drew on various schools of economic thought to challenge Keynesianism. One is the emphasis on the price mechanism as a means of allocating resources, discovering new ways of providing services, and facilitating comparisons between different products and services and rival providers of goods and services. A second borrows from the Austrian School of micro-economics, associated with Menger and von Mises, which emphasized that economic decisions are made by individuals and that it is marginal adjustments in prices and costs that influence decisions.

A third is the monetarist interpretation of inflation, a view that has influenced politicians more than academics. In the 1970s only a minority of British economists—including Harry Johnson, Alan Walters, and Brian Griffiths at the London School of Economics, David Laidler and Michael Parkin, then at Manchester, and Patrick Minford at Liverpool—challenged Keynes's ascendancy. The IEA's greater interest in the problems of micro- rather than macro-economics also brought the ideas of the public-choice school to a wider British audience. The most prominent exponents of the approach have been Professors Buchanan and Tulloch, formerly of the University of Virginia at Charlottesville, and now of George Mason, USA. Their writings challenged the view that a decision of government, or a collective choice, is the activity of some disinterested group. Politicians and bureaucrats have their own vested interests, just like any pressure group, and budgets and bureaucracies grow in large part because of the ambitions and mutual interests of the people involved—of vote-seeking politicians, selfish interest groups, and expansionist bureaucrats.

This 'economic' theory of the political process, and of how the role of government employment, spending, and taxation grows, was eagerly taken up by the right wing, which wanted to reduce all three and promote the free market. There was no point in curbing the power of the producers, only to increase that of bureaucrats and politicians. The market was more responsive to popular choice than to the political process. Public-choice advocates have been less concerned with specific policy recommendations than with pointing to the negative side effects of government as decision-makers. The IEA has also shown some interest in political reforms and imposing constitutional limits on governments, which would allow a greater scope for free markets.

Much of the IEA's work starts from the belief that tax-financed services by government often conceal the costs of these services, do not respond to consumer choice, and place no constraint on demands for the services. It is also critical of the government monopoly or near monopoly of the provision of many services and the consequent denial of choice. Its pamphlets have advocated such policies as education vouchers, negative income tax, greater use of pricing as well as vouchers in health and education, the sale of council houses, the abolition of exchange controls, an independent university, and the privatization, contracting-out, and deregulation of many government services, particularly in welfare. Where these were achieved, the IEA had often made the case long before. Its very first pamphlet, published in 1957, questioned the state's dominance in the field of pensions. It has also commissioned public opinion surveys which, it claims, show widespread support for its ideas in reforming the welfare state, not least by introducing competition and pricing.

There is no official IEA view. It regards itself primarily as a publishing house, and the published opinions are those of individual authors and in no way commit the IEA. (It is quick to claim that it publishes work by non-monetarists, non-marketeers, and non-

Conservatives.) But there are two recurring themes across the IEA publications. One emphasizes the need to limit the role of government (central and local) in those areas where markets can supply services; government should concentrate on providing essential public goods, such as defence or clean air. The other canvasses the benefits of markets and competitive pricing—'the daily referendum of the market'. Publications have been critical of the state's near-monopoly provision of health and education which, combined with the avoidance of economic pricing, limits the scope for redistribution from the poor and the rich and provision of adequate help for those in the greatest need.

The IEA undoubtedly played an important role in changing the climate of opinion from the mid-1970s onwards and in turn profited from the change in climate. Enoch Powell in the early 1960s and later Sir Geoffrey Howe and Sir Keith Joseph were among the few senior politicians to show an interest in its work. But until the early 1970s it was regarded as eccentric by the political and economic establishments. When the Conservatives were in opposition again after 1974, Sir Keith and Mrs Thatcher were supportive and Sir Keith founded the CPS in 1974, to build on the IEA's work. The ideas gradually gained a wider hearing in the late 1960s and early 1970s, largely through the newspaper columns of people like Samuel (now Sir) Brittan in the *Financial Times*, Peter Jay in *The Times*, and later (now Lord) William Rees Mogg, the paper's editor. Bosanquet warns that the IEA, having begun as David, has become Goliath, and now 'is in danger of becoming an orthodoxy in itself'. Arthur Seldon claimed in an interview in 1984: 'Sceptics would say to us, in defence of the collectivist policies: "Give them time, they'll work in the end." By the mid-1970s they had been saying it for thirty years and could no longer ask for more time.' In challenging fashionable views across so many areas, Seldon explicitly asked his authors not to be limited by 'considerations of current administrative practicability or political acceptability'. So often these are advanced by politicians and interest groups as a smoke screen to preserve the status quo.

More recently the IEA has broadened its interest beyond economics. It has established a health and welfare unit and one on the environment. It has published studies on health reform and how the breakdown of the family might be reversed, and critiques of the government's 1990 health reform, which rejected vouchers for patients. This followed its failure by 1985 to persuade Sir Keith Joseph to introduce school vouchers. By 1989 Seldon and Ralph Harris had stepped aside and the torch passed to Graham Mather, who was appointed Director General in 1987. Mather had previous experience of think-tanks, good contacts with Whitehall, and had been a Conservative parliamentary candidate. He sought to broaden the remit of the institute, encompass constitutional reform, regulation, and the civil service, and address politicians directly. This shift of emphasis caused tensions in the IEA, which anyway were exacerbated by the fall of Mrs Thatcher in 1990, and, under some pressure, Mather resigned in 1992. Under a new Director General, John Blundell, the institute reverted to its former role, while maintaining its interest in constitutional reform and encouraging greater economic liberalization within the European Union (Muller 1996).

The Adam Smith Institute

The ASI was conceived in 1976, and established the following year to develop free-market policies. According to its charter, its task is to further 'the advancement of learning by research and public policy options, economic and political science, and the publications of such research'. Hayek was chairman of its advisory board and it is run by Madsen Pirie and Eamonn Butler, two graduates from St Andrews. A number of other St Andrews graduates who became Conservative MPs, such as Christopher Chope, Michael Forsyth, Robert Jones, and Michael Fallon, have authored papers for the Institute. Both Michael Portillo and John Redwood have also written ASI papers. American influences were also important, particularly the example of the Washington-based right-wing think-tank, the Heritage Foundation. Pirie and Butler have described themselves as 'scholar activists' and 'policy engineers', proposing policies which could translate their ideas into practice (Heffernan 1996: 77).

In contrast to the IEA, the ASI has been more concerned with policy implementation, and its target audience is primarily decision-makers in government, rather than opinion-formers. It was an early advocate of privatization, deregulation, the contracting-out of services from Whitehall and local government, and a reduction of the powers of access to private property enjoyed by public officials. An early interest was in quangos, and it provided an exhaustive listing of budgets and terms of reference and the government's record in abolishing them. *The Omega File* (ASI 1986) contained over 600 free-market proposals for ministers. They included privatization of the nationalized industries, pensions, most local-authority services, and even prisons. It called for private insurance to replace the welfare state and greater use of private health insurance and charges. It wanted parents to be given a greater choice over schools and, via school boards, to determine a school's policy. It advocated the replacement of domestic rates by the poll tax.

The ASI has been skilful at attracting media coverage for its causes (Pirie is a frequent writer and broadcaster) and has claimed to exercise influence in Whitehall. A number of its proposals have been implemented, but this may have been a case of anticipating the policy concerns of ministers (see pp. 153–4 on poll tax) and one sceptic claims that any direct impact 'was at the margin of public policy rather than at the centre' (Heffernan 1996: 82). For example, it published a series of papers to coincide with Mrs Thatcher's working party which reviewed the health service in 1988 and its conclusions were very similar to those of the working party—of which Pirie was a member (see p. 155). The reforms of the civil service and measures adopted in the Citizen's Charter also fit in with much of the ASI's work on market-testing and contracting-out. Pirie was also a member of John Major's Citizen's Charter committee between 1992 and 1996.

The Centre for Policy Studies

The CPS was established by Sir Keith Joseph in August 1974, with the permission of the Conservative leader Edward Heath, shortly after the Conservative Party's defeat in the February election. The original inspiration was Sir Keith's desire to learn from the party's experience of government between 1970 and 1974 and from the successful social-market economies of countries such as Japan and West Germany. Sir Keith became chairman, Margaret Thatcher president, and Alfred Sherman (later Sir) the director. The Conservative Research Department had long reflected the views of R. A. Butler and One-Nation Conservatism, a situation which Sir Keith wished to question. Challenging established views and widening the range of free-market options for a future Conservative government and providing a base for people who held these views was, Sir Keith's backers argued, best done by an organization which had some distance from the party machine.

The political importance of the CPS for internal Conservative politics became apparent in September 1974, when Sir Keith openly broke with the leadership on economic policy. In his famous Preston speech in that month he emphasized the important role of the money supply as well as incomes policy in any attack on inflation (see below). Sir Keith's speech was widely viewed as a bid for the leadership, even though it was Mrs Thatcher who later toppled Mr Heath. As party leader Mrs Thatcher turned to the CPS for support, and for a time it became a rival to the party's Research Department. But when the party was in government, its importance stemmed largely from the work done by CPS-connected people acting in their own capacity and later in advising ministers and Mrs Thatcher. Among its early associates were Alan Walters (later Sir) and John Hoskyns (later Sir), who were to work for Mrs Thatcher at 10 Downing Street, and David (later Lord) Young, who became a Cabinet minister. Hugh Thomas (later Lord Thomas of Swynnerton), who became chairman in 1979, and Alfred Sherman were active in speech-writing for Mrs Thatcher. These were all Conservative outsiders, disillusioned with the direction of the Conservative Party under Heath.

Initially, the CPS's main task was helping to prepare and publish the speeches of Sir Keith Joseph and Margaret Thatcher, presenting evidence to parliamentary and select committees and establishing study groups to examine particular issues. Each group's task was to translate ideas into practical policies and was disbanded when its work was finished. The reports usually favoured market-oriented policies, and its study group on nationalized industries was a pioneering advocate of the privatization of the nationalized British Steel, British Telecom, and British Leyland. Another study group campaigned for sweeping reform of the state pension, and successes included portable pensions, abolishing the Inner London Education Authority (ILEA), and increasing the parental voice on the governing bodies of schools. It invited the American academic Charles Murray in 1986 to talk about his work on welfare 'dependency' and the emergence of an 'underclass' in the USA and the possible lessons for Britain. In his *Losing Ground: American Social Policy, 1950–1980* (1984), Murray had argued that existing levels of welfare provision undermined the work ethic and encouraged a culture of poverty. The idea was taken up by Conservative ministers, including John Moore, the Secretary of State for Health and Social Security in 1987.

As with the IEA, there developed a conflict over the future direction of the CPS. How free was it to think the unthinkable? How should it strike a balance between intellectual independence and serving the party, particularly when it was in government? Sherman's original idea was that the CPS should be distinct from the Conservative Party, to provide a forum for the exchange and development of ideas, cultivate public opinion, challenge prevailing assumptions, and advise ministers. He wanted, however, to retain what he regarded as its original ginger-group function of freedom to criticize the government from the free-market point of view and attract supporters who were not necessarily pro-Conservative. In a radio interview, after his departure, Sherman commented: 'I saw it in the first place as an outrider. An organization that would not be in the party and therefore would be able to ask questions, to think the unthinkable, to question the unquestioned' (Sherman 1983). Lord Thomas had a more modest view of the Centre's role and thought any criticism which its publications made of the government should be measured and constructive. Links with the Tory party are close. When Mrs Thatcher resigned the party leadership, John Major succeeded her as CPS President and for a time David Willetts was Director until he was elected to the Commons in 1992. Under Willetts the CPS provided influential inputs for the NHS reviews and further privatization.

The Social Affairs Unit

The SAU was founded in 1980 with a remit in social affairs broadly similar to that of the IEA in economics. 'We were impressed with how the IEA operated,' the SAU director Digby Anderson explained in an interview. 'Just as it attacked a sclerotic consensus in economics, we wanted to do something similar on social policy.' Its authors are drawn from all areas within the social sciences—criminologists, philosophers, educationists, and theologians—but rarely include economists. According to one self-description, the SAU sought to build 'a systematic literature on the practical outcomes of government attempts at social engineering in the field of education, health, social welfare, discrimination, and criminal rehabilitation'. Many authors have been highly critical of the assumptions which dominated the public sector in general and social policy and the welfare state in particular. A repeated theme of the publications has been scepticism about social engineering. They have questioned and often debunked the alleged expertise of various welfare professions, especially in social welfare and teaching, the more exaggerated analytic and predictive claims of various social sciences, particularly of social work, sociology of education, and criminology.

The SAU is not a primary research institute or a policy centre. The publications are designed, written, edited, and promoted to make such academic debate available to a wider audience. Authors usually select an issue of concern and then report on how it has been covered in the academic literature. Often authors find that the received view in academe has a poor evidential base, or may even fly in the face of evidence. Anderson's high-media profile provides a platform for the views. According to Anderson in an interview, 'the solution is not in politicians, but in a better informed public opinion'.

The flavour of some of its authors' standpoints is reflected in the title of such hard-hitting collections as *Breaking the Spell of the Welfare State* (by Digby Anderson, June Lait, and David Marsland), which advocated swingeing cuts in state welfare spending, or *Pied Pipers of Education*, which argued for vouchers and fixed-term contracts for teachers. Publications have covered police accountability, criminal deterrence, social-security reform, positive discrimination, the role of the Church of England, the family, public-sector housing, the curriculum, nutrition policy, and the need for individuals and families to exercise greater responsibility for their own welfare.

The work of the unit's authors has sounded many favourite New Right themes. One has been the questioning of social engineering, on the grounds that social reformers or interveners know less than they assume about what they are doing and little about the effects of their interventions. In many areas of social work and health education, SAU authors observe that the reformers lack an assured knowledge base and in consequence have difficulty in evaluating the results of their programmes and justifying public expenditure on them. Apologists for the programmes usually point to the need for yet more inputs of resources (of money, staff, and research), more time, and a redefinition of the programme's goals; or they offer an explanation of failure by pointing to other factors which are beyond the control of policy-makers. Anderson in particular remarks on the unassessable, unstoppable, irreducible character of state welfare—a system which he argues is literally out of control.

Some SAU authors have also criticized the poor quality of much social science as it bears on social policy, pointing to studies, for example, in poverty, welfare, or industrial relations which are shot through with relativism and value judgements. The argument that the study of society is not and cannot be truly scientific is a familiar part of the New Right approach.

The Social Market Foundation

The Social Market Foundation (SMF) began in 1987 as a think-tank for the Social Democratic Party—ironically, just when the party was on the verge of being wound up. The moving spirit was Robert Skidelsky, an academic at Warwick University and the biographer of John Maynard Keynes. His deputy was Danny Finkelstein, at the time an adviser to the party leader, Dr David Owen. The SMF was relaunched in 1990 as a non-libertarian free-market body. It distinguished between the social and the free market because it insisted that the outcomes of the free market have to be socially acceptable (Baston 1996). According to a strategy statement: 'Experience shows that market systems are most secure, and work best, if they are embedded in institutions and practices generally regarded as "fair".'

Like other think-tanks, it publicizes its ideas through conferences, seminars, and commissioned pamphlets. It has also invited a number of prominent US figures to talk about policy matters. These include James Pinkerton (a member of Ronald Reagan's White House staff) to talk about the new directions of American conservatism and the New York Police Commissioner to talk about inner-city policing. The Foundation has been successful in getting its ideas discussed on air and published in quality newspapers, particularly *The Times*. Its interest in applying the social-market approach to public services—particularly, education, health, housing, and transport—and developing internal markets is close to the heart of John Major. Indeed, both Skidelsky and Finkelstein joined the Conservative Party, and the latter became Director of the party's Research Department. Although the SMF is free of party attachment, David Willetts is a member of its board, and a number of Conservative Cabinet ministers, including John Major, have either given speeches or attended seminars at the SMF. It has concentrated on applying commercial and customer-oriented disciplines to the public services. This fits in well with John Major's Citizen's Charter initiatives.

The above list is only a selection of the New Right groups which emerged in the 1970s and 1980s. The National Association for Freedom, formed in 1975, used the law against trade unions and shared with the think-tanks a wish to limit the power of the state. The Institute of Directors emerged as a more combative advocate of free enterprise than the Confederation of British Industry (CBI), which was associated with tripartism. Groups were formed to advance greater choice and standards in education (e.g. the Hillgate Group, the National Council for Standards in Education, and FEVER, or Friends of the Education Voucher). The Conservative

Family Campaign was formed in 1986 to promote a Christian pro-family stance in the Conservative Party. Lord Harris helped to found the Bruges Group to advance the case for a free-market EC, in line with Mrs Thatcher's views.

Conclusion

Many of the 'New Right' figures in Britain for long gave the impression that they were outnumbered in the mass media and academe by spokesmen for leftist and collectivist values. In 1942 Joseph Schumpeter had anticipated this development when he argued that capitalism, by creating an anti-capitalist culture, would destroy itself. He claimed that the intelligentsia, the offspring of an affluent society and expanded higher education, would be critical of entrepreneurial values, the profit motive, the free market, and materialism. They would turn for employment to the professions, the media, and academe, but not to business. Large corporations would nourish a bureaucratic rather than an entrepreneurial outlook amongst their leaders. Businessmen would not be persuasive advocates for capitalism and would be selective in their support for the values of competition and free enterprise, abandoning them when it was convenient.

Thirty years later, Schumpeter's concern was echoed in the USA by the New Right attacks on the 'new class', which is highly educated, well endowed with communicating skills, and disproportionately employed in the mass media, universities, and cause groups, but not in business or finance. According to Irving Kristol (1978), members of the new class are predominantly anti-business, permissive, and even anti-patriotic.

In Britain, leading Conservatives, including Mrs Thatcher (in an interview with the author), also complained that their supporters were not naturally 'political', certainly when compared with the greater commitment shown by activists on the political left. They claimed that the party had lost the initiative in the 1960s and early 1970s in schools, universities, and even churches to proponents of collectivist, egalitarian, and anti-capitalist values. They faced an alleged politically centrist establishment, 'the world of senior civil servants, lawyers, top bankers, university lecturers and pundits' (Riddell 1989: 17). A survey of journalists by Tunstall (1970) found that many specialist journalists were to the left of their organizations and more likely to vote Labour than Conservative. University teachers in the 1960s, according to Halsey and Trow (1971), were more left-wing and more supportive of the Labour Party than were other middle-class groups. Later there was to be strong evidence of the dominant Keynesian outlook among British economists at universities. In a letter to *The Times* in 1981, 364 economists, including four former chief economic advisers to the government, stated that the government's policy of decelerating the rate of growth of money supply would worsen the economic depression, harm the industrial base, and threaten social and political stability. Other policies, by implication Keynesian, should be tried.

The Conservative concern about the drift of ideas was well expressed by Ronald Butt, a sympathetic commentator, in the *Sunday Times* on 20 October 1974. 'In the past decade, the whole vocabulary of political and social debate has been captured by the Left, whose ideology has fundamentally remained unanswered by the Conservatives. Where the Conservative Party has answered back, it has done so by conceding half the case that it should have been rebutting and has usually sought to appease the trend.' He stated that the party 'needs, even at the risk of being called reactionary, to react. With the language of politics so largely monopolized by the Left and with the intellectuals whose activities have so much influence on society mostly talking that language, the Conservative Party needs politicians with strong persuasive power and clear ideas who are utterly committed to the Conservatives' historic role.'

But this claim by Conservatives that the new class was helping to shift the middle ground in favour of the left coexisted with a belief in the existence of a silent majority which was not represented by the opinion-formers. Indeed, there was ample survey evidence that the electorate was well to the right of the major parties on issues such as immigration, law and order, discipline and standards in schools, capital punishment, and trade unions; policy in these areas was made by a parliamentary élite which did not reflect public opinion. David Robertson (1984) monitored changes of public opinion on many questions that were asked in identical form in the general elections in October 1974 and May 1979. Of seventeen questions that can be directly compared, he showed that the electorate moved to more right-wing positions on fifteen and to the left only on the question of increasing cash for the NHS. He claims that 'the brute evidence is that rightwards shift of the Conservative policy in the 1970s was at least matched by a similar shift in mass opinion' (1984: 236). The voice of this silent majority could be strengthened by such policies as increasing parental influence in the management of schools, holding frequent elections of trade-union officials and pre-strike ballots, reducing the size of the public sector, curbing the power of powerful producer groups, and, above all, by the Conservative Party adopting a bolder and more populist right-wing leadership. In providing that voice, the think-tanks and their intellectual heroes helped to prepare the ground for Mrs Thatcher.

6 The Legacy

To date there have been a number of audits of the Thatcher record. As noted in Chapter 1, many commentators were so impressed by the radical agenda and longevity of the Thatcher premiership that they considered it worthwhile to conduct major studies even while she was still in office. The flow of studies has only increased in the years since her departure in 1990. Mrs Thatcher's memoirs and those of many of her former Cabinet colleagues employ such triumphalist terms as 'revolution', 'turning-point', or 'miracle' to describe her achievements. More ambitiously, her record has been merged with Fukuyama's (1992) celebration of the triumph of Western capitalism and the collapse of the USSR.

Not surprisingly, revisionists have been at work. They claim, variously, that the policies of the 1980s did not make much difference, or that some of the changes are explained by other factors; or that many of the changes would probably have occurred anyway. So much of the record has been overlaid by myths, hyperbole, and partisanship that her successor (who has been a casualty of the myth-making) exploded in an unguarded moment in July 1993 about 'a golden age that never was'. Revisionists can point to the similarity in the figures for public spending and taxation as shares of GDP in 1979 and 1990, or note that industrial-relations reforms, curbs on local government, monetarism, cash limits on departmental programmes, and sale of state assets were all tried between 1970 and 1979. Claims that Thatcherism failed to have a distinct impact have come from: (*a*) critics who are usually, but not exclusively, on the Conservative party's free-market wing, for whom she was not radical enough, and (*b*) political scientists who are impressed by the constraints operating on any government (Rose 1984; Marsh and Rhodes 1992), notably the inheritance of so many policies and spending programmes (Rose and Davies 1995). They also argue that her governments operated in a traditional British top-down manner (Tant 1993), or in a traditional Conservative way of protecting the central government's autonomy on issues of 'high politics' (Bulpitt 1986). In other words, Thatcher was not *exceptional*.

The view taken by this author is that the Thatcher Government produced such a large number of far-reaching changes across much of the policy spectrum, that it passes *reasonable* criteria of effectiveness, radicalism, and innovation (cf. Moon 1994).

Commentators have also been divided over whether Thatcherism was a coherent project, inspired by a clear philosophy, or whether it was, for the most part, *ad hoc*, inconsistent, and improvised. Accounts by some ministers and Mrs Thatcher herself give the impression of a deliberate, carefully planned programme. According to Peter Riddell, it was, however, 'essentially an instinct . . . an approach to leadership rather than an ideology' (1989: 2). Clearly, there were different emphases over time. The economy and trade union reform dominated the 1979–83 Parliament, trade unions and privatization that of 1983–7, and education, health, and the poll tax, that of 1987–90. Political scientists are also more impressed with the inconsistency, improvision, and opportunism. However, one does not have to accept an 'either/or' position. The reality of governing a pluralistic society, adapting to changing circumstances and responding to public mood is that politicians have to compromise some of their original plans, or even reverse them.

As a leader dedicated to changing the political agenda, Mrs Thatcher had several political advantages, compared to other government leaders in a Western democracy or indeed in Britain. As Conservative party leader she had the final say on policy and had control over appointments to the party machine, the Shadow Cabinet and the Cabinet. A Labour Party leader has no comparable formal powers. She started out with a comfortable parliamentary majority (43) in 1979, and then enjoyed landslides (144) in 1983 and (100) in 1987; the last two majorities were the largest for any government since 1945. She was not encumbered by the necessity to make deals with coalition partners, or constrained by a separation of powers, a powerful second chamber, a strong local-government system, or a written constitution. Moreover, for the first half of her premiership, the Labour Party was at its weakest and most discredited for over fifty years and among the electorate the opposition forces were split between the Labour and Liberal parties. Finally, she was in office for eleven continuous years, the longest period enjoyed by a British Prime Minister in modern politics. This tenure provided ample opportunity for policy learning, or incremental development of policy (for example, on industrial relations, privatization, the economy policies, and local-government structure and finance), and the large parliamentary majorities (combined with the executive's dominance in the legislative process) assured an untroubled passage for most legislation for virtually the entire period. The advantages provide a more than reasonable basis for testing if parties make a difference in British politics.

A criterion of the effectiveness of a radical government is that the changes it makes in policy, laws, or institutions survive its period in office. For example, a testimony to General de Gaulle's influence on French politics is that the Fifth Republic's constitution, created in 1958, still endures. Similarly, many of the post-war Labour Government's policies and programmes were still in place thirty years later. By contrast, the 1970–4 government of Ted Heath left the smallest legacy of any post-war administration, as much key legislation was quickly scrapped by the succeeding Labour Government and the structural reforms of local government and the health service were short lived (see p. 74). Even British membership of the European Community was thrown into question until the 1975 referendum was completed (Kavanagh 1987, 1996).

This chapter attempts to assess the legacy of the Thatcher years in the following areas:

- policy-making
- the Conservative Party
- the electorate
- economic performance
- the civil service
- local government
- the market
- interests
- public opinion
- leadership style.

Objectives

It is worth reminding ourselves at the outset of the main objectives which Mrs Thatcher set for her ministers in 1979. Essentially they were threefold:

1. *To reverse the country's relative economic decline.* This has been a goal of most British governments for the past thirty years, as evidence has mounted of the country's worsening economic performance, relative to other Western countries. In her memoirs Mrs Thatcher claims: 'we fell further behind them [our European competitors], until by 1979 we were widely dismissed as "the sick man of Europe" . . . And as the 1970s wore grimly on, we began to fail in absolute as well as relative terms' (1993: 7). In fact, concern over Britain's industrial decline *vis-à-vis* the USA and Germany goes back for at least a century.

2. *To reverse policies which, far from arresting decline, actually contributed to it.* The main culprit for Mrs Thatcher was the post-war consensus, which she described as social democracy, or Butskellism. This was: 'a controlling, managerial, bureaucratic, interventionist style of government'; 'a miserable failure in every respect' (1993: 6, 7). Her Conservative predecessors were not exempt from blame, for the Heath Government's statutory control of prices, incomes and dividends, and corporatism, 'proposed and almost implemented the most radical reform of socialism ever contemplated by an elected British Government' (1993: 7). She promised to promote the free market, exercise tight control of public spending and taxation, and encourage the 'vigorous virtues' of self-reliance and prudent finance.

3. *To restore the authority of the state.* This has long been a concern of Conservative statecraft, but by 1979 it had a particular resonance because of the paralysis of government which preceded the party's defeat in February 1974, and then Labour's in the 1979 elections. The defeats of both governments were associated with the collapse of their incomes policies at the hands of the trade unions. Governments were compromising their authority because they had become overloaded with

expectations and demands. As the achievement of many of their policies depended on the cooperation of key groups, so the bargaining power of the latter increased. Ministers should henceforth concentrate on essential tasks and shed inappropriate responsibilities, such as trying to deliver full employment and to control prices and wages. Mrs Thatcher promised to provide strong leadership and resist the selfish claims of interest groups, particularly those unions in the public sector who wanted to increase total public spending funded by the taxpayer. The politics of economic liberalism and the strong state were both means and ends.

Policy-Making

Apart from changes in particular policy areas, there was also an intended shift in how policy was made. Particularly notable was the emergence of a stronger Number 10 imprint on policy-making. Mrs Thatcher and her private office were interventionist in changes in industrial relations, education, and health (she chaired the 1988-9 Downing Street working party on the NHS), and the memoirs of Lords Lawson and Howe acknowledge her persistent lobbying over a wide range of economic and foreign-policy issues. Mrs Thatcher also convened *ad hoc* seminars at Number 10 or Chequers to inform herself on such diverse topics as broadcasting, the cinema, football violence, Russia, South Africa, and German national character.

In seeking to combat what she regarded as the inertial effects of Whitehall and the 'cosy' policy networks between departments and interest groups, Mrs Thatcher often turned elsewhere for ideas, including free-market think-tanks (see Chapters 4 and 7). She abolished the CPRS in 1983 and strengthened her own Policy Unit. She did not appoint any royal commissions, regarding them as a device which had too often been used to postpone necessary if unpalatable solutions and too often produced recommendations which were the lowest common denominator of the commission members. In the seventeen years before 1979, fifteen commissions had been appointed to report on various topics. In her eleven years of office Mrs

Thatcher did not appoint any (and in his six years John Major appointed only one). It is too soon to say if this will prove to be an enduring feature.

Policy-making with Thatcher was usually confined to a circle of the already converted, conducted in house rather than in public, and concerned less to research and consult than to find ways of implementing desired policies. This was particularly the case with the poll tax and many of the education and health reforms. By tradition, such far-reaching changes would have been preceded by royal commissions or committees of inquiry. Instead, Whitehall usually allowed limited periods for consultation and proposals and virtually sidelined the affected interests and the good and the great. In retrospect, it can be seen that ministers paid a price for this approach, as defects—in the poll tax or the schools' core curriculum to name but two areas—were exposed and had to be either abandoned or significantly revised.

The forceful Number 10 thrust to policy relied largely on Mrs Thatcher's personality—her energy, well-known views on most policy questions, and appointment of appropriate ministers. Ferdinand Mount, head of her Policy Unit between 1981 and 1983, recalled in an interview that she would follow up proposals at departmental level, 'like a dog after a bone'. In June 1996 a Treasury official, again in an interview, contrasted the atmosphere prevailing under Mrs Thatcher with that under John Major: 'A memo from Number 10 stating that "the Prime Minister wishes . . . " made people sit up in Whitehall under Mrs T, but has little effect under John Major'. Harold Wilson and James Callaghan encouraged their Policy Units to propose radical reforms for the professions, schools, and council-house sales. Yet Bernard Donoughue (1987: 108), the Head of the Policy Unit at the time, reports that they had little impact, in large part because the department ministers could go their own way unless pressed by a strong Prime Minister.

Incrementalism and learning were seen in the gradual approach to industrial relations, where five major acts were passed between 1980 and 1990. Privatization, as often noted, hardly figured in the 1979 Conservative manifesto, but loomed large in those for the 1983 and 1987 elections. The original intention had been to apply strict financial discipline to the nationalized industries. When this proved too difficult to achieve and public spending was still increasing as a share of GDP, ministers turned to the more radical step of selling them off (Swann 1993: 139).

The Conservative Party

Historians have often commented on the Conservative Party's tradition of loyalty to its leader, as well as its ruthlessness in dispensing with him or her when this is judged to be in the party's interest. Conservative Prime Ministers, not least Mrs Thatcher's predecessor Ted Heath and her successor John Major, have had their troubles with the parliamentary and party conferences, and she was forced to stand down by MPs. From 1970 onwards Conservative MPs became more willing to dissent from the leadership. During Heath's period of government, the proportion of Conservative MPs defying the party whips in the division lobbies was the highest in the party's modern history (Norton 1978). It is worth recalling that Mrs Thatcher did not convert the party to her vision of politics; the Conservative Party was not Thatcherite. Her election as party leader in February 1975 was largely for reasons other than her beliefs: many MPs voted for her on the first ballot as a means of ousting Ted Heath, who had led the party to a defeat in three out of four general elections. Over the two leadership ballots she attracted minuscule support from members of the Shadow Cabinet. Her election as party leader was largely a revolt of the backbenchers against the party establishment.

It was also well known, not least by Mrs Thatcher (1993: 123, 149), that a good part of her economic agenda was not shared by her first Cabinet. Only seven of its twenty-two member ministers had not been in a previous Cabinet. It was a Cabinet of Heath-men and proved to be particularly divisive, notably over economic policy. She changed this over time, largely by removing 'wet' opponents of her economic policy in Cabinet reshuffles between 1981 and 1983. The Cabinet formed after the 1983 election victory saw the appointment of sympathizers in Parkinson, Tebbit, Lawson, and Cockfield, and by the end of 1985 these were joined by Ridley and Lord Young of Graffham. Yet it would still be difficult to think of the Cabinet at any time of her premiership as being largely Thatcherite, and it should not perhaps be surprising that on the fateful night of 21 November 1990 some two-thirds of her Cabinet ministers advised her to resign. A mark of the lack of a successor who would carry on the torch was that she had to throw her weight behind John Major, not because he was a Thatcherite, but because the alternatives were so clearly not of her persuasion (see p. 198).

Conservative MPs were no more Thatcherite. In a remarkably prophetic article, 'The Lady's Not for Turning. But What About the Rest?', Philip Norton (1990) calculated that in 1990 only 15 per cent of Conservative MPs could be regarded as true Thatcherites. These included the *Tory right* (who felt strongly about discipline and law and order, and supported capital punishment) and the *neo-liberals* (who supported the free market and were generally sceptical of the European Community). Most MPs were *party loyalists* and would support her—or any Conservative leader—as long as she provided party unity, economic success, and the prospect of general election victory. Although she may have gained more votes than Michael Heseltine in the first round of the leadership election in 1990, it was telling that she was opposed by 40 per cent of MPs.

What did change over the 1980s was the greater willingness of her supporters to organize themselves in such bodies as the 92 Group, No Turning Back, the Bruges Group, and the Fresh Start group, the last formed after Maastricht. The first two clearly supported her outlook on market economies, law and order, and Europe. Ironically, it was after her departure that a growing number of Conservative MPs came to share her hostility to the European Union (EU), which replaced the EC at the Maastricht Treaty. This created problems for her successor.

Mrs Thatcher's appearances at the annual party conference always produced an effusive display of affection and admiration by party representatives. She was perhaps the first post-war Conservative leader who clearly reflected their strong views on such issues as trade unions, high taxation and public spending, law and order, and immigration. Her populist authoritarian stance was also backed by the Tory tabloids. Many of her predecessors gave the impression that they found the annual Conferences vulgar, even distasteful, occasions. She also had a clear view of who 'our people' were—the middle class, small-business proprietors, shopkeepers, and striving members of the working class. But how typical of the broader membership were the conference representatives? In the 1980s party membership sharply declined and there was a de-energizing of local Conservative political activity. These failings were not confined to the Conservative Party but reflected broader problems of contemporary mass political parties. Surveys showed that Conservative members were predominantly elderly (two-thirds were over 56) and had fairly progressive views on poverty, giving workers more say at their place of work, and spending more on the NHS (Whiteley, Seyd, and Richardson 1994).

The Electorate

Over the period 1979–92 the Conservative Party clearly forged a new electoral plurality, one which was sufficient to deliver election victories on the back of a minority of votes. With a regular 42 per cent share of the vote in a two-and-a-half party system it was able to gain clear majorities under the first-past-the-post electoral system. Although these were the lowest vote-share figures with which the party had secured office in any election since 1922, they might be considered an achievement, given the multi-party context. The 42 per cent average share for the four general elections (1979–92) is on par with the party's average of 42.6 per cent for the four previous elections (1966–74). The Conservatives usually gained around 60 per cent of the Lab.–Con. vote, the largest share of the two-party vote in the post-war period. What was not clear was whether there had been a realignment of the party system or to what extent the Conservative lead was largely a product of temporary disillusion with Labour.

Conservative supporters between 1979 and 1992 were drawn quite widely across the social spectrum. The party's share of the working-class vote held remarkably steady, although it fell slightly in

TABLE 6.1. *Vote by class, 1992, compared to 1987 and 1979*

	Con.	Lab.	Lib. Dem.	Con. lead over Lab.	Swing to Lab.
Professional/managerial (ABs)					
Vote in 1992	55	23	22	+32	+5.5
Change from 1987	−1	+10	−9	−11	
Change from 1979	−9	+2	+6	−11	+5.5
Office/clerical (C1₂)					
Vote in 1992	50	29	21	+21	+1.0
Change from 1987	+2	+4	−6	−2	
Change from 1979	−4	−1	+5	−3	+1.5
Skilled manual (C2s)					
Vote in 1992	41	40	19	+1	+3.0
Change from 1987	−2	+4	−2	−6	
Change from 1979	0	−4	+4	+2	−2.0
Semi-skilled/unskilled manual (DEs)					
Vote in 1992	31	55	14	−24	+4.5
Change from 1987	−1	+8	−7	−9	
Change from 1979	−3	+2	+1	−5	+2.5

Source: see Crewe (1992: 5).

the professional and managerial groups (ABs) (see Table 6.1). It retained a narrow lead over Labour among the skilled manual workers (C2s), and in three of the four general elections (1979 to 1992) actually led Labour among the southern working class. The party has also made inroads among the petty bourgeois, the ranks of the self-employed and small business, but lost ground among the middle class, particularly the professions. The accumulated effect of the four general elections was to tilt the nation's geographical axis to a more Conservative south and east and a more Labour north and west. Over the four elections the Conservatives lost seats and vote share in Scotland, the north, and Wales. Indeed, the weakness of Conservatism in Scotland and Wales (17 out of 110 seats in 1992—a fall of sixteen since 1979)—called into question the continuity of the UK, as seats returned a large majority of Labour to a House of Commons dominated by Conservatives. The Conservatives were also virtually wiped out in the major cities. The party gained in the south-east and the Midlands, which reflected the greater economic prosperity and population growth in the latter regions (Crewe, Norris, and Waller 1992). In the 1987 general election only one of the 181 constituencies with the highest rate of unemployment was represented by a Conservative MP.

The Conservative Party also increased its lead over Labour as the party with which people identified. A 2 per cent lead in 1979 (38 per cent to 36 per cent) increased by 1992 to 11 per cent (42 per cent to 31 per cent), according to the British Election Studies series, and was the party's highest share since the surveys were first conducted in 1964.

Economy

The figures hardly bear out ministers' claims that the 1980s saw a dramatic relative reversal of the country's economic decline. The Thatcher premiership began and ended with the economy in recession. Before the 1979 election, the party claimed that cutting taxes and public spending would be the criteria of economic success; in government, ministers modified this by reducing them as shares of GDP. By 1990 taxes as a share of GDP had increased compared to 1979 (from 35.5 per cent to 37.5 per cent), although within that figure income tax as a percentage of GDP actually fell from 11.2 per cent to 10.3 per cent. Public spending also increased as a share of GDP until 1983, and then steadily declined until 1987/8, when it fell below the figure for 1978/9. By 1990 it was still below the figure the government inherited, but rose again after Mrs Thatcher's departure. Public spending as a share of GDP rose and fell as the economy prospered and faltered by affecting the outlay on unemployment benefits and income from tax receipts. Public spending remained high in spite of receipts from privatization sales and North Sea oil, the decision in 1980 to update benefits (including pensions) in line with whichever figure was lower for the annual increase in earnings or in prices, and the imposition of tougher conditions for receipt of unemployment and other benefits.

Apologists suggest that these figures would probably have been higher under Labour, or without the determination of Number 10 and the Treasury to bear down on both spending and taxes. Most other OECD countries performed worse on these Thatcherite criteria of good economic management, and virtually all of them shifted from taxing income to taxing spending and cut back top rates of income tax. During the 1980s, out of twenty-four OECD countries, only Belgium and West Germany managed to cut total tax as a share of GDP, and by 1990 the UK's tax share of GDP was the lowest of EC member states.

The recessions also reduced the average rate of economic growth. From the second quarter of 1979 until 1990 the annual figure for economic growth averaged 1.8 per cent, a figure below that for the 1960s and 1970s and below the OECD average, in spite of the dividends from North Sea Oil. The figures improve if one starts from 1981. Although productivity, or output per head, was better than over the previous decade (but not over the 1960s), other countries also improved and the UK still lagged behind France, Japan, and Germany.

Inflation at 10 per cent in 1990 was the highest in the G7 countries and virtually the same as it had been in 1979. In both years the figures were above the OECD average. By 1982 the inflation rate had fallen to the OECD average of 5 per cent and fell further to 2.6 per cent in July 1986, the lowest figure for nineteen years. Beating inflation was the first objective of economic policy, and, to quote the 1987 manifesto: 'There is no better yardstick of a party's fitness to govern than its attitude to inflation.' Thereafter, the return of inflation, and the regime of high-interest rates required to conquer it, damaged the economic record.

The government's many revisions of the unemployment figures—which had the effect of reducing the numbers recorded as out of work—limit the usefulness of comparison of official figures after 1979. Over the eleven years, the official number of unemployed doubled and the true figure was much higher. The regime of high interest rates and the effects of North Sea oil on the value of the pound squeezed inflation but also fed through into higher unemployment figures. Treasury ministers regularly claimed that demand management and budgeting for full employment were beyond the power of governments. Sir Geoffrey Howe, in his first 1979 Budget, stated: 'There is a definite limit to our capacity, as politicians, to influence these things for the better.' But not all Cabinet ministers accepted the relentless increase in unemployment in the early 1980s as the price for the credibility of the anti-inflation strategy. Howe and Thatcher had to face a Cabinet revolt in 1981 (Young 1989: 218–19). Howe's 1981 Budget had actually cut the PSBR at a time of high and rising unemployment. Maintaining policy in spite of previously unthinkable levels of unemployment became a test of 'resolute leadership'.

The government's medium-term financial strategy (MTFS) was of limited help. It was announced by Sir Geoffrey Howe in his 1980 Budget and set steadily reducing targets for money supply and public borrowing (PSBR) as a means of achieving lower inflation. Sterling M3 was planned to decline by 1 per cent per annum between 1980/1 and 1983/4 and the PSBR from 4 per cent of GDP to 1.5 per cent. The targets were the government's anchor for managing the economy. Although inflation fell rapidly, it was not because of the MTFS—the targets for which were regularly exceeded—but because of a fall in commodity prices. By 1982 government spokesmen talked less about money supply and more about monetary growth and the exchange rate. Controlling the monetary aggregates proved difficult to achieve and the Treasury therefore sought to control them indirectly by the exchange rate. In 1984 the target was concentrated on M0, the narrower measure. The next year the Chancellor, Nigel Lawson, abandoned M3 and, though emphasizing M4, or broad money, did not set a target range. Monetarism was effectively dead. Management of interest rates and the exchange rate were regarded as more promising policy instruments.

The Civil Service

Over the Thatcher years there was considerable change in the structure and ethos of the British civil service. Mrs Thatcher's dislike of the public sector (except for the police and armed forces) had been well signalled beforehand. She frequently expressed admiration for wealth-creators and risk-takers; civil servants, like academics, had to remember their dependence for funding on the wealth-making sector. According to Sir Frank Cooper, a former Permanent Secretary to the Ministry of Defence (1976–83), 'I'm not sure she dislikes civil servants in their own right. I don't believe she does. But I don't think that she regards them as a group of people who are contributing to the wealth of the nation' (Young and Sloman 1986: 49). She regarded much of the senior civil service as upholders of the consensus politics associated with the country's post-war decline and was also deeply suspicious of departmental cultures. Too often senior civil servants appeared to her to be closely tied with the producer lobbies—the Ministry of Agriculture with the farmers, the Department of Education with the teaching unions, the Department of Health with the British Medical Association—and conspired to boost public spending on their programme at the cost of the hard-pressed taxpayer (on education, see Baker 1993: 172).

There were several indicators of change. One was the 20 per cent reduction in the size of the service by the time she left office in 1990. Another was the abolition of the Civil Service Department in 1981 and transfer to the Treasury of responsibility for the service's pay and conditions of employment. There was also a new emphasis on achieving value for money and good-management practice. This started with Sir Derek Rayner's 'scrutinies' to eliminate waste in departments, the Financial Management Initiative in 1982, and the gradual extension of cash limits (introduced in 1976) to more Whitehall programmes. The thrust of these measures was to encourage among officials a greater consciousness of costs, to curb the growth of spending and to reinforce Treasury control. The Next Steps programme (the idea of Robin Ibbs) was inaugurated in 1988 and was designed to separate issues of strategic management and policy from those of service delivery, with responsibility for the latter gradually being transferred to executive agencies. It was reinforced by the extension under John Major of market-testing (via competitive bids from other suppliers for Whitehall work), contracting-out and privatization. By 1996 some 75 per cent of civil servants worked in agencies. Not surprisingly, these changes and the attempts to overturn so many established policies tested traditional relationships between ministers and civil servants.

Equally upsetting for civil servants was that many of these initiatives were spawned from outside, sometimes from free-market think-tanks. Interestingly, both Rayner (from Marks & Spencer) and Ibbs (from ICI) were outsiders. Some critics called for more radical changes. Sir John Hoskyns, the first head of Mrs Thatcher's Policy Unit, urged the appointment of more outsiders to top positions in the civil service and of officials who would support ministers committed to radical policy changes. This amounted to a call for the politicization of the service and was rejected by Lord Bancroft, head of the service until 1981. In a public lecture in 1983 he argued that a civil servant who could answer 'yes' to the question 'Is he one of us?' should retire and become a party politician.

By the late 1980s Mrs Thatcher had had a hand in the appointment of all senior civil servants then in post. She was inclined to promote so-called 'doers' and problem-solvers rather than masters of the traditional art of dispassionate advice. She was, she says, 'determined to change the mentality exemplified in the early 1970s by a remark attributed to the then head of the civil service, that the best the British could hope for was "the orderly management of decline"' (Thatcher 1993: 46). She also had little time for the CPRS, viewing it as redundant when a government, like hers, had a clear philosophical doctrine (1993: 30). But in 1988 the Royal Institute of Public Administration ruled out complaints of politicization; it found that it was the officials' style more than their ideology which affected their promotion prospects under Mrs Thatcher. Yet the enthusiasm with which officials backed the poll tax; reports of officials helping to draft replies to Parliamentary Questions to mislead MPs; and evidence of their complicity in the illegal sale of arms to Iraq in 1988 constituted a warning to civil servants to retain a measure of detachment.

Local Government

Traditional Conservative praise of local government as part of a pluralistic political order, a potential check on an overweening central government, and a means of advancing civic life has been abandoned since 1979. A contemporary defence of the role of 'little platoons' in public life is more likely to invoke alternatives to local government, such as voluntary groups and the market (Waldegrave 1994). The Conservative onslaught on local government in the 1980s was triggered both by changes in local government and by the growing concern of the centre to control public spending. Local government (accounting for 25 per cent of total spending) was bound to be a target for ministers looking for cuts. And, as a quasi-monopolistic and heavily unionized provider of such services as state education and rented housing, it was also a target for Thatcherism. But concern over local government, as with trade unions and the public sector, did not just start in 1979. The 1974–9 Labour Government had already curtailed local choice in education, by making comprehensive schooling mandatory, and curbed local spending. It is doubtful that even a Labour government or a Conservative one led by somebody other than Mrs Thatcher would have allowed local government to remain unscathed, though it might not have followed the complete Thatcher line. National economic policy, particularly the government's goals of reducing inflation and public borrowing and public spending, shaped ministers' attitudes to local government. As Rhodes (1992: 61) comments: 'Economic problems provided the stimulus to interfere,' although it was ideology that led to the adoption of such specific policies as the poll tax, contracting-out, privatization, and opting out of schools.

The legacy of the 1980s has been a political system which is even more centralized, and a system of local government which is severely limited in its financial autonomy, both for raising and for spending money, with a diminished role in education, housing, and urban development. The government was the first to curb the authority of local authorities to increase their rates in the Rates Act (1989); it then abolished the rates, assumed powers to 'cap' the poll-tax replacement to rates (1990) and its successor, the council tax (1993), and also imposed a uniform business rate. The effect of measures to allow the sale of council houses, opting-out of schools and tenants from local authorities, and of competitive tendering for services such as refuse collection and street-cleaning, has been to reduce the dominant position of local government as a provider of these services. Central government directly funded the opted-out schools and took some control of state schooling by imposing a national curriculum in 1988. Local government was also sidelined by the creation of urban development corporations, charged with the regeneration of inner cities, and run largely by local business people. On some calculations there were over fifty pieces of legislation affecting the role of local government during the 1980s. Such legislative hyperactivity might be seen as a mark of the government's mounting frustration at the successive failures to achieve its aims. But at the end, local government was squeezed in a pincer between greater control over finance from the centre, and pressures from Whitehall-created quangos and consumers.

The Market

A target of the Thatcher Government's economic policy was the economic interventions of the state, which were condemned for draining the country's productive capacity, increasing the burden of taxation, and 'crowding out' private investment. 'Rolling back the state' was regarded as essential to creating an enterprise economy. Much of this was done by privatization (or the sale of assets and shares owned by the state) and liberalization (the relaxation or abolition of a service's statutory monopoly).

Ministers took the view that, if the demands from the public sector could be reduced, the government could tax less and spend less, so allowing the market to extend consumer choice. Consistent with this policy was the rejection of a formal or even informal pay policy, price controls inherited from the outgoing Labour Government, reduction in the number and scope of wage councils, abolition of exchange control, and creation of enterprise zones. Privatization, or the sale to the public of the assets or shares of state-owned companies and utilities, became the flagship of the Thatcher project. It began almost immediately in 1979 with the sale of a 49 per cent stake in Cable and Wireless, but the first major privatization was not until 1984, with the sale of 50 per cent of British

Telecom. By 1990 two-thirds of the assets which were publicly owned in 1979 had been sold off. The privatization programme also helped to boost private share ownership (from 7 to 25 per cent of adults). As noted, this programme emerged as a response to frustration with the financial demands from loss-making nationalized industries. Critics pointed to the lack of competition faced by monopoly services and the resultant absence of commercial discipline and the low pre-tax real rates of return on the capital employed. The refusal, however, to break up the utilities such as British Gas or British Telecom, prior to sale, did little to promote competition. The revenues from the sale of state assets were an unanticipated boon to the Treasury. Between 1979 and 1990 £60 billion was raised from sales of state industries, utilities, and council houses, a sum that was useful for funding tax cuts and reducing government borrowing.

The marginal rates of income tax were cut substantially (the standard rate from 33 to 25 per cent), most dramatically at the top (to 40 per cent), and a large share of government revenue was raised from higher indirect taxes and national insurance contributions. Whitehall also cut back on regulations over firms and its subsidies to industry and the regions. Banks, building societies, and the City were deregulated. The NHS and local government were compelled to put a number of services out to competitive tender. Home ownership was extended, assisted by the sale of over one million council houses in the 1980s. This continued a party tradition of the sale of council homes under Conservative local authorities and the Heath Government. But the property-owning democracy turned sour by the end of the decade as there was a collapse in the housing market, and in the early 1990s some two million homeowners were caught in a negative equity trap, i.e. the value of their houses was less than the outstanding mortgage debt.

Interests

The adoption of many new policies and rejection of traditional methods of policy-making disturbed many interests. The hostility of ministers to interest groups, particularly those in the public sector, reflected in large part the New Right critique of the links between Whitehall departments and producer lobbies and the tendency for the latter to 'capture' the former. Taxpayers were poorly organized, not least because a programme's costs when dispersed among millions of taxpayers were so slight that there was no incentive to organize. But, because gains to members of the group were concentrated, there was an incentive for members to join a group and campaign. According to Mancur Olson (1982), interest groups (what he calls 'distributional coalitions') could become so entrenched that they could veto policy change which they regarded as disadvantageous to them but might be desirable for the national interest. He regarded Britain as a severe case of 'institutional sclerosis', because the continuity of the regime had allowed the interests to become established. In Germany and Japan, by contrast, many interests had been either smashed or severely weakened by the totalitarian governments or by defeat in the war. Olson did not find it surprising that these last two countries had achieved such high rates of economic growth in the post-war period and that Britain had done so badly.

That a Thatcher Government would try to curb such collectivist-orientated groups as the trade unions and local government was fairly predictable, and the preceding Labour Government had tangled with them. Formal incomes policies were hardly politically credible after the 1978 breakdown: the Winter of Discontent had strengthened the Conservative dismissal of the incomes-policy approach to curbing inflation. The unions were as unpopular as they had been a decade earlier (for the closed shop, unofficial strikes, and mass picketing). Conservatives under Mrs Thatcher were more outspoken in blaming the unions for overmanning, restrictive practices, low productivity, and strikes, particularly in the public sector, where they would often exploit their monopoly position.

A sharp contrast between the politics of the 1970s and of the 1980s was the marked decline in the unions' political influence and bargaining power, culminating in the effective removal of the trade-union question from the political agenda and the demise of tripartism and corporatism. On the positive side, the introduction of pre-strike ballots and regular elections of union officials made trade-union leaders more accountable to their members. Political contributions by unions had to be made through a fund approved by members in a secret ballot and these usually supported the creation of the fund. Union power was weakened by the effects of legislation outlawing secondary action, ending the closed shop, and removing immunity for union funds in cases of illegal action. The creation of a legal framework ended the voluntarist approach to industrial relations. The legislation was reinforced by growing unemployment, particularly in the manufacturing sector, changing patterns of work (notably the decline of manufacturing and the rise of part-time work and jobs in services which are less unionized), and a steep fall in membership (from 13.3 million to 9.9 million between 1979 and 1990 or from 50 per cent to 35 per cent of the workforce). In contrast to the experience of the Heath Government, the rolling programme of legislation in four Employment Acts (1980, 1982, 1988, and 1990) and a Trade Union Act (1984) was made to 'stick' and contributed to redressing the balance in bargaining between employers and unions. Another effect of the legislation and unemployment was to reduce sharply the number of strikes and days lost due to industrial disputes. During the 1990s figures for strikes and working days lost due to strikes were post-war lows. The twelve-month strikes by the National Union of Mineworkers (NUM) against pit closures ended in April 1985 in failure and with the NUM split. The open-door policy of Number 10 in the 1970s ended; Mrs Thatcher met TUC leaders only twice in her twelve years in office, compared to the frequent visits to Downing Street under her predecessors.

Less predictable was the Thatcher Government's willingness to tackle established middle-class interests as well. It challenged the professions' claims to possess an expertise, which had for long been used to limit ministers' scope to regulate and scrutinize their activities and, in the public sector, justify demands for more spending. Restrictive practices by the professions were offensive to supporters of the market, and the IEA had long campaigned against them. Professional autonomy was challenged by managerialism and economy. Schoolteachers found that their national pay-bargaining rights were scrapped, and a curriculum, national testing of pupils, and contracts of service were imposed upon them. University teachers lost tenure, the quality of their teaching and research was regularly assessed by independent bodies, and higher education was increasingly regulated from the centre. The University Grants Committee was replaced by a Funding Council, consisting of a higher proportion of business figures, and this was carried further with that body's replacement by a Higher Education Funding Council. The education minister also assumed far-reaching powers to instruct the Council. Whitehall imposed new contracts upon doctors, limited their budgets, and linked a greater part of their pay to the number of patients they treated. Opticians lost their monopoly on sale of spectacles. Although changes to the legal profession were more modest, barristers lost their exclusive rights of audience in the higher courts and the solicitors lost their monopoly over conveyancing. The culture of performance pay, competition, value for money, and external audit and inspection has been imported to much of the public sector and to some of the professions. The new government hero in the public sector was the businessman or the management consultant. Such unprecedented interventions were justified by ministers on the grounds that breaking the power of groups was necessary to make the market work and to empower the consumer/customer. In her memoirs, Mrs Thatcher dismissed the objections of the professions as 'special pleading disguised as high-minded commitment to some greater good' (1993: 634).

The government also confronted the so-called Establishment, for long associated with the Conservative Party. Particular targets were the Church of England (traditionally the 'Tory party at prayer') and the BBC. During the 1980s various bishops spoke in thinly veiled terms about the need for the government to follow less socially divisive policies and to tackle unemployment and poverty more vigorously, and for a politics of consensus not confrontation. Bishops Jenkins of Durham, Hapgood of York, and Sheppard of Liverpool were prominent critics. The report of the Archbishop of Canterbury's committee on the inner cities, *Faith in the Inner City* (1985), was widely interpreted as an implicit criticism of government policy. It, in turn, was dismissed as 'Marxist' by a government spokesman and assailed by a number of Conservatives. The views of the membership of the General Synod of the Church of England confirm the breach and suggest that the churches, along with the universities and intellectuals, became a platform for the old left–liberal consensus (Martin 1989). In the 1992 general election, 45 per cent of the clergy and 43 per cent of bishops voted Liberal Democrat, compared to 23 per cent and 28 per cent respectively who voted Conservative (*Guardian* 1996).

Tensions between the government of the day and the BBC are now a given of political life. The radicalism of the Thatcher Government and its free-market thrust, not surprisingly, brought it into conflict with the public corporation. The government put pressure on the BBC to withdraw programmes which it regarded as hostile to government policy. The Home Office requested the BBC to withdraw its 'Real Lives' documentary on Northern Ireland, approved a police raid on the BBC's Glasgow Studios to seize material relating to a defence project, prevented the broadcasting of a Radio 4 series about espionage, and used its power to ban all radio and all broadcast interviews with the IRA. Ministers also attacked the BBC for its coverage of the war with Argentina in 1982 and coverage of the US bombing of Libya in 1986.

Public Opinion

Mrs Thatcher claimed that support for the free market, a low tax regime, and the cultivation of self-reliance depended for their long-term success on a change in public mood, particularly about the role of government itself. Her most unconservative ambition was to remake the culture, for 'Economics are the method: the object is to change heart and soul' (Holmes 1985: 209). To this end, she used the bully pulpit of her office to lecture the nation as no other Prime Minister has done this century. She advocated what commentators called middle-class or Victorian values, but what she regarded as the 'common sense' she had learnt during her Grantham childhood. Party spokesmen reiterated the themes that it was not the government's job to solve as many problems as heretofore; that government should be more attentive to the interests of taxpayers when considering demands for public spending, that 'real' jobs would be created and sustained not by government subsidy but by workers making goods which people would buy, and that people should reduce their expectations of what government could achieve. How successful was it?

Surveys show that there was a significant change on attitudes to the balance between public ownership and denationalization. Between 1979 and 1983 large majorities favoured denationalization, but thereafter there was a steady fall in the number of supporters. This shift almost certainly took account of the reduction in the number of firms and services in public ownership, as more voters approved of the new status quo. Over time bad publicity relating to the performances of some water companies and the soaring remuneration packages awarded to some of the directors in the privatized utilities discredited the privatization alternative. On industrial relations there has been a steady increase in the proportion thinking that trade unions are a good thing and that they do not have too much power, a sharp contrast to the public mood in the 1970s. In 1979 voters agreed by a majority of 41 per cent that the trade unions were too powerful; by 1987 they disagreed by a majority of 20 per cent. The changed mood took account of the reduced number of strikes and days lost due to industrial disputes.

Ministers also managed to break the link between levels of unemployment and the popularity of government. Psephological wisdom held that governments would be punished at the ballot box for high levels of unemployment. By 1983 Conservative ministers persuaded the public that the doubling of unemployment since 1979 could be blamed on international forces and the trade unions, and won a decisive election victory. Their case was also helped by the fact that, although surveys showed that Labour was widely preferred by voters on the issue, the party simply lacked credibility as a potential government.

The evidence is more ambiguous if we turn to the so-called Thatcherite values of thrift, reliance, and enterprise. Surveys showed that during the 1980s a growing majority preferred more spending on public services, even if this involved tax increases, over cuts in taxes and in services. In 1979 a third preferred the tax-cuts option and a third the tax-increase option. By 1981 there had been a shift in favour of the latter, and it increased steadily during the decade. A majority also regularly thought that it was more important for firms to take care of their workforces than to pursue profits. The minority support, according to surveys, for profit-driven capitalism and a low tax economy was a clear repudiation of Thatcherism. Although Mrs Thatcher once memorably claimed that there was 'no such thing as society', the British public were not becoming a nation of individuals.

If we consider harder data, it is also difficult to argue that more people became more self-reliant. By 1990 dependency, in the form of higher unemployment and numbers of households in debt, had increased. The number of people relying on income support increased by 60 per cent between 1979 and 1990. Ivor Crewe (1991: 18) comments: 'The real symbol of social change in the Thatcher years was not the stock certificate or property title deed but the credit card.'

Mrs Thatcher was not a popular Prime Minister (see Table 6.2). Over the course of her premiership, her mean 'satisfaction'

TABLE 6.2. *Popularity of post-war Prime Ministers*

Question: Are you satisfied or dissatisfied with —— as Prime Minister?

Period	Prime Minister	% satisfied		
		Mean	Low	High
1945–51	Attlee	47	37	66
1951–5	Churchill	52	48	56
1955–7	Eden	55	41	70
1957–63	Macmillan	51	30	79
1963–4	Douglas-Home	45	41	48
1964–6	Wilson	59	48	66
1966–70	Wilson	41	27	69
1970–4	Heath	37	31	45
1974–6	Wilson	46	40	53
1976–9	Callaghan	46	33	59
1979–82	Thatcher (pre-Falklands)	36	25	46
1982–3	Thatcher (post-Falklands)	47	44	52
1983–7	Thatcher	39	28	53
1987–90	Thatcher	38	23	52

Source: Gallup.

score among the electorate on the monthly Gallup poll was 39 per cent, making her their second least popular Prime Minister since 1945 (only Heath had done worse). She divided the public more than any other British leader in the post-war period. Few people were indifferent; they either admired or disliked her. They agreed on her qualities of strength, courage, and outspokenness and being 'good in a crisis'. But they also saw her as divisive, condescending, and out of touch. The Falklands War was important in increasing public respect for her. To the end people disliked her lack of 'compassionate qualities' but respected her 'warrior qualities'. Crewe (1991) points out that, until Nigel Lawson's resignation in October 1989, her popularity score regularly ran a little ahead of or equal with that of her party, after which she ran 3 or 4 per cent behind. When the economic record turned sour, her lack of popularity made her into an electoral liability. After her downfall, MORI found that 52 per cent agreed that 'On balance she had been good for the country' and 44 per cent that she had been 'bad'.

The changes in public attitudes have not been all in one direction. Some of the shifts, particularly about trade unions and nationalization/privatization, have been a consequence of changes in the real world of industrial relations and ownership of the utilities. Changing responses to similar questions over a number of years reflect a change in the status of the subject under question. Much of the survey evidence shows a resistance to Thatcherite values, and one exhaustive analysis (Rentoul 1989) has bluntly dismissed Thatcherism as a failure. There was more popular support for Thatcherite values between 1975 and 1979 than when she was Prime Minister. Electoral success came in spite of, not because of, her values. Victories owed more to a divided opposition and public perceptions that the Conservatives were more likely to deliver prosperity than Labour.

The public likes orderly trade unions, well-run utilities, and a well-funded NHS. Values change only slowly. After all, studies of political culture in Eastern Europe showed a strong resistance to communist values, even when the regime exercised strong control over the mass media and schools.

Leadership Style

Reference was made earlier to the *mobilizing* and *reconciling* styles of political leadership. Effective political leaders have to take account of both role demands. In the inter-war years Stanley Baldwin and Ramsay MacDonald, by temperament and conviction, were reconcilers. Gladstone, Lloyd George, and Joseph Chamberlain were classic mobilizers, concerned with changing things. They were not respecters of party lines, and the last two in particular were widely distrusted by parliamentary colleagues. The mobilizing style has a greater appeal when there is a national crisis or acute dissatisfaction with the status quo and a demand for new change.

In Britain the character of being a mobilizer or a reconciler has not been related to party or being in opposition or government. At times, the movement between the last two may be cyclical, with one style breeding a reaction in favour of the other—Lloyd George was followed by Bonar Law, Churchill by Attlee, and Thatcher by Major (Hirschman 1982). A leader may also start out as a mobilizer but end as a conciliator, as happened with Harold Wilson and Ted Heath.

Mrs Thatcher remained a mobilizer to the end. Talk of policy U-turn or reversal, associated with Mr Heath, was expunged from the political vocabulary. She prided herself on her reputation as an 'Iron Lady', a term applied pejoratively to her by Soviet leaders in 1977. She also reacted against the political 'fixer' style of leadership, associated with the Labour Prime Ministers Harold Wilson and James Callaghan in the 1970s. She believed in strong leadership, disparaged consensus politics, and boasted of giving a lead. Her reliance on her Number 10 advisers, the taking of decisions outside Cabinet in *ad hoc* committees, the reduction in the number of Cabinet papers and meetings, the dismissal of senior ministers, and a willingness to display in public her disagreement with colleagues or an agreed Cabinet line can each be found in other Prime Ministers. What matters is the totality of these features in the Thatcher style of premiership. Political style is, of course, personal, ephemeral, something that disappears with the removal of the politician. Yet it is also a model that can be followed or rejected by successors. Mrs Thatcher did not transform the role of Prime Minister in British politics. Although the office is not highly institutionalized—and she made only minor changes in this respect—incumbents can do the job in different ways.

Anthony King suggests that her significance was that she pushed her authority to the outer limits. 'The repertory of available prime ministerial styles has been extended' (1985: 137). In fact, because the outer limits of authority are not clearly defined, she was able to involve herself closely in many areas which her predecessors had downgraded. King warned that, if she were a successful leader, then future Prime Ministers would be tempted to draw on her style. On the other hand, if her premiership ended in disaster—and the disaster seemed to be a consequence of flaws in the style—then they might draw a different set of inferences. Indeed, the increasingly negative reaction to the forceful way she presented her views and the circumstances of her downfall triggered a reaction among colleagues. She seemed to thrive on confronting an enemy, external or within. Her leadership style was destabilizing the Cabinet, producing spectacular resignations, and she could no longer lead a united team. A style that had once made her an effective leader ultimately proved her undoing. As noted, the public also grew tired of her style, and by the end she was an electoral liability. This was a warning: John Major was more collegial, restored Cabinet government, was less inclined to lecture the public, and disowned attempts by advisers to foist an 'ism' on him.

The next chapter argues that John Major has carried on with much of the Thatcher agenda and in a number of areas has actually advanced and consolidated changes begun under her. Labour's rhetoric and policies are available for analysis. The party has accepted so many of the Conservative policies, not least on the economy, that many commentators talk about a new consensus in British politics. Chapter 10 explores in more detail the policy areas in which Labour has moved in the direction of a Conservative party. Sir Keith Joseph's complaint of the socialist ratchet has been reversed. Election defeats, social and economic changes, and the entrenchment of legislation have forced Labour to camp on ground largely dictated by the Conservative Party.

The growing debate about the decline in political accountability and checks and balances is also a testament to the controversial nature of the Thatcher reforms as well as the uncompetitiveness of the party system. Labour's Richard Crossman once praised the 'battering ram' of a single-party majority in the House of Commons and the sovereignty of Parliament which enabled Labour to achieve changes. Subsequently, Lord Hailsham criticized this system as an 'elective dictatorship'. The long period of Conservative government (with large majorities in the Commons on a minority of the popular vote), the ease with which it was able to centralize power and rule relatively unchecked, and the growth of the quangos, largely appointed by and accountable only to ministers (and distributing some £50 billion of public money by 1996) stimulated Labour's interest in constitutional reform Liberals had long been committed to reform: what was new was Labour's shift. In promoting a constitutional agenda of proportional representation, a Bill of Rights, a reformed House of Lords, and devolution for Scotland, the opposition parties could look to Hayek for support. He deplored the unchecked sovereignty of Parliament as inimical to the values of limited government and constitutionalism, which he associated with good government.

Mrs Thatcher's (and John Major's) ministers, however, were and have not been much interested in constitutional reform. Mrs Thatcher's memoirs recall that, when appointing Conservative policy groups in 1982 to work on themes for the election manifesto, she rejected one on 'constitutional reform' because 'I felt that there was really nothing of note to say on that subject' (1993: 282). That remained her position to the end. The sovereignty of Parliament was defended against claims from bureaucrats in Brussels trying to forge a European 'super-state', and the quangos, school-governing bodies, and training councils provided new opportunities for accountability. The same is true of their approach to government machinery. In Whitehall, the Department of Prices and Consumer Protection was merged into the Department of Trade in 1979, Trade and Industry were re-merged after the 1983 election, and Health and Social Security were separated in 1988. In Downing Street the Policy Unit was strengthened after the CPRS was disbanded in 1983. Compared to the Wilson and Heath years, however, this was modest tinkering. By contrast, local government and the civil service and much of the part of the public sector have been subject to what can fairly be termed constant upheaval.

Conclusion

There are difficulties in assessing the impact of any government. To compare a government's initial manifesto promises and statements of intent with outcomes in government seems straightforward enough. But this approach has shortcomings. Achievements may be due to other factors—for example, favourable economic circumstances—or be unanticipated consequences of other policies. Britain's exit from the Exchange Rate Mechanism (ERM) in September 1992 was followed by a remarkable improvement of many macro-economic indicators, most of which had been dismissed as impossible to achieve outside the ERM by government spokesmen. Similarly, adverse circumstances may blow a government off course and force changes in policies. As is often noted, British governments with an assured House of Commons majority are well placed to deliver their legislation; not surprisingly, the Thatcher Governments achieved virtually all their legislative intentions. But legislation is only an input to the policy process. What of social and economic outcomes?

Some commentators are sceptical that the Thatcher Governments made much long-term difference. They claim that a British government's alleged strength is only *vis-à-vis* Parliament, and outcomes are shaped more by 'ongoing reality', in the form of interest groups, the permanent civil service, external factors (for example, the quadrupling of Arab oil prices in 1974), the decisions of international groups such as the European Union, as well as the constraints which stem from the country's modest economic performance. Richard Rose has demonstrated that changes in party incumbency during the post-war period have had little impact on economic conditions—rates of inflation, unemployment, economic growth, and prosperity. 'Reality' also expresses itself in the inheritance of many public-policy and public-spending commitments from the past. In 1990 almost three-quarters of public spending went on policy programmes introduced by governments before 1945 and only a tenth on programmes introduced in the 1980s (Rose and Davies 1995). Although the Thatcher government managed to shift the trend of some economic outcomes—for example, inflation and manufacturing productivity—even these changes broadly followed trends in OECD countries. It might also be argued that radical changes in industrial relations, privatization and state utilities, ending the social partners' approach to inflation, and curbing local government were only inputs to the policy process. This is a statement on the limits of British government in general rather than a critique of the Thatcher Government.

A different critique of the Thatcher record is provided by Marsh and Rhodes (1992). They claim, in a nutshell, that, once we look at outcomes, the Thatcher Governments failed to achieve as much as they promised or has been claimed on their behalf. Some outcomes were unintended—for example, the liberalization of the credit system and the 1988 tax cuts encouraged an unsustainable housing boom, and when this collapsed it resulted in a substantial increase in house repossessions and personal indebtedness. The big increase in manufacturing unemployment in the early 1980s was partly a consequence of too high an exchange rate, but it increased demands on the social-security budget and boosted public spending, both of which were unanticipated and unwelcome. Marsh and Rhodes (1992: 181) explain much of the government's failure in terms of ineffective implementation strategies. Too often ministers lacked clear and consistent objectives, a stable socio-economic environment, and cooperation or acquiescence from key interests. Some failures followed on ministers' refusal to consult and negotiate with affected interests. Some stemmed from a lack of appropriate and accurate information or from shortcomings in theory—for example, inflation fell in spite of a rapid increase in money supply and in borrowing, both contrary to what monetarist theory predicted.

This analysis of government failure is worth further consideration. Given the many advantages which the Thatcher Governments enjoyed, one is tempted to say that, if they failed, then intended political change may be well nigh impossible. Is the implication that, in the absence of all of the conditions specified by Marsh and Rhodes—in other words, being virtually omnicompetent and omniscient—then governments should simply abstain from radical action?

How feasible is it for any government in a democracy to enjoy these favourable conditions? How attainable are these conditions anyway in a democratic political order and pluralistic society, where governments are expected to compromise and respond to changing circumstances and shifting public mood?

A more reasonable standpoint is to adopt a comparative perspective on the Thatcher record and examine how it compares with its predecessors. On this basis, the Thatcher Governments may be regarded, along with the 1945 Attlee Government, as one of the two most successful post-war periods in Britain (Moon 1994). Achieving a slowdown in the rate of growth in public spending (from 3 per cent per annum in the 1960s and 1970s to 1 per cent per annum in the 1980s, a sharper reduction than in most OECD states) can be regarded as an achievement. The privatization programme, outcomes of the reforms in industrial relations, changes in the delivery of public services, the reduced role of local government, and the shift in the balance of taxation from direct to indirect were all intended outcomes. Moreover, the Conservative Party's successful general-election record is also something that should not be ignored. Doubtless a number of external factors contributed to the government achieving many of its objectives. But, if the claim is made that the Thatcher Government made little or no difference, then it is difficult to envisage any government in Britain making such a difference. In that case, the crucial questions should be posed not by policy analysts but by theorists of representative democracy and constitution-makers.

7 Ideas into Policy

Although the major think-tanks of the political right have all been interested in shaping the political agenda and promoting policies, they differ in their priorities and approaches. Some range widely across the policy front—for example, the IEA and the ASI—while some are specific—for example, the Conservative Family Campaign, the Hillgate Group on education, or the Bruges Group on Europe. The IEA directs its efforts primarily at opinion-formers and shifting opinion in the longer term, while the ASI tries to address the immediate concerns of policy-makers. The CPS and ASI have taken pride in their access to Whitehall, something to which the IEA and SAU attach less importance. Madsen Pirie of the ASI has distinguished between the roles of policy *architects*—concerned to shape the climate of opinion—and *engineers*—interested in providing policy prescriptions. The first two groups have resembled the *policy engineers*; the last two the *architects*.

This chapter assesses the impact of the policy advocates covered in Chapter 5. It studies the ways the ideas have been transmitted to the public and the policy-makers—the process of permeation—and the conditions which make for successful translation from, say, a pamphlet to a policy. A change in policy is usually the chief goal of most think-tanks and we examine their impact on three policy areas in the 1980s—education, health, and the poll tax. But the think-tanks have other uses and functions, such as providing a network of sympathizers, a launching pad for a political career, a means of flying kites, and so on. Finally, the chapter examines relevant similarities and differences between Britain and the USA, the two exemplars of New Right politics in the 1980s.

Permeation

No matter how striking or 'obviously' attractive an idea may be, it has to get into the heads of politicians. The early Fabians pioneered the classic tactics of permeation, *via* pamphleteering, journalism, ensuring that sympathizers were appointed to key committees, and lobbying policy-makers. Keynes followed suit and, of course, had to persuade his fellow economists. James Cornford claims that, to be successful, advocates of new ideas have to acquire 'the temperament of the salesman rather than the scholar' (1990: 28); Keynes, Friedman, the Webbs, and the think-tanks examined in Chapter 5 were all skilful publicists.

We do not know a great deal about how ideas germinate in the so-called policy communities of relevant officials, interest groups, and specialist commentators in a particular field, or how the climate of opinion influences decision-makers. Dicey seemed to take for granted that there was a harmony between legislation and the dominant tendencies of the public mood in the nineteenth century. Proof of the influence of ideas was to be found in legislation and vice versa; the ideas were 'in the air', a response to the era. In the middle of the century Bentham's ideas were influential in finance, law, penology, and administrative practice (particularly in India, then a *tabula rasa* for the enthusiastic reformer). Finer's (1972) suggested means by which the Benthamite ideas were transmitted to decision-makers remain relevant today. These included *irradiation*, through personal contacts at salons and clubs, *suscitation*, or stirring public opinion through the press, Royal Commissions, and parliamentary select committees, and *permeation*, through the appointment of sympathizers to commissions and committees. Finer (1972: 13) notes the interconnection of these different methods: 'IRRADIATION made friends and influenced people. Through them, SUSCITATION proved possible. SUSCITATION led to official appointments and hence PERMEATION. And permeation led to further irradiation and suscitation: and so on *da capo*.'

Although academics figure prominently among authors and members of the governing bodies, and some of the papers are subject to a sort of refereeing process, report empirical research, and cite academic sources, some publications might be found wanting on strict scholarly grounds. Much of the published output is value-driven, addressed primarily to policy-makers, and commissioned by organizations which have a policy agenda. The ASI, for example, has tended to 'evangelize' among the already converted, according to Denham and Garnett (1996: 47). Many of the think-tanks operate with very small research staffs—less than the size of a typical university economics department—and therefore have to commission work from outsiders. In 1990, for example, the combined budgets of the IEA, ASI, and CPS totalled £1.2 million; in contrast, the budgets of the three major US think-tanks exceeded £30 million (Hames and Feasey 1994: 218).

Denham and Garnett observe that think-tanks come in different forms. Some are academic bodies dedicated to scholarly research, some focus on contract research, and some (for example, the free-market bodies) are primarily 'advocacy tanks', akin to pressure groups. The latter want to publicize their work, shape the agenda, and influence policy. Seminars, conferences, pamphlets, and press conferences help to get their ideas picked up by the media. Their work attracts more publicity than purely academic research. Papers can be published in a matter of weeks, compared to the lengthy time span that academic journals seem to require. Producers and editors have turned to think-tank leaders as authoritative spokesmen for a free-market point of view. Digby Anderson, Danny Finkelstein, Graham Mather, Madsen Pirie, and Arthur Seldon have appeared regularly on radio and television or written for the press.

Also important have been *sympathetic journalists* who have a regular column in a newspaper or weekly. Particularly supportive throughout the 1970s was the *Daily Telegraph*, under the editor, Maurice Green, a supporter of liberal economics. His staff included Frank Johnson, John O'Sullivan, and Peter Utley, and the last two helped Mrs Thatcher with speeches. All three also worked for a spell on *The Times*. Arthur Seldon of the IEA managed over the years to place forty-seven articles in the *Daily Telegraph* (Muller 1996: 97). Two of the most influential economic commentators, Samuel Brittan of the *Financial Times* and Peter Jay of *The Times*, were among the first (in the early 1970s) to be persuaded by the IEA of the monetarist case. William Rees-Mogg, as editor (1967–81) of *The Times*, was another convert to monetarism and opened the columns of the paper to advocates of monetarism and free-market politics, as did Evans's successor as editor, Charles Douglas Home.

Prominent academics also canvassed New Right themes (Cowling 1989). Some of the most forceful were those who had shifted their political allegiance to the right in the 1970s, including the prolific Paul Johnson (a former editor of the *New Statesman*), who broke with Labour and showed all the zeal of a political convert, as did the ex-Labour MP, Woodrow Wyatt. The latter wrote regularly for *The Times* and the *News of the World*. Professor Hugh Thomas, the historian, also moved to the right, became a foreign-policy adviser to Mrs Thatcher, was in due course ennobled by her, and became Director of the CPS. In addition, the philosopher Professor Roger Scruton for a time had a regular column in *The Times* in the mid-1980s and edited the pro-Tory *Salisbury Review* (founded in 1982). The historians Norman Stone and Robert Conquest wrote on foreign affairs and defence.

A good example of the formative role of academic research was the volume *Britain's Economic Problems: Too Few Producers* by Roger Bacon and Walter Eltis (1976) (see p. 65). In fact, the major impact came when the *Sunday Times* provided the analysis with extensive coverage over four weeks in 1975, along with commentary from twenty senior politicians, businessmen, and union leaders, and published a large number of letters. The three substantial articles were headlined by the paper's editor as 'Declining Britain'. The book resonated with the talk of voters' growing resistance to paying more taxes, and complaints that the public sector was overmanned and that there was a public spending crisis. Harold Wilson remarked in the House of Commons, immediately after the 1975 articles, that Whitehall had 'too many chiefs and too few Indians'. The articles and the debate helped to crystallize the views of policy-makers in both main parties (Thatcher 1977; Barnett 1982) and even senior trade-union leaders (Minkin 1991: 170). Eltis later claimed that he and Bacon would 'hardly have written such a striking one [book] without the stimulus of writing the first three chapters for a mass readership' (letter to author, 6 March 1997). Given the pressures on politicians' time, economists have to write papers which are short and non-technical if they want attention. Articles in newspapers are a good medium through which an advocate can have an effect (Eltis 1993: p. xxi).

The tabloids, though less interested in politics, were generally hostile to such New Right targets as high taxation, abuses of trade-union power, 'loony-left' local councils, and 'welfare scroungers'. The *Sun* ran a regular column from Professor John Vincent, the historian at Bristol University, and the *Daily Express* one from George Gale. The political imbalance of the daily press in Britain is well known and has long been anti-Labour Party, particularly to its left wing. But in the 1980s it accelerated, and by 1987 three-quarters of the British electorate were reading a pro-Conservative daily at general elections. The left-of-centre *Guardian*, *Mirror*, and the weekly *New Statesman* hardly competed with the agenda-setting forums available to New Right publicists.

It would be far-fetched to say that New Right ideas swept British universities. Indeed, the government's relations with academe were generally poor. Partly this was because of financial pressures on higher education and partly because of a clash of intellectual styles. Mrs Thatcher was interested in ideas, but ideas which had a practical application, and expressed her views in a manner that was both didactic and abrasive. She had little time for the 'on the one hand, on the other' approach of liberal academics. Conservative electoral support among university dons, already modest by 1970, plummeted in the 1980s (Harrison 1994). In the three general elections of 1983, 1987, and 1992, Conservative support among dons averaged 16 per cent, a remarkably low figure for such a middle-class group compared to about 35 per cent for the Alliance and 40 per cent for Labour.

Harrison (1994: 214) notes that, of the twenty-six influentials discussed in John Ranelagh's *Thatcher's People* (1991), only four were university teachers and several had not been to a university at all. A few monetarist economists (e.g. Professors Patrick Minford, Tim Congdon, Alan Walters, and Brian Griffiths) stood out, and, at the LSE, Professors Kedourie, Letwin, and Minogue supported some parts of the new thinking (the last two were also directors of the CPS). Even as late as 1990, very few academic economists supported the ideas of New Right economics and the majority clung to many ideas of the 1960s (Ricketts and Shoesmith 1990). St Andrews University was obviously a seedbed for the ASI, and its founders,

Pirie and Butler, were both St Andrews alumni. There was also the so-called 'Peterhouse Right', drawn from former students and dons at the Cambridge college; they included academics Roger Scruton, Maurice Cowling, John Casey, and Edward Norman, and journalists such as George Gale, Charles Moore, Simon Heffer, Colin Welch, John Vincent, and Peregrine Worsthorne (Cowling 1989).

In so far as this group had a collective view, it was more worried by an alleged excess of democracy and permissiveness, and threats to British nationhood. The *Salisbury Review* and Scruton's *The Meaning of Conservatism* rejected the free market and defended the authority of the state and 'a view of legitimacy that placed public before private, society before individual, privileges before rights' (1980: 150).

A final and classic tactic of permeation was the appointment of sympathizers to Conservative party or government committees. Several think-tank members worked on the policy groups which the Conservative Party formed to prepare the party's election manifesto. In 1995 Danny Finkelstein of the SMF served on two such groups, David Willetts of the CPS and Madsen Pirie of the ASI were members of Mrs Thatcher's working group which reviewed the future of the health service in 1988, and the latter also served on John Major's Citizen's Charter Committee.

But, for the new agenda to make headway, there was also a need for a prominent political figure to carry the torch. The media were more likely to report the speeches of a politician of substance. Sir Keith Joseph was the torch-bearer, the first Conservative frontbench figure to offer a sustained and broad-ranging challenge to the direction of post-war British economic management and to the record of the 1970–4 Conservative Government (see p. 79).

Conditions for Success

John Kingdon's study of how political agendas change refers to ideas floating around in 'a policy primeval soup' and compares the survival and success of some ideas to a natural selection system (1984: 123). Our suggestion of the conditions which determine the likelihood of an idea's success are not dissimilar to Kingdon's (also see Seldon 1996).

The conditions include:

1. *Good timing*. This is not an entirely satisfactory term. There is a risk of tautology in claiming that an idea succeeds because its time has come or the climate of opinion is ready for it; proof that the climate of opinion is receptive is that the idea succeeds! It is worth recalling that most proposals have little impact and disappear from view. Occasionally, an idea may be revived as the policy community shows more interest as circumstances change or new priorities emerge. For example, maintenance loans for university students were canvassed in 1962 and again in 1966. But it was not until the mid-1980s that a more right-wing government, public-spending pressures, and expansion of numbers in higher education combined to undermine the traditional form of support for students in higher education. The spirit of the industrial-relations reforms of the 1980s had been preceded by discussions in the Eden Cabinet in 1956, a failed attempt to legislate in 1969, and a law in 1971 that was soon rendered inoperative because of union non-cooperation. Various government committees and an IEA paper had supported the abolition of resale price maintenance—which fixed the retail prices of goods—but no action had been taken. In 1963 a Conservative Government was anticipating a general election, and its local associations, which included a number of small businessmen, were not sympathetic to abolition. But political pressures—a private member's bill proposed abolition and forced the Cabinet to take a view, and the eagerness of Ted Heath, the new minister at the Board of Trade, to make his reputation—forced the issue. A measure of denationalization/privatization (for iron and steel) was enacted in 1953, but this was regarded as a 'one off' and even the full scale of the post-1979 privatization programme was not envisaged at the outset of the Thatcher Government. As ministers found that the political opposition was hardly formidable and the sell-offs were popular with voters, so the programme gathered steam.

Reflecting on his own experience as head of the Institute of Public Policy Research (IPPR), James Cornford (1990) warns that a think-tank needs to think five to ten years ahead to allow new proposals to gestate, infiltrate public opinion, and persuade key political actors. Hayek, after all, propagated his ideas about markets and the role of money supply in inflation for thirty years before they were taken seriously by senior politicians. Describing the revival of interest in his ideas in the mid-1970s, Hugo Young (1984) writes: 'the man and his ideas finally met their moment. They collided with a party traumatized by defeat, guilty about its failure and vengeful against a leadership which had distanced itself by a succession of U-turns from the policy set out in 1970'. Much the same might be said about the earlier influence of Keynes. Peter Hall (1989: 372) claims that in the USA the appeal of Keynes's ideas was mainly to young economists and graduate students. Because senior economists had invested much of their careers and reputations in earlier theories, it took some twenty years for the young generation to achieve positions of authority, and spread Keynes's ideas.

2. *Discrediting of the status quo.* Hood (1994) suggests that an existing policy, and the interests and values which support it, can be overturned by an alternative theory or destroyed from within by failures and contradictions; it can be more effectively terminated by a combination of the two. The build-up of dissatisfaction with the status quo can reach a stage in which an alternative policy moves from being 'unthinkable' to the possible and then, given the right circumstances, to the desirable. In 1992 Sir Keith Joseph, reflecting on the change in the climate of opinion he had helped to bring about, said in an interview: 'another factor . . . is essential: the existing culture must fail' (Harrison 1994: 214).

Dissatisfaction, on its own, however, is not enough to guarantee success. The presence of some of the other conditions mentioned earlier is also vital. To date, such long-advocated New Right ideas as negative income tax, school vouchers, widespread use of vouchers or private insurance in health, and banning strikes in so-called essential public services have not been acted on. Treasury opposition to spending implications, concern over voters' reactions, worry about administrative upheavals, and fear of controversy can still tame radicalism.

3. *Feasibility*, or the 'doability of' a policy. Much academic research may not have obvious consequences for action or not be applicable in policy terms. A learned paper may invite the sceptical 'so what?' question from the policy-maker. An advocate has to go further and address concerns about implementation, even if it means straying beyond his area of expertise. The ASI, for instance, makes a point of accompanying policy recommendations with suggestions of how to counter or appease interest groups which may feel threatened by the proposal. New Right ideas in the 1970s made progress because their exponents were prepared to reach out and relate their work to a political agenda covering not just economic but also industrial and social issues. As the work of 'professional' academic economists became more quantitative and abstract, so it appeared to be less relevant to broader issues of social policy and the concerns of politicians (Bosanquet 1983). Sir Alan Walters, as economic adviser to the Prime Minister, spoke in 1981 of the need to take account of social and political constraints and possibilities: 'I believe that it is incumbent on an economic adviser always to make sure that the policy advice he gives is *administratively* feasible. Policy prescriptions must always be *practical*. . . . it is simply a waste of time if he (the adviser) pursues policies and provides detailed advice on matters which cannot be said to have any political chance of acceptance' (1981: 8, emphasis in original).

4. *Addressing the concerns and values of politicians.* To resonate with British policy-makers, a proposal has to take account of the prevailing mood in Whitehall and Number 10. Does it fit in with the broad policy thinking of ministers? If it will cost money, is the mood hostile or sympathetic to additional public spending? Is it a priority for the relevant department? Will it lose votes or divide the party? In the 1980s the Treasury welcomed privatization proposals because the proceeds raised would help to fund tax cuts and reduce the public-sector deficit. The sale of council houses and opt-outs by schools were also attractive to ministers who wished to curb local government and extend home ownership. The cult of managerialism and the ideas of internal markets and performance indicators were grasped by a government which wished to improve public services

but curb public spending. On the other hand, proposals for introducing vouchers or private insurance in education and health, respectively, made little progress because of ministers' fears of electoral opposition (Thatcher 1993: 591).

Given the abundance of social-science theories and policy recommendations it is not surprising that policy-makers are usually more receptive to research findings which support their preferences. Many Conservatives became interested in New Right ideas in the 1970s in part because they reinforced their own values and prejudices (Midwinter 1993: 81). Mrs Thatcher was known to have her 'favourite' economists who were predominantly monetarist, such as Patrick Minford, Alan Walters, and Tim Congdon, and other academics whose work supported her views. British politicians are not unique in this. In the absence of a consensus in particular disciplines or policy fields, a politician or policy-maker will have little difficulty in finding a theorist who can support his or her predispositions.

5. *Support from heavyweight political actors.* Peter Gourevitch (1989: 89) points out that, without influential backing, good ideas will fail; with support, bad ideas can still shape policy. To be translated into policy, ideas must link up with politics. Joseph Chamberlain tied his own considerable political reputation to promoting protective tariffs in the first decade of the century, Enoch Powell almost single-handedly injected immigration on to the political agenda in 1968, and Tony Benn took up the cause of reforming the Labour Party after 1979. Such ideas did not, of course, originate with these politicians. But the weight of the politician attracted media attention for each cause. Particularly important in producing the policy changes in the 1980s was the interest in the 1970s of Mrs Thatcher and Sir Keith Joseph in free-market economics, monetarism, and privatization, and the commitment of the former to implementing such policies. It helped that they were in key positions, one as party leader and then Prime Minister, the other as Chairman of the party's Advisory Committee on Policy and someone close to Mrs Thatcher. Case studies of reform show how decisive is the commitment of a minister and the support of Prime Minister—for example, Kenneth Baker at Education, Norman

Tebbit at Employment, and Sir Geoffrey Howe and Nigel Lawson at the Treasury.

A Cabinet Office memo which states that the Prime Minister (particularly if a strong figure like Mrs Thatcher) wants action is likely to galvanize Whitehall. Given the modest administrative resources (in comparative terms) in Number 10, much depends on the Prime Minister's energy and determination. It was often claimed that Mrs Thatcher appeared at times to have an agenda separate from that of much of the Cabinet. This exaggerates, but she relentlessly followed up policies and harried ministers who, she suspected, might lack enthusiasm about reform.

6. *Access.* To have influence, the policy advocate requires the attention of the decision-makers. In turn, an advocate who shows awareness of the financial, ideological, and electoral constraints on politicians is more likely to gain and maintain access. Think-tanks differ in the importance which they attach to access. Those who wish to influence public opinion or promote their causes across the political spectrum may prefer to maintain some distance between themselves and politicians. Academics may be concerned, in the short term at least, to acquire or safeguard a reputation for independence and the esteem of academics colleagues. As noted, a clash over the roles of the CPS and IEA—in particular, how close they should be to Conservative ministers—led to the departure of Sir Alfred Sherman from the CPS in 1984 (see p. 103) and of Graham Mather from the IEA (see p. 100) in 1992.

Impact on Policy

As in many studies of political power, it is difficult to judge the extent, relative to other factors, of a group's influence on policy or the climate of opinion. The IEA, for example, published papers advocating floating the pound, abolishing resale price maintenance, and ending full-employment Budgets, before they were achieved. But many other minds were also turning in these directions, and, outside the think-tanks themselves, no authoritative source has attributed decisive influence to their role. That a group or policy advocate recommends a course of action which is subsequently adopted is not proof of cause and effect. Cynics have suspected that some of the proposals advanced by the ASI were triggered by an awareness of what Whitehall was privately considering. An ASI proposal which 'anticipated' Whitehall could demonstrate its influence. The claims to influence which groups make may be repeated uncritically by the media and academics. A feature of Richard Cockett's *Thinking the Unthinkable* (1994) is that the claims to influence by the New Right think-tanks are frequently stated but not demonstrated. Communications with ministers and officials or photographs of meetings, however insubstantial or fleeting, with the Prime Minister are reported and prominently displayed in the group's promotional literature. A reputation for influence adds to credibility and can in turn improve access to policy-makers and an ability to attract funds. Two of John Major's closest advisers in Number 10 have dryly observed how virtually all the free-market think-tanks have claimed parentage of the Citizen's Charter (Hogg and Hill 1995: 103).

A potential pitfall of a think-tank's or advocate's promotional activity is that it may cause jealousy among rivals, including civil servants, other advisers, and politicians themselves. Sir Alan Walters's frequent claims to have decisively shaped the 1981 Budget have been disputed by the then Chancellor, Sir Geoffrey Howe. According to Sir Geoffrey, Walters was 'never happier than when he was making some exclusive input into the Prime Minister's thinking, except when he was taking (or claiming) the credit for having done so' (Howe 1994: 187). Media reports that Mrs Thatcher paid more attention to Walters's views on the defects of ERM than of her Chancellor's support for it contributed to Nigel Lawson's resentment of Walters and, eventually, his resignation.

The poll tax, health reforms, and education reforms were three policy areas in which radical ideas were canvassed. Below we examine the three areas.

Poll Tax

The origin of the poll tax (known officially as the community charge) is still surrounded by controversy. Fortunately, the whole episode has been the subject of a detailed study, revealingly titled *Failure in British Government* (Butler, Adonis, and Travers 1995). When introduced in Scotland in 1989 and then in England and Wales the following year, the tax was celebrated by the ASI as yet another example of its influence on government policy. However, when it turned out to be a political disaster, many of those associated with the birth of the tax rapidly distanced themselves from it.

The impetus for a reform of local-government finance lay in the widespread dissatisfaction with the existing system of household rates. Margaret Thatcher had pledged herself to abolish them in 1974, although when she became opposition leader and then Prime Minister other issues took priority. But there was no doubt of her feelings on the subject. Dissatisfaction led to a search for alternatives. The government-appointed Layfield Committee had considered and rejected a poll tax in 1976. In November 1979 Tom King, her Minister for Local Government, raised the tax as a possible alternative to rates. Michael Heseltine, the Secretary of State for the Environment, issued a Green Paper in December 1981 which acknowledged that rates might be replaced by a poll tax. In October, a few weeks before the publication of the Green Paper, Madsen Pirie of the ASI had proposed a *per capita* tax in the *Daily Mail*. The idea was rejected by the Environment Committee of the House of Commons in 1982, and the following year a government White Paper, *Rates*, concluded that there was no alternative to domestic rates. That seemed to be the end of the matter; there was no satisfactory alternative to the rates.

The search for an alternative returned to the agenda in 1984 because of the hostile reaction to a revaluation of rates in Scotland. This had the effect of sharply increasing bills for many households. Conservative ministers were nervous about the impact of an imminent revaluation in England and Wales, and Mrs Thatcher set up a Cabinet committee in 1984 to look again at alternatives. William Waldegrave and Kenneth Baker were key members and both had reputations to make. The committee began work in the autumn and a decision to move to a poll tax was taken at a Chequers meeting in March 1985. In April, six months after the committee began its work, the ASI published Douglas Mason's paper, *Revising the Rating*

System (1985), which proposed a flat-rate tax, and was followed by Michael Forsyth's *The Case for a Poll Tax* (1985), published by the Conservative Political Centre. By the time the idea was officially launched in public by Baker's 1986 Green Paper, *Paying for Local Government* (DoE 1986), it had been widely canvassed. The poll-tax proposal was included in the 1987 Conservative election manifesto and became law in 1989.

Notwithstanding its claims to parentage of the tax, few insiders gave credit to the ASI. Indeed, the authoritative *Failure in British Government* (Butler, Adonis, and Travers 1995: 30–1) suggests that the members of the Cabinet committee were more influenced by the book *Local Government Finance in a Unitary State* (1980) by the LSE Professor Chris Foster, and that pressure from senior ministers for an alternative to the rates 'was far more important than the overtly ideological attachment to the poll tax', or the contributions of Mason or Forsyth (ibid. 72). Crick and van Kleveran (1991: 407) state that some ministerial members of the committee claim never to have heard of the ASI, and Kenneth Baker does not refer to it in his memoirs. Cynical observers suggest that this was a case of the ASI jumping on a bandwagon (Heffernan 1996: 84). One might conclude that the ASI's main achievement was to fly the poll-tax kite and demonstrate to civil servants that the idea had support in Tory circles.

Health

Britain in the 1980s, in common with a number of other Western states, faced spending pressures from the growing costs of health care. The pressures were a consequence of an ageing population, developments of new medical technology, and rising expectations for better care. Health was a demand-driven service and obviously a matter of concern to Conservative ministers, who wished to curb the growth of public spending. They were inclined to regard the calls by doctors, consultants, and nurses for more money and more staff as white-collar trade unionism. In a search for greater value for money, ministers borrowed the devices of audit, performance indicators, and competitive tendering from the private sector. Think-tanks floated other ideas. The IEA supported charging and vouchers, on the grounds that these would give patients more choice, facilitate the injection of more funds into high-demand services, and help to cut waiting lists. The ASI favoured the extension of private health care backed by tax relief. Both proposals foundered on Treasury opposition. Ministers were also cautious because they knew that hostility from the medical profession was supported by distrust among voters who did not think that the NHS was 'safe' in Conservative hands. Surveys regularly showed that voters suspected ministers of wanting to privatize health care and of creating a two-tier service, with the NHS providing an inferior service.

Faced with another funding crisis after the 1987 general election, Mrs Thatcher decided to set up a ministerial working group chaired by herself. She rejected the idea of a royal commission or a departmental inquiry. The group's remit was to review the financing of health, but it soon took in questions of the structure of the NHS. It considered submissions from a number of groups, including the IEA, the CPS, and the ASI, and Madsen Pirie of the ASI and David Willetts of the CPS were members of the working party. The ASI advocated the merits of a version of US health maintenance organizations (HMOs) in which subscribers pre-paid to provide comprehensive health care for an agreed period. HMOs had an incentive to keep charges down so that a subscriber would remain loyal. Other radical suggestions, including a hypothecated health tax, vouchers, or extending private insurance, were rejected. Universal free care would remain.

The key element in the eventual scheme, revealed in the government White Paper (Cmnd 555) *Working for Patients* (January 1989), was the establishment of a managed internal market in which GPs, consultants, and health authorities would purchase care on behalf of their patients from hospital trusts. There would be a separation of health providers from health purchasers, and the former would have to compete for custom. Giving doctors budgets, it was hoped, would enable them to influence the behaviour of hospitals (Thatcher 1993: 614), and so to drive down costs. The idea of the internal market was the work of Professor Alan Enthoven, of Stanford University, California, whose work was brought to wider attention by Norman Macrae's (1984) lengthy survey of health reform in *The Economist*, and Enthoven's 'Revolution in the Management of the NHS' (1985).

Mrs Thatcher claims (1993: 617) that, had she remained in office, she would have extended incentives for private health care and in certain cases provided patients with a credit from their district health authority for use within the NHS or the private sector. The effect of the think-tanks on policy was modest (Williamson 1993) and was primarily to popularize ideas from the USA—either Enthoven's work on internal markets or the experience of the HMOs.

Education

In the 1960s Conservative critics of state education were variously *preservationists*, who wished to retain the best of the traditional school curriculum and education methods, and more market-oriented *reformers*, who wished to extend choice and make schools more accountable to parents (Raab 1993). The authors of the *Black Papers*, launched in 1969 (Cox and Dyson 1969), were among the earliest critics of progressive teaching and elimination of streaming in comprehensive schools, and supported a return to a traditional curriculum and the introduction of testing.

The main counter-attack from the right came in the mid-1970s. In his *Crisis in Education* (1975), Rhodes Boyson, a Conservative councillor, headteacher, and member of various education groups, advocated greater parental choice and a national curriculum. Another pacemaker was Stuart Sexton, an adviser to Boyson, influential member of various groups, and a special adviser to two Conservative education ministers after 1979. He argued, additionally, for schools of excellence and a monitoring of standards. Interestingly, all these reforms were to be achieved in the 1980s (Knight 1990: 112).

The think-tanks were slower to tackle education. The IEA, perhaps predictably, argued for education vouchers as a means of increasing parental choice while maintaining a universal system. The idea had been launched in a Bow Group paper in 1959 by Brendon Sewill, subsequently Director of the Conservative Research Department (1965–70). It was also considered by the Conservatives in opposition after 1966 and rejected because of fears of the disruption it would cause (Knight 1993: 92). In 1975 the CPS established a study group on education which provided a platform for radicals such as Caroline Cox, John Marks, and Stuart Sexton. As well as advocating the above reforms they also favoured the abolition of the ILEA. In time, the first two moved on to establish the Hillgate Group to campaign for education reform and Sexton created the Education Unit at the IEA. Concern was not confined to the right. In his call for a 'great debate' on education at Ruskin College in 1976, the Labour Prime Minister Jim Callaghan supported a core curriculum, steps to monitor standards, and greater links between education and industry. To an extent, schooling was being made a scapegoat for economic failure (Raab 1993: 231).

By the time of the 1979 general election dissatisfaction with schooling was found across the political spectrum, although most reformers were concentrated in the Conservative Party. Conservative critics complained of a lack of choice (exacerbated by mandatory comprehensive education and the elimination of grammar schools), poor results in tests, the emphasis on equality instead of excellence, and 'producer capture' of education, as the interests of teaching unions, local government officials, and professionals outweighed those of parents and students.

The 1980 Education Act took steps to widen parental choice and give parents representation on governing bodies. Another Act in 1986 went further in requiring schools to provide greater information about their performances and reduce local authority representation on school governing bodies. The thrust of these reforms was consolidated in the 1988 Education Reform Act. This introduced a core curriculum, extended parental choice, brought in local management of school budgets, and allowed schools to opt out of local-authority control and become grant maintained. Mrs Thatcher's commitment was reflected in her decision to chair the Cabinet committee on education. Although the voucher scheme was looked at on a number of occasions and rejected (Arthur Seldon 1986), open enrolment and *per capita* funding achieved some of the purposes of the voucher system and have been called a quasi-voucher (Raab 1993: 233). Mrs Thatcher claims that with these measures her government had gone as far as possible towards a 'public-sector voucher' (1993: 280), but her final, 1990, party-conference speech still hinted at vouchers (ibid.: 591).

State schooling, like health, continues to be provided out of taxes for the vast majority of the population. Proposals for charging or hints of privatization have frightened the politicians. Instead of privatization, they have used internal markets backed by performance indicators (and, inevitably, league tables). The 1988 Act combines the strong state with a free market, exemplified in the core curriculum and the extension of parental choice. 'The state is thus "rolled back" where possible and brought to heel where not' (Raab 1993: 238). The think-tanks have certainly promoted debate about state education, have canvassed reforms and have had a strong impact on legislation. It is a case of committed individuals who have also been active in local government (important for the Conservatives in the late 1970s) and the Conservative Advisory Committee on Education. They were able to table resolutions at annual Conservative conferences and provide an input to the Research Department. In some respects the groups have operated as internal party think-tanks. But perhaps even more important in forcing change were events and mounting public concern.

For what it is worth, the memoirs of virtually all Mrs Thatcher's Cabinet ministers make very few references to the think-tanks (Heffernan 1996: 83), and studies of policy initiatives in the 1980s rate their influence as no more than modest compared to broader circumstances (Hames and Feasey 1994: 227). The opportunities and pressures presented by the oil shocks in the 1970s, the splits in the Labour Party, and the Winter of Discontent were crucial to the acceptance of the new ideas. As one shrewd Conservative insider (pre-Thatcher) comments: 'A revolution in policy requires more than people prepared to think the unthinkable' (Douglas 1994: 245). For the most part, New Right ideas seem to have been taken on board only when they served the purposes of politicians. Central to many policy shifts was the practical experience of politicians; many existing policies had shown themselves to be unworkable at the levels of Conservative Party interest and effective government. As

Harrison's thorough study comments: 'Political philosophy (Hayek) and monetarist theory (Friedman) chimed in with, articulated, and provided a framework of action for sentiments that arose from personal instincts and practical situations' (Harrison 1994: 217).

The verdicts of recent studies specifically designed to examine the impact of ideas on the shaping of policy in post-war Britain reinforce this scepticism:

- we can be reasonably confident in saying that, although both ideas and practices have changed, the history of social policy in the post-war period is not primarily one of changing ideas shaping a changing political practice. (Pierson 1996: 162)

- what is surprising about the impact of ideas on post-war British history is just how limited rather than great their impact has been. Even where their influence is demonstrable, they need to be seen in the context of the interplay of interests, individuals and circumstances. To understand what has shaped post-war Britain, ideas on their own are not enough. (Seldon 1996: 289)

- politicians . . . will rarely be able to afford the luxury of treating ideas too seriously as ideas. On most occasions, ideas will form part of the manipulative mechanisms of British governing. As such, they will be variably employed as weapons of attack, defence, praise or denigration. (Bulpitt 1996: 226)

- As for UK deregulations, it is all too obvious that the originating forces were diverse. (Swann 1993: 141)

- [It] . . . is difficult to resist the conclusion that the 'New Right' phenomenon as such has had a fairly vague and indeterminate role in the causation of social changes and that the impact of the 'New Right' and its ideas has been fairly indirect, unsystematic and fragmented. (Welsh 1993: 54)

- It is mistaken to suggest that think-tanks provided in themselves the ideas that give intellectual weight to Thatcherism. Any direct impact that they had was at the margin of public policy rather than at the centre. (Heffernan 1996: 82)

One does not have to look far for the constraints imposed by other political actors. In government the influence of the permanent civil service, fears of the reaction of interest groups, and concern about electoral reactions may all induce second thoughts among politicians.

Mrs Thatcher was a great reformer, but on numerous occasions her own caution or opposition from colleagues held her back. In her memoirs she claims that resistance from colleagues prevented her from proceeding with school vouchers, doing more on private health insurance, and keeping Britain out of the ERM in 1990 (Thatcher 1993: 591, 615, 697). Lawson and Howe go further and accuse her of outright timidity on occasions—for example, on proposals to abolish the NEDC in 1987 and the National Dock Labour Scheme in 1989 (Lawson 1992: 718). Alfred Sherman and John Hoskyns retired from the ranks of her advisers in some frustration at her failure to follow up some of their more radical proposals.

Other Influences

Yet think-tanks can have other functions which may, indirectly or eventually, show up in policy outcomes. They include:

1. *Influencing the climate of opinion.* Anthony King (1992) notes that in the twentieth century the three periods of major agenda change in British politics—1906–14, 1945–50, and post-1979—were all preceded by a ferment of new ideas. The ideas helped to create a new climate of opinion and were picked up by policy-makers. For much of the post-war period Keynesianism and assumptions about the benefits of government intervention in the economy and provision of welfare prevailed in Whitehall. In the 1970s, however, there was a revival of neo-liberal ideas which shaped perceptions of government being borne down with excessive expectations, entitlements, and public-spending commitments.

Respectable academics can provide arguments and evidence to controvert conventional wisdom and question existing policy. Both Nigel Lawson (1992: 606) and Sir Keith Joseph (1987) admitted that their thinking on the educational system was influenced by Correlli Barnett's *Audit of War* (1986), a study of Britain's relative economic decline in the post-war period. Thatcher (1977) paid tribute to the work of Robert Bacon and Walter Eltis, which argued that the growth of the public sector was 'starving' the private sector of investment and workers. Many policy-makers have paid tribute to the work of Hayek on markets, Friedman on the money supply, and the Virginia School on the public-spending consequences of budget-expansionist bureaucrats, vote-buying politicians, and public-sector trade unions.

2. *Reinforcing the instincts, values, and policy agendas of politicians.* At times this role may take the form of acting as a ginger group to combat the alleged obstructiveness of civil servants. One popular link with Whitehall for think-tanks is via ministers' special advisers. These were introduced by Wilson's Labour Government in 1964 and extended under Mrs Thatcher. In 1974 Wilson also created a Policy Unit in Number 10 for the Prime Minister. Under both Thatcher and Major, members of the Unit and ministers' special advisers maintained close links with think-tanks. A number of Secretaries of State encouraged policy advocates to debate issues with their senior civil servants; at Education, for example, Sir Keith Joseph invited Arthur and Marjorie Seldon to argue the case for school vouchers with his senior civil servants. Advocates have also been able to take advantage of the working parties established by departments and Number 10 to review particular policies. Mrs Thatcher's memoirs acknowledge her reliance on Walters to counter the pro-European thrust of the Treasury and the Foreign Office and on Sherman and Hoskyns to toughen industrial-relations policies when Jim Prior was Secretary of State of Employment (1979–82). Sir Geoffrey Howe admits that he was irritated by Mrs Thatcher's frequent invocation of remarks (usually critical) from 'my people'—outside the party—such as Sherman, Lord Wyatt, David Hart, and Brian Crozier when she was arguing a point with him. Howe objected to her tendency to cite their dismissal of his department's policies, not least when their opinions could not be tested by his officials.

3. *Supplying a vocabulary for politicians.* The think-tanks were certainly important in promoting the political 'buzzwords' of choice, incentives, enterprise, welfare dependency, and self reliance. The CPS was important in its early years in recruiting help for Sir Keith and Mrs Thatcher to write speeches. This opposed the 'old' lexicon of social justice, redistribution, incomes policy, planning, and state intervention, as politicians pressed levers to shape behaviour. John

Vaizey (1983: 5) characterizes this view as resting on the belief that 'if politics could be got "right" then . . . the economy, business, social and racial problems would all be straightened out'.

4. *Providing networks and mutual support.* The offices of the groups are located within a few square miles of each other in Westminster, close to Parliament, Whitehall, and Conservative Central Office. Regular study lunches, seminars, and other social gatherings provide social and intellectual support for participants. Until 1979 many New Right advocates regarded themselves, probably correctly, as a beleaguered minority, not just in the universities, but in the media and even in the Conservative Party. 'In the early days we reassured the handful of free marketeers that they were not alone,' said IEA's Arthur Seldon in an interview.

The CPS was a meeting-point for like-minded people. Alfred Sherman who was working as speech-writer and adviser to Sir Keith Joseph at the CPS, introduced John Hoskyns and Norman Strauss (then at Unilever) to each other in 1974 and then to Sir Keith and to Mrs Thatcher. Although advocacy of free-market ideas was oriented to the Conservative Party, the party's Research Department between 1974 and 1979 was headed by Chris Patten and was not sympathetic to many of these suggestions. After 1979, and Patten's departure from the department, this changed. Some of the key think-tank figures were appointed in Whitehall as advisers and were able to provide a direct input to policy. There has been a remarkable degree of overlap in the memberships of the boards and study groups and authors of the pamphlets of the various think-tanks. The close links between the activists have helped to develop what has been called 'a free enterprise solar system' (Graham Mather, interview). But many of the contacts were informal. According to John Burton, at one time an economist with the IEA, the influence of the groups cannot 'be represented in informal organizational charts by listing government appointments. There are also basic social realities such as patterns of friendship, think-tank networks, and behind-the-scenes intellectual milieux' (1993: 110).

5. *Flying kites.* A group's independence from a political party gives it a freedom that a party's research department lacks; it can

'think the unthinkable'. Whatever emanates from a party body is regarded by the media as a statement from the party; if a think-tank raises a controversial idea, it can be disowned by a party. In fact, sections of the media and the political opposition are still likely to regard a think-tank as a 'front' for a party and headline a report or statement from a free-market think-tank as a 'Tory proposal' or even a 'hidden agenda', as Labour used ASI's Omega File in the 1987 general election. In the 1990s the closeness of the Institute of Public Policy Research (IPPR) to Labour meant that it was sometimes seen as a front for the party.

6. *Supplying a take-off for a career in politics and government.* Increasingly, MPs are drawn from the para-political ranks of special advisers, party officials and researchers, lobbyists, and members of think-tanks (Riddell 1993). David Willetts, once of the Policy Unit, then of the CPS, became a Conservative MP in 1992 and a minister in 1995. The CPS indeed was a remarkable feeder for the Thatcher Government. Apart from John Hoskyns's transition to head of the Policy Unit, other alumni include Walters, Lord Young of Graffham, and John Redwood, who later headed Mrs Thatcher's Policy Unit, before joining a merchant bank and becoming an MP and then Cabinet Minister under John Major. Graham Mather (once of the Freedom Association, the Institute of Directors, the IEA, and since 1993 the European Policy Forum) became a Conservative MEP in 1994.

The US Example

Britain and the USA, under Thatcher and Reagan, were the pioneers of the New Right politics in the 1980s (Adonis and Hames 1994). The first sought to combat the collectivist consensus, dating from the 1945 Labour Government, the second to undo F. D. Roosevelt's New Deal agenda dating from the 1930s. The sense of a shared Anglo-American enterprise was reinforced by the two leaders' close personal relationship and the links between the Conservative and Republican parties. There is no doubt that the USA under the Reagan Presidency (1981–9) was an inspiration for much of the

British New Right. The role of think-tanks and the academic work on monetarism and public choice were more advanced in the USA and there was an even more powerful growth of libertarian and free-market ideas. Bodies such as the American Enterprise Institute, the Hoover Institution, and the Heritage Foundation were generously endowed and in many respects set the agenda for some of the British groups. Common New Right themes in both countries included hostility to the scale of government intervention in the economy and provision of welfare, as well as to the growth of taxation, bureaucracy, and regulations, and support for a strong stand on defence and law and order. The smaller public sector and lower public spending and tax GDP ratios in the USA meant that it had a less developed form of the collectivist polity found in Britain and Western Europe. There was also a deeply rooted historical and cultural suspicion about the role of central government itself.

One may point to some influences on the British right from Western Europe, such as Austrian economics (on the IEA) or social-market thought in post-war Germany (on the SMF). But the sum total pales in comparison with the US contribution. A number of West European states, with their emphasis on corporatism or the social-partnership approach to economic management, and the EU with its pursuit of a fixed exchange rate and social protection and regulatory aspects of the social chapter, have been a negative model for many Conservatives.

In the USA the opinion-forming and policy roles of think-tanks have been helped by various factors, including the profusion of radio and television channels, opportunities to purchase air time, and the sheer variety of newspaper and journal outlets which provide a platform. Heritage, for example, provides policy briefs for Washington politicians, consultants, and media reporters, and New Right ideas are discussed sympathetically in journals such as the *American Spectator*, *Public Interest*, and *Commentary*. They are backed by powerful lobbies such as the Moral Majority, the National Taxpayers' Union, and various tax-cutting groups and organizations, such as the Conservative Caucus, the National Conservative Political Caucus, and the Committee for the Survival of a Free Congress. These have exploited the new technology of television and computerized mailing to build up lists of supporters and raise funds. The groups have lent support to the many single-issue pressure groups which are sympathetic to right-wing causes—for example, the anti-abortion group Life Amendment Political Action Committee (LAPAC) and Gun Owners of America (Peele 1984). They were also associated with an electorally successful President and with the economically dynamic and politically influential 'sunbelt' of the West and South.

Yet there were significant differences between the two countries. Reagan's tax cuts, for example, were advocated and defended largely on supply-side grounds; it was claimed that the cuts would pay for themselves because the incentives would make people work harder, increase earnings, and boost tax revenues. Tax reductions in Britain were a part, but not a major part, of New Right economics and were advanced as a means of promoting efficiency and enhancing personal choice. The British Treasury showed more interest in controlling the money supply and balancing the budget. The American New Right was also willing to make use of state and local government as a counter to federal government; returning funds and power to the states was seen as part of a conservative agenda to roll back government. This is a stark contrast to the major curbs which Conservative governments imposed on local government (Jenkins 1995). The cornerstones of the Thatcher project were privatizing state utilities, curbing local government powers, and reducing the influence of trade unions. In contrast, such concerns were only minor features of the Reagan project.

Another difference between the two countries lies in the political importance of morality and religion. American religious groups have advanced the issues of abortion, pornography, and school prayers to the heart of politics; but these hardly figure at all as political issues in Britain. A related Anglo-American difference lies in the role of judiciary and attitudes to the constitution. Although the right in Britain has long attacked 'lenient' sentencing by judges, there is a greater recognition in the USA of the judiciary's wide policy-making role. This in turn heightens public interest in the views of candidates for judicial office, particularly to the Supreme Court. The courts and judges have been attacked for their 'liberal' bias on such issues as racial integration, mandatory school bussing, quotas, defendants' rights in courts, and abortion. The American right has also been more interested in constitutional measures like a balanced budget amendment to the constitution—to curb deficit spending—or a call for tax-cutting referendums at local and state levels. Their British counterparts have had little to say about checks and balances on the executive; indeed, a sovereign Parliament (with a Conservative majority) was the means of achieving much of the Thatcherite agenda.

Bosanquet (1983) has claimed that the ideas of the New Right have had a greater impact in Britain and the USA than in Western European countries because of the relative weakness or absence of strong social democratic or Christian Democratic traditions in the first two countries. In the USA, the right has also been able to invoke a liberal consensus which includes a suspicion of government and its potential threat to liberty. In Britain, the combination of relative economic decline, which undermined the established policy consensus, and the crisis of the Labour Party provided the New Right with its opportunity. In both countries the groups gained intellectual respectability, media attention, approval from influential politicians, and electoral support.

Many of the New Right ideas have not been confined to Britain and the USA. Governments in many countries are striving to contain the rise in costs of public services without reduction in quality, improve economic performance, curb inflation, restrict borrowing, and make government more efficient. There has been a good deal of policy transfer across borders, as policy-makers and policy advocates have sought lessons from abroad. New Right reformers in Britain looked to the USA and Sweden for labour-market policies, to New Zealand for improvements in the civil service, and so forth. In the field of health-care reforms, to take one example, there are many similarities between the mixture of competition and regulation adopted by governments in Britain as well as in Sweden, Germany, and the Netherlands, regardless of the political complexion of the government. Many Western countries have experimented with allowing the money to follow the patient, separating purchasers of health care from providers, and increasing competition between providers. Williamson comments: 'the reforms in Britain appear much more part of an international movement which is attempting to come to terms with escalating costs than some neo-liberal experiment' (1993: 209). Much the same could be said of reforms in schools and higher education.

Conclusion

In so far as the New Right approach is about limiting the role of government, it can in theory affect all policy areas. In practice, it has to date largely concentrated on the economy, the privatization of state utilities, industrial relations, and reforming the public services, and has largely ignored constitutional and foreign-policy questions. This neglect is being remedied. The IEA, not surprisingly in view of its support of a liberal economic agenda, has shown an interest in political reform and even a written constitution—a traditional means of achieving limited government. Europe has emerged as a major source of concern to the think-tanks. Developments in the European Union and rulings of the European Court of Justice increasingly infringe on British domestic policies and, at times, work against the free market.

We return again to the perennial question of the relationships between ideas and circumstances. It is not possible to say which of the two is more important; one without the other is hardly likely to produce policy innovation. The two connect as circumstances colour the perceptions of policy-makers, and ideas can indirectly shape circumstances, not least by helping to discredit the status quo. Any study of particular cases is likely to conclude that ideas influence policy outcomes only when they work in conjunction with interests and circumstances. In the cases of the poll tax, privatization, monetarism, and curbs on the unions, the dissatisfaction with the status quo increased the receptivity of policy-makers to new ideas. John Stuart Mill put it well in his essay 'The Claims of Labour' (1845): 'But when the right circumstances and the right ideas meet, the effect is seldom slow in manifesting itself.' Even if many of the measures of the Thatcher Governments are judged to have been *ad hoc* and pragmatic, rather than part of a grand hegemonic project, we should not neglect the advantages which Conservative ministers could gain from them. Indeed the public-choice approach would urge us always to be sensitive to the self-interest (or 'rent-seeking' behaviour) of all politicians (cf. Jenkins 1995). It so happens that each of the three policies examined above—and one could add to their number—suited the political designs of Conservative ministers. They had the effects of weakening local government, trade unions, and the nationalized industries—all three of which were seen by ministers as anti-market institutions.

8 The Taming of Labour

In a democracy, political parties operate in a competitive environment. If politicians are not quite like profit-seeking businessmen in a market, they do seek office and, therefore, votes. With office, they will have the opportunity to put their policies into effect. In a competitive system, a party's policies are in part necessarily reactive, shaped by the actions of rivals and the actual or anticipated responses of voters. Party leaders seek to satisfy their activists, sympathizers, and, sometimes, non-supporters, and appealing to these groups may be in conflict. Parties also have to compete against their rivals, not least to ensure that they do not concede issues. Before 1914, the Liberals were pacesetters on social reform, in part to head off the infant Labour Party's appeal to the working class. After 1945, the Conservatives were compelled to come to terms with the welfare and full-employment policies of the Labour Government. In 1974 Labour embraced Scottish devolution as an answer to the rise of nationalism north of the border. The need to win votes is an incentive to adopt or abandon particular policies.

A party in government has many more resources to shape the political agenda than does one in opposition. Such devices as the Queen's Speech, Prime Minister's Question Time, ministerial statements, the annual Budget, and control of the parliamentary timetable all provide opportunities. The media are usually more interested in reporting what the party in government is doing or saying. The opposition has to react; will it accept, amend, or reverse the government's proposals? Governments can act, oppositions can only talk. After each election defeat in 1979, 1983, 1987, and 1992, it has had to review its image and policies in the light of the electorate's rejection of them, and after each defeat accept fresh tranches of the Conservative programme, including policies that it had resolutely opposed. Changes have been such that the Blair leadership now refers to the party as New Labour. To what extent is this attributable to Thatcher?

It is worth restating the novelty in the twentieth century of a British government:

(*a*) having a coherent political project,
(*b*) seeking to dismantle much of the policy status quo, and
(*c*) winning three consecutive general elections, each with commanding parliamentary majorities.

Mrs Thatcher created problems for many traditional Conservatives; she created even more for Labour, the official opposition. During the 1987 election she declared that her objective was the destruction of socialism, but that Labour would never disappear in her lifetime. This meant forcing the party to abandon its attachment to policies of high taxation, borrowing, and spending, and its hostility to free enterprise. In other words, she wanted a Thatcherite policy consensus to prevail even after she had left the political scene. This chapter concludes that her objective appears to have been largely achieved.

Labour, like any defeated party, had to come to terms with the scale of its defeat in the 1979 general election and what it signified about its record in government. Initially, the party made a sharp turn to the left. This was a consequence less of a reaction to Thatcherism than dissatisfaction with the record of the Callaghan Government. For much of the Labour left, the enemy was the party's right-wing leadership. They regarded 1979 as a watershed. The party's electoral decline and the weakness of the British economy were interrelated. Trying to make capitalism and the mixed economy work was doomed and Labour's pursuit of the electoral middle ground had failed. The critics successfully argued that Labour should adopt left-wing policies, break with the consensus, and become more responsive to its activists. The Labour right had a different analysis. They had dominated the leadership and blamed the left (and the Conference and National Executive on which the left was well represented) for making unreasonable demands, and the unions, whose strikes against the pay policy had weakened the government. The right lost the argument.

The reaction of voters to this analysis turned out to be quite different from that anticipated by the left. In the short term, the changes led to a Labour split, acceleration of electoral decline, and relegation to its longest period in opposition since it was created as a national party in 1918. In the longer term, however, the party had its most right-wing policies in its history. Anthony Downs (1957) has elegantly argued that in a competitive two-party system the losing party will 'rationally' move towards the policies of the winning party so that both parties will pursue the 'floating' voter who is assumed to favour policies in the middle (see p. 47). If this analysis applied in a competitive two-party system with a largely consensual electorate, the parties would end up with pretty similar policies. In the case of the Labour Party, this is indeed what occurred after the 1959 election defeat and, as will be argued, happened incrementally after election defeats in 1983, 1987, and 1992.

It is not inevitable, however, that the losing party will move towards its opponent. At times, the Labour leadership has reacted to election in a non-Downsian manner, *particularly when it has just lost office*. After Labour governments lost elections in 1931, 1970, and 1979 there was a move in the opposite direction, as influential critics blamed the party's recent record in government for alienating its supporters.

The crisis of the Labour Party in the 1980s was compounded of four interlinked features—the failure of revisionism as a political strategy, electoral decline, the left's success in reforming the party's institutions, and a split which led to the creation of the Social Democratic Party in 1981. An examination of Labour's decline is important for understanding the weakening of the post-war consensus and the opportunities provided for Mrs Thatcher.

Revisionism

Many Labour supporters took much pride in the achievements of the Attlee Government of 1945. It still remains the only government in the party's history which is widely regarded in a positive light. But after it lost office in 1951 what was to follow? On public ownership in particular there was intense debate whether the 1945–51 nationalization measures should be the first instalment towards the achievement of a more state-managed economy or whether the party should now consolidate the mixed economy. In large part this was a battle between the party's left and right wings, although the factionalism extended to other issues, notably, attitudes to the American alliance, German rearmament, and Britain's role as a nuclear power.

The major theorist of the Labour revisionists was Anthony Crosland. His book, *The Future of Socialism* (1956), was their Bible. The term was originally applied to the ideas of the expatriate German Socialist Eduard Bernstein. At the end of the nineteenth century Bernstein had noted that capitalism, contrary to Marxist predictions, was not on the verge of breakdown and that a working-class revolution and a socialist breakthrough were not imminent. He argued that socialists could and should work through the existing political system and introduce reforms rather than plan for the revolution. Crosland similarly reminded his readers that changes in management and the blurring of lines between public and private industry meant that now 'capitalism was reformed almost out of recognition' (1956: 517). Managers had become more socially responsible, as much interested in creating a stable economic environment as the pursuit of profits, and Keynesian macro-economic techniques equipped the government with sufficient leverage over demand to deliver full employment and influence the decision of firms without directly controlling them. Public ownership was no longer important, although the industries that had been nationalized should remain so. Modern socialism should be about achieving greater social and economic equality, through programmes of state spending to improve public services, progressive income taxation, and measures to narrow unearned differences in income. Economic growth and a larger economic pie were important if greater equality and redistribution in favour of the less well-off were to be achieved without conflict. The Conservatives had realized this and the shift in the political agenda to the left could therefore be regarded as permanent. Labour had won the argument.

As noted in Chapter 2, Labour became less ambitious in its plans for public ownership after 1951. Following the party's third successive election defeat in 1959, the party leader Hugh Gaitskell argued that the party had to come to terms with affluence and full employment and their effects on the working class. In particular, he wished to amend the party's Clause 4, which proclaimed the party's objective of comprehensive public ownership. The clause enabled their opponents to say that Labour believed in taking every corner shop into public ownership and slighted the party's other objectives. Gaitskell was defeated in this attempt to attack the core part of Labour's ideology. In practice, however, Labour governments between 1964 and 1970 proved to be revisionist. Apart from rationalizing iron and steel, they acted as though capitalism, subject to controls, was succeeding.

Yet the record of the Labour Governments of 1964–70 and 1974–9 presented a problem for the revisionists who occupied many of the Cabinet positions. The slowdown of economic growth in the West in the 1970s—what the left called a crisis of capitalism—called into question the validity of their analysis. Crosland had always argued that popular support for greater social spending and redistribution depended on economic growth. Without growth, taxes would have to increase to fund public services; in turn, this would generate demands for wage increases; and, in the absence of economic growth, inflation. The Wilson Governments (1964–70) quickly abandoned the pursuit of economic growth, made the balance of payments the top priority, and brought many low-paid workers into the tax net. Surveys showed that by 1970 support for more spending on social services had dropped more sharply among voters who were most disappointed by the Labour Government's economic record (Butler and Stokes 1974: 296–302). Affluence was required to make people feel sufficiently well off to support 'altruistic' social policies (Alt 1979: 381). There was also growing evidence in the 1970s that increases in the so-called social wage (i.e. on public services and welfare benefits) did not serve to dampen pressure from employees to maintain or increase wages and salaries. Indeed, in his last work Crosland (1975) was no longer so confident that expanding public spending was the route to greater equality. He complained that much spending promoted middle-class interests and he advocated giving priority to public spending which would benefit the working class.

Revisionists had also claimed that, because their policies would bring economic and electoral success, they could defy the party's Conference. But what if successive Labour governments failed to improve the social services and promote economic equality? What if their policies divided the party and led to quarrels with the unions (for example, over incomes policies and proposed reforms of industrial relations)?

The Wilson Government started out in 1964 with high hopes. It promised to boost economic growth, expand the social services, and plan the British economy. From the outset it chose to make the balance of payments and the exchange rate of sterling a priority. The position of sterling as an international currency made it vulnerable to international flows of funds. Because of the weakness of the British economy, holders of overseas funds lacked confidence, particularly when Labour was in office. Labour ministers after 1964 and 1974 found that foreign funds were attracted only by high interest rates (which inhibited home investment) and squeezing public spending (cf. Callaghan 1987: 167). Devaluation in 1967 was followed by a series of spending cuts to turn around the balance of payments. Much the same occurred under the Callaghan Government.

The intervention of the IMF to save the pound in 1976 was a significant watershed in post-war economic policy. A loan was arranged on condition that the government cut planned public-spending totals, increased the excise tax, and sold off some British Petroleum shares; all were steps designed to cut the PSBR in spite of the high level of unemployment. This was the opposite of Keynesian policy and, ironically, was based on calculations which were subsequently shown to have overstated the deficit (Healey 1989). The policy worked in that interest rates and inflation fell steadily and the pound recovered (Dell 1996). More significantly, the key elements of Thatcherite economics were in place: according priority to low inflation over low unemployment, squeezing public spending, cutting the PSBR, accepting the limits to high rates of taxation of incomes, and curbing the growth of the money supply.

One result of the disillusion with the Wilson and Callaghan governments was electoral decline. Another was that the influence of the left grew in the extra-parliamentary party, as did the influence of the latter—the constituency activists, trade-union delegates, and the National Executive Committee (NEC)—*vis-à-vis* the parliamentary party. (Seyd 1987).

Electoral Decline

Over the thirty-four year period, 1945 to 1979, the Labour and Conservative parties were each in government for seventeen years. Electorally, Labour was one of the most successful centre left parties in Western Europe. Compared to a number of its continental counterparts, it had many advantages; the British trade unions were not split politically or industrially, and there was no rival socialist party or strong Communist party competing for working-class votes. Moreover, it was usually the only centre-left party in Western Europe able to form a government on its own because it was unencumbered by operating in a multi-party system or a proportional electoral system. The first national survey of the British electorate (Butler and Stokes 1974) argued that Labour was becoming the party of the majority. The effects of social class (the working class was twice as large as the middle class and largely pro-Labour) and inheritance of party loyalties meant that, other factors being equal, it entered elections as the 'natural' majority party. The Conservative Party could still win general elections, but it would need skilled leadership, good luck, and Labour misfortunes to overturn an increasingly disadvantageous social and political context.

Politics, however, is not subject to such strict economic and sociological determinism. By 1979 Labour had undergone the most spectacular electoral decline of any socialist party in the post-war period. Between 1951 and 1979 it lost vote share at every general election bar 1966 and tumbled from 47 per cent in 1966 to 37 per cent in 1979. The steady erosion of support over these years among its core constituency, the working class, is seen in Table 8.1. Between 1964 and 1979 its share fell from 64 to 50 per cent and its lead over the Conservative Party from 36 to 15 per cent. In 1964 a clear majority of Labour identifiers supported the party's position on three important tests of socialism: extending public ownership, spending more on social services, and disagreeing with the proposition that the trade unions had too much power. By 1979, however, only a third of Labour identifiers supported these positions (see Table 8.2). Indeed, manual workers were more in sympathy with

TABLE 8.1. *Decline of Labour working-class vote (or percentage of popular vote)*

Votes	1959 Non-manual	Manual	1964 Non-manual	Manual	1966 Non-manual	Manual
Conservative	69	34	62	28	60	25
Liberal or minor party	8	4	16	8	14	6
Labour	22	62	22	64	26	69

Votes	1970 Non-manual	Manual	Feb. 1974 Non-manual	Manual	Oct. 1974 Non-manual	Manual
Conservative	64	33	53	24	51	24
Liberal or minor party	11	9	25	19	24	20
Labour	25	58	22	57	25	57

Votes	1979 Non-manual	Manual	1983 Non-manual	Manual
Conservative	60	35	58	33
Liberal or minor party	17	15	26	29
Labour	23	50	17	38

Source: Crewe (1984: 194), and sources cited there.

many Conservative than Labour manifesto proposals. Even on issues on which Labour was united, such as restoring trade-union rights, preventing council-house sales, public ownership, nationalization, comprehensive education, and providing more social-service benefits, working-class voters were divided. Labour was losing touch with its traditional voters.

There was also decline among Labour's grass roots. If we discount the trade-union affiliations (many of whom were reluctant or

TABLE 8.2. *Long-term trends in support for Labour Party policies amongst labour supporters (%)*

	1964	1966	1970	1974	1979	Change 1964–79
Percentage of Labour identifiers:						
In favour of nationalizing more industries	57	52	39	53	32	–25
Who do not believe that trade unions have 'too much power'	59	45	40	42	36	–23
In favour of spending more on the social services	89	66	60	61	n.a.	–28 (1964– Feb. 1974)

Sources: 1964, 1966, 1970: Butler and Stokes Election Surveys; Feb. 1974, Oct. 1974, 1979: British Election Study cross-section surveys.

involuntary members and indeed did not even vote Labour), individual membership fell from over a million in 1952 to less than 300,000 in 1979 and remained around this level throughout the 1980s. The decline of mass political parties is part of a general trend in Britain and elsewhere and coincides with the spread of affluence, television, and new forms of recreation and greater mobility. Interestingly, membership in many other voluntary organizations has actually increased over the same period. One result was that some smaller Labour parties in city centres were easy targets for 'takeovers' by left-wing activists. There was a significant radicalization of the Labour Party in local government in a number of cities. The heavy losses suffered by the party in the local elections in 1968 and 1969 swept away many senior Labour councillors, and in Manchester, Liverpool, Sheffield, and London boroughs they were replaced by younger, more assertive, and more left-wing councillors. Many of the councillors were employed in neighbouring local authorities or were officials in local public-sector trade unions or organizations. After 1979 they were frequently in conflict with the

Conservative Government because of their 'high' spending and 'high' rates. They were local socialists, spending money in part to regenerate their local economics, while the central government was pursuing a very different policy (Gyford 1985).

Although we have no long-term evidence on the point, it may be that the smaller Labour membership was both more left wing and more unrepresentative of Labour voters. A survey by Whiteley and Gordon of Labour Party delegates at the 1978 conference found that the majority of delegates were middle class (though self-described working class) and employed in the public sector (see Table 8.3). By large margins they supported Tony Benn as party leader, favoured a broad range of left-wing policies, and vigorously denounced the party leadership for its 'betrayal' of socialism. On all counts they were markedly out of line with the views of Labour voters. Within Parliament a new 'hard' left emerged, one which was much less respectful of parliamentary traditions. The replacement of sitting MPs over time through retirement and reselection due to constituency redistributions helped the left. The culmination of this trend was the election of Michael Foot as leader of the party over Mr Healey in 1980.

TABLE 8.3. *1978 Labour Conference delegates*

Occupational status	%
Public sector	60
Skilled workers	22
White-collar workers	70
Among white-collar workers:	
self-described working class	72
self-described middle-class	22
objectively clearly middle-class	57

Source: Whiteley and Gordon (1980).

Power in the party

Even before 1979 a number of critics could point to a recurring cycle of power relationships in the Labour Party's history. In opposition, the extra-parliamentary bodies, particularly Conference, usually became more assertive and influential, the policies often shifted to the left, and the party leader, lacking a Prime Minister's authority and patronage, was more beholden to them. In government, however, Labour leaders were more concerned with policies which they judged to be politically acceptable, administratively practicable, and economically affordable. Labour ministers were surrounded by civil servants and had to take account of the expectations of the financial markets and business. Conference, the party executive, and the trade unions were pressure groups, no more no less. At times the policies of a Labour government led to conflict with Conference and the NEC. As members of a 'national' government and with responsibilities to the national electorate, ministers could become less oriented to the party membership. After 1964 the Labour Government increasingly defied Conference, which was supposed to speak for rank-and-file party members.

Effective party leadership had long rested on cooperation between party leaders and the major trade unions, or at least acquiescence by the latter (Minkin 1980). This relationship broke down spectacularly in the outbreak of industrial unrest in 1979. Tony Benn was the most articulate spokesman for the thesis of 'betrayal' of the movement by its parliamentary leaders. Addressing the 1979 annual conference, held after Labour's election defeat, he proclaimed:

We have seen twenty years of surrender. Since 1959 the Parliamentary leadership of the Labour Party has been going along with the idea that the postwar consensus built upon full employment and the welfare state was a permanent feature of life in Britain and that the trade unions would be brought into a position where it helped to run it. That response has failed to command the support of our people, because they have seen at first hand that it did not contain within it any element whatsoever of transformation and second that even by its own criteria it failed. That policy could not bring about growth and could not extend freedom.

The lesson which the activists learnt from this history was that there was little point in winning policy battles when the party was in opposition, if Labour in government abandoned or diluted them. They therefore concentrated their energies on reforming the structure of the party. Making the parliamentary party subordinate to the

Conference might ensure that party policies were carried out. The call for greater party democracy was mounted by the left wing to make the Parliamentary Labour Party (PLP) more accountable to Conference and MPs more accountable to local party activists. Shifting the balance of power in the party became the left's preferred way of closing the gap between Conference and Labour MPs and forestalling 'betrayal' by the latter. Party democracy was a means of making Labour safe for socialism. Spearheaded by the Campaign for Labour Party Democracy, the activists circulated model resolutions, had them adopted by sympathetic constituency parties and trade-union branches, and successfully exploited the party's tradition of rank-and-file participation and the myth of Conference sovereignty.

Pressure for party reform centred on three demands: NEC control of the manifesto, mandatory reselection of MPs within the lifetime of Parliament, and election of the leader by party members, not just MPs. After a year of in-fighting the proposals were submitted to the 1980 conference at Blackpool. Votes for mandatory reselection and the election of the party leader by some form of electoral college were carried, but the proposal to give the NEC control of the manifesto was lost narrowly. A further conference was held at Wembley in January 1981 to decide on the details of how the party leader would be elected. The scheme eventually adopted granted the trade unions 40 per cent of the vote, MPs 30 per cent, and constituencies 30 per cent.

The reforms primarily concerned the relationships between the different party institutions and had been promoted and resisted by the left and right wings as a means of advancing their respective ideologies and interests. If there had been a greater agreement in the party on policy, then the debate over reforms would have been less divisive. As an exercise in making the party more democratic, the new system was flawed. Many other issues related to party democracy—such as the block vote of the trade unions, ballots using one member, one vote (OMOV), and the methods by which trade unions and constituency parties actually decided their votes at Conference—were ignored. This reform agenda was left to Kinnock and his successors.

When Mr Callaghan announced his resignation as party leader in October 1980, Denis Healey was the clear favourite to succeed him. Michael Foot was Deputy Leader but, because of his age (67) and his assumed support for Peter Shore, he was not regarded as a likely candidate. In the end he stood, in response to heavy pressure from trade-union leaders, constituency parties, and his own assessment that he would do better than any other left-winger against Mr Healey. On the first ballot Mr Healey ran ahead of Mr Foot, and Peter Shore and John Silkin were eliminated. But on the second ballot Mr Foot won by 139 votes to 129. His election was widely regarded as a vote for reconciliation and unity—he certainly gained a handful of votes from MPs on the centre and right who thought that he offered the best chance of avoiding a split in the party, as well as from some who hoped that his election would hasten a split. He was the first party leader from the left to be elected since George Lansbury in 1933.

The new machinery for electing leaders was tested fully in the election for the deputy leadership in 1981. The contest was another blow to the cause of party unity. In 1980, under the old system, Denis Healey had been elected to the post unopposed by MPs, but now he was opposed by Mr Benn and Mr Silkin.

The election campaign was a drawn-out and bitterly contested affair. When the votes were finally cast, Mr Silkin was eliminated on the first ballot and Mr Healey eventually defeated Mr Benn by a mere 0.8 per cent of the electoral college vote. His lead among MPs (137 to 71) and trade unions (3.9 million to 2.3 million votes) just overcame the 4-to-1 support of the constituency parties for Benn. A number of 'soft' left MPs who had supported John Silkin on the first ballot for the deputy leadership refused to vote for Tony Benn on the second round. To the fury of the latter's supporters, thirty-seven MPs, including Mr Kinnock, abstained. This was a decisive moment, both for the left, which fragmented into 'soft' and 'hard' groups, and for establishing Kinnock's leadership credentials.

The Split

The 1979 Parliament was significant for a split in the Labour Party and the emergence of a substantial 'third force' in British politics.

The exit of the Irish Nationalists from Parliament in 1918 and the rapid decline of the Liberals after 1929 had meant that Britain effectively had a two-party system. Although the Liberals made a gradual recovery in the 1960s and reached 18 per cent of the vote in February 1974, the British electoral system was a barrier to achieving a breakthrough in seats. In spite of episodic talk since the 1960s of a realignment on the centre left, involving a fusion of Liberals and Labour right-wingers, nothing came of it.

During 1979–80, however, two forces combined to assist the creation of the Social Democratic Party. The first factor was the growing unhappiness of a number of substantial Labour figures with what was happening in the party. In the end it was the 'Gang of Three'—Shirley Williams (out of Parliament), Bill Rodgers, and David Owen—who opened the path to a breakaway party. These were all members of the previous Labour administration and could reasonably have expected to hold office in a future one. They were unhappy at the party's repudiation of so many of the last Labour Government's policies, but it was the left's success in forcing through the constitutional changes that was the final straw for them. They feared that the left had captured the party for good.

The second factor was the availability of Roy Jenkins, whose term of office as President of the European Commission was due to end in January 1981; he was looking for a means of re-entry to British politics. Jenkins had left a post in the Labour Cabinet in 1976 to take up the Presidency, but was now disenchanted with what was happening to the party. In March 1981 the new Social Democratic Party was formally launched, supported now by fourteen Labour MPs and one Conservative. Within twelve months the number of MPs had grown to twenty-nine, thanks to further defections from Labour and by-election successes. Ivor Crewe and Anthony King (1995) show that the breakaway group was not primarily a revolt by the pro-European or the right wing of the party. Most defectors may have been of this persuasion (and Jenkins and the Gang of Three had resigned from Labour's front bench in 1972 over the decision to support a referendum on EC membership), but the majority of Labour's pro-European and right-wing MPs stayed in the fold. The key factor in swaying the defectors was that their roots in the Labour movement were shallower and their connections with the constituency more famous than those of the members who remained.

During 1981 and 1982 the electoral alliance of Social Democrats and Liberals emerged as the most formidable threat to the two-party system for over fifty years. But the major problems for the Alliance was that it did not mobilize a clearly defined social or geographical constituency and did not have a distinct agenda. Within its first twenty months support in opinion polls for the new party and the Alliance fluctuated between 20 and 50 per cent, a telling indicator of the 'softness' of its base. Once the element of novelty had disappeared, the Alliance found it difficult to secure mass-media attention. In early 1982 a downturn in support was apparent, even before the Falklands episode drove it from the front pages.

Labour entered the 1983 general election with a manifesto which did not command the support of many of its leading figures. One shadow minister termed it 'the longest suicide note in history'. It called for the reintroduction of exchange controls, the introduction of selective import controls and, not surprisingly, British withdrawal from the EC. It promised the abandonment of nuclear weapons, the restoration of privatized assets to public ownership, repeal of the Conservative industrial-relations measures, an end to compulsory council-home sales, a big rise in public spending, and a reduction of unemployment to one million within five years.

At the 1983 general election Labour's electoral decline accelerated. Its 27.6 per cent share of the vote was a fall of over 16 per cent from its clear defeat in 1959 and of 12 per cent from its last victory in October 1974. It finished 15 per cent behind the Conservatives— the biggest gap in the vote shares of the two main parties for over fifty years and only just ahead of the SDP. In terms of votes cast per candidate, it was the party's worst result since its creation in 1900. It was now a party of a section of the working class, supported by only 38 per cent of the manual workers and 39 per cent of trade unionists. The Conservatives had an eight-point lead (40 to 32 per cent) among the skilled working class according to Gallup. Labour could draw on the support of majorities only of workers in Scotland and the north of England, and of those who were employed in the public sector, and were council-house tenants. But affluent workers, who were car-owners, buying their own homes, and employed in the private sector, clearly preferred the Conservatives and had economic incentives for doing so. Labour's share of the vote in 1983 trailed behind that of socialist parties in virtually every West European state. From being an electoral leader, it was now a laggard (Crewe 1984).

Although the result was a disaster for the left, Tony Benn was consoled that eight million people had voted for socialism and the new model Labour Party. This ended the first phase of Labour's reaction to Thatcherism.

It is interesting to speculate why the Labour Party turned out to be so out of touch with its supporters. Why did the Downsian model, which assumes that party leaders seek office and therefore adopt policies which most voters want, not operate? One explanation must take account of the revival in the 1970s of the idea of inner-party democracy. The reforms of 1981 decentralized power to the activists in the constituencies and the trade unions. Downs assumed that power is concentrated in the hands of the elected politicians, who therefore have an incentive to be responsive to voters. In Labour's case power was dispersed to small numbers of activists who, on many issues, were out of sympathy with the views of the MPs and voters. But activists were not elected by the voters and no electoral sanctions could be wielded against them. The radicalization of the party found little echo in the country. The 'gap' between the party's policies, increasingly shaped by a left-wing Conference, and the views of Labour voters was wide in 1979 and 1983. On many key issues in the 1979 general election the Conservatives were more representative than Labour not only of the electorate but also of the working class. The same was true in 1983. Labour had become a vanguard party, rejecting the assumption that the voters knew what was good for them.

The charge that the Labour leadership betrays socialism has been a persistent theme of the left wing. After 1979, however, it was more sustained and widely articulated throughout the movement, and linked to demands for constitutional changes. The view that revisionist and consensus policies had been tried and failed gained ground. Changes in the trade unions—particularly the shift to the left in many executives—made them less reliable allies at Conference for a right-wing parliamentary leadership. The fact that Labour governments since 1964 had also trespassed on the unions' sacred ground of free collective bargaining only added to the tensions. The Winter of Discontent, the election defeat in 1979, the steady decline in the authority of the PLP, and then the exit of right-wing leaders to the SDP shifted the balance in the party. Defenders of the mixed economy and the records of previous Labour governments were relatively isolated (Seyd 1987).

Kinnock

Neil Kinnock has joined a long list of Labour leaders who rose as men of the left, but moved to the right once they had gained the leadership. His trajectory followed those of Ramsay MacDonald (1922–31) and Harold Wilson (1963–76), two of only three leaders in the party's history to win a general election. In Kinnock's defence it can be claimed he inherited a party in decline and that electoral pressures and changing economic and security conditions forced him to abandon many of his earlier policy positions.

The leadership rules adopted in 1981 were tailor-made for a politician like Kinnock. He spent much of his early political career courting the rank and file in the constituencies and addressing fringe meetings at Conference, rather than making speeches in the House of Commons. This profile was oriented to the activists, gained him election to the NEC in 1978, and was a surer route to the top. Kinnock easily won the party's leadership contest in 1983, gaining 91 per cent of the constituency vote and 73 per cent of the trade-union vote. Under the new rules for electing the leader, activists in the trade unions and constituency parties were given more weight than MPs.

In his nine-year spell as party leader, Kinnock changed his mind on many of the significant political issues of the day, including Europe, defence, public ownership, industrial relations, and taxation. Each one involved an abandonment of his left-wing past. These changes contributed to a portrait, eagerly fostered by the tabloids and political critics, of a man who was lacking in principle and driven by shifts in public mood. The party's gradual passage—often hesitant, ambivalent, and even forced—from the left to the right was expressed in his own personal political evolution.

Neil Kinnock's 'project' of modernizing the Labour party was a grand term for making the party electable. It involved three steps. The first was to change the institutions of the party so as to empower the leadership and make the party more representative of and responsive to the electorate at large rather than the activists. The second was to change the party's policies, in particular to ditch the unpopular ones. But achieving this would require the prior reform of the party. He has recently recounted that even by the time of his election as leader in 1983 he knew that shifting the policies on Europe, defence, and public ownership would be necessary. These had been drawn up with a view to pleasing different elements in the party rather than the electorate (1994). Finally, there was a need to alter the party's image, which in turn required actions on policy and party institutions. The greatest symbol of unreconstructed Labour turned out to be Clause 4 and its commitment to widespread public ownership. In effect, Labour under Kinnock abandoned the policy, although it was left to Tony Blair to kill off the symbolic clause (see p. 218).

Neil Kinnock had a clear idea of the obstacles to his strategy. One was the Bennite left. In 1983 he compared Benn's supporters to the Bourbons, who had learnt nothing and had forgotten nothing (1994: 535). Another was the habit, which he termed *impossibilism*, whereby the extreme left set the party leaders objectives that could not be realized in a democratic process or in a reasonable span of time—and then condemned the leadership for failure or even betrayal. Kinnock's task was to make Labour electable and everything was subordinate to that. His major party speeches invariably contained references to the importance of Labour gaining power and doing what was necessary for this. But he knew the party was not electable with the policies and the image that he had inherited.

As party leader, Kinnock proved to be cautious, though there were outbursts of boldness. His first task was to build a coalition for change. But how could he do this, when there were over 600 constituency parties and numerous trade-union delegations, many of whom were ignorant of or hostile to the changes in British society and values? At the outset, he lacked an assured majority on the NEC, and the party's structure of checks and balances had constrained previous reforming leaders. Under the party constitution, drawn up before Labour was a potential party of government, the NEC and annual Conference each claimed a share of sovereignty, and the party's ethos combined anti-élitism, a tradition of questioning and even distrusting the leadership, and a respect for the voice of the grass roots (Minkin 1980). Across the party, suspicion of political marketing, of studying the views of voters, and of using modern communication methods to present policies hindered the leadership's ability to adopt electorally responsive policies.

Kinnock's first attempt at reform proved to be a salutary experience. He wanted the local parties to move from a delegate system to a membership system for the selection and reselection of candidates, calculating that this measure would weaken the influence of zealots in the local parties. He supported the proposal for one member, one vote. But the proposal was defeated at the 1984 conference; it attracted hostility from a number of trade unions whose power would be diluted. The defeat dented his authority, gave ammunition to his opponents in and out of the party, and fed the image of the party as being in hock to the trade unions and lacking strong leadership.

In future, Kinnock would have to be a Fabian, proceeding cautiously and building assured majorities for a reform before putting it to the test of a vote on the NEC or at Conference. All this took a good deal of his time and energy. Some of his targets, particularly the Liverpool Militant, were litigious, and he had to ensure that the party followed all the proper procedures when expelling members. A good part of Kinnock's tenure as leader was tied up in unheroic work in party headquarters and in back rooms, sorting out inner-party squabbles, rather than selling the party to the public. He had to 'square' key colleagues and trade-union leaders before key votes and involve himself in the minutiae of votes of various NEC groups and union conferences. He dismissed speeches, resolutions, and behaviour which did not take account of their effects on the electorate as mere self-indulgence. Many key groups in the party had other goals than making Labour electable; some took the view that it was better for Labour to lose and be socialist than sacrifice its principles in pursuit of office. One critic of the reforms, the London MP Ken Livingstone, warned the party against changing policies after the 1983 election disaster: 'We must not compromise with the electorate' (Mitchell 1983: 133).

Subsequently, Kinnock wrote of the difficulties created by 'an element (in the party) which has treated realism as treachery, regarded appeals to party unity as an excuse for suppression of liberties and scorned any emphasis on the importance of winning elections as a contaminating bacillus called "electoralism"' (1994: 540).

Over time, Kinnock gradually gained control of the NEC. By 1986 he could just get a majority if he spent time coaxing a few 'swing' members, and by 1989 he had an assured one. He was assisted by a number of constituency parties which responded to the NEC recommendation to allow party members to vote in the elections for NEC candidates. This produced a shift to the right in elections for the constituency section.

Reforming the party was important to demonstrating Labour's competence; if the leaders could not run the party effectively, then how could they govern the country? Labour had been damaged by the Winter of Discontent in 1979, the internal divisions which led to the creation of the SDP in 1981, the bitter Benn–Healey contest in 1982, and the activities of 'loony-left' local authorities. These were all well publicized by a hostile media and contributed to an image of division and extremism. The making of the new party was done by centralization at the top but also by extending participation at the grass roots. There were many reasons for making Labour a mass party, but weakening the power of small groups of activists in the constituencies was significant. This was the purpose of Kinnock's appeal for the party to raise its individual membership to over one million; in fact, membership remained under 300,000.

By the time of the 1987 general election modest changes had been made in Labour's policies, particularly on Europe, public ownership, and industrial relations. The 1983 manifesto pledge to withdraw from the EC was replaced by an acceptance of membership, but this was accompanied by a refusal to allow EC interference in Labour's policies for national economic recovery. Earlier ambitious proposals for extending public ownership, renationalization, and taking a government stake in key economic sectors were reduced to a pledge to restore privatized British Telecom and gas to public ownership. The pledge to repeal the Conservative employment laws gave way to a promise to introduce new industrial-relations legislation, but retain pre-strike ballots and election of union leaders. The party still clung to its non-nuclear defence policy.

The scale of Labour's 1987 election defeat—its share of the vote was 11 per cent behind the Conservatives'—showed how far it was from achieving power and how little actual progress had been made since 1983. Skilful presentation had failed to compensate for shortcomings in policies and image. Labour was widely seen as unable and unwilling to stand up to powerful trade unions; as a tax, borrow, and spend party; as running risks with inflation; as doing little to improve living standards; and, finally, as unsafe on the country's defence.

Following the election defeat, the party launched a wide-ranging review of policy. After three successive election defeats, radical action was required. Labour was in a weak position, but Kinnock in a strong one. The party had to recover the support of skilled workers, particularly in the south and the Midlands, develop an acceptable alternative to Thatcherism, and formulate economic policies which did not alienate business and finance. Both British society and the international economy had so changed that 'old' Labour's appeals and policy prescriptions would no longer work. Could the policy review do for Labour what the Bad Godesberg conference had done for the German Social Democrats in 1959? That party responded to a series of election defeats by breaking decisively with its Marxist past and embracing the market: 'As much competition as possible, as much planning as necessary.'

The conduct of the policy review gave more scope to the parliamentary party, particularly the leader's private office, at the expense of the NEC. Mr Kinnock and his associates decided each policy group's remit, chairman, and members, and the final drafting of many of the reports was overseen by his office. The first results of the review were expressed in the policy document *Meet the Challenge—Make the Change* (1989), and showed a continuing shift to the political centre. The party now praised the merits of markets and competition, acknowledged the role of private ownership, and asserted the rights of consumers of the public services. It welcomed closer cooperation with the EC and favoured entry, given the right conditions, to the European Monetary System. As Patrick Seyd comments (1993: 79), the policy review managed to detach the party from such electorally unpopular policies of public ownership, unilateral defence, and the legal immunities of trade unions. The party also moved to new ground in canvassing constitutional reform, including an elected Scottish Assembly, a reformed second chamber, and a charter of civil rights. But plans to return British Telecom, gas, water, and electricity to public ownership remained, and the party was still wedded to quangos in the form of a British Investment Bank and a British Technology Enterprise to assist new technologies. Clause 4 was still intact.

The review provided a qualified welcome for markets and competition. The state would intervene to 'compensate' for market failures and ensure that companies were more responsive to the consumers. As Seyd concludes: 'There was still a place for collective, co-operative and community action. In addition the Thatcherites regarded the market as morally right, whereas the policy review took a pragmatic view; the market was efficient and fair, but there would still be many occasions when intervention would be required' (1993: 85).

An important part of the Kinnock project was to increase central or leadership control over the party organization, as a means of changing policies and altering Labour's image. A shadow communications agency, drawn largely from the public-relations industry, was established and given a key role in developing campaign strategy and marketing the party. Indeed, the policy review and the creation of such leader-driven bodies as the campaign management team, the campaign strategy committee, and the agency were used to bypass the NEC. In 1988 the NEC took powers to intervene in the selection of by-election candidates. This power was used to exclude candidates of which the leadership disapproved, usually because they were too left wing. It also expelled members regarded as infiltrators.

Kinnock returned to his plans to introduce one member, one vote for the selection and reselection of parliamentary candidates. The 1987 Conference agreed that, in the selection of parliamentary candidates, trade unions would be restricted to a maximum of 40 per cent of the vote, while 60 per cent or more would be allocated to individual members. Crucially, all party members would now be entitled to participate in the election process. The dual thrust of the leadership was to take more power in its own hands and enfranchise ordinary members, with the objective of weakening the power of activists. Subsequently, the principle of one member, one vote was extended for the election of the constituency representatives to the NEC. Throughout it was assumed that individual members were more representative of Labour's electoral supporters than were party delegates.

Labour entered the 1992 election with high hopes. It failed yet again, finishing sixty-four seats behind the Conservatives and 7.6 per cent behind in the share of the popular vote. The Conservatives' winning margin was greater than that achieved by any party in general elections between 1950 and 1979. With just over 34 per cent of the vote, Labour had still not regained its 1979 vote share. Many leading party figures believed that there had been a last-minute swing away from the party. The closer it got to the voting decision, and the prospect of a Labour government, so a crucial number of potential Labour and Liberal supporters drew back. Fear of Labour was still significant after the election. John Smith's shadow budget was blamed for feeding suspicions that the party was still wedded to high taxes and spending to pay for improved pensions and child benefit. Smith proposed to raise the top tax rate from 40 to 50 per cent and lift the ceiling on national insurance contributions, pensions, and child benefits. As party strategists became convinced of the electoral damage of perceptions of their policies on spending and taxes, so they were determined to be conservative in future.

Neil Kinnock resigned the leadership soon after the election defeat. He could reflect that, compared to 1983, when he became leader, Labour's policies were now firmly in the mainstream of West European social democracy. The party advocated partnerships between the public and private sectors, was pro-European, promised constitutional change and, as a consequence of supporting Britain's membership of the ERM, favoured 'prudent' policies on public spending and tax.

It was a comment on the extent to which so much of Kinnock's energy had been concentrated within the Labour Party that his main achievements had been to change the party structure so fundamentally. The changes included:

- distancing the party from the trade unions, notably by reducing the trade-union vote at the annual conference to 70 per cent;
- weakening the power of party activists in constituency parties by the introduction of membership ballots for the selection and re-selection of parliamentary candidates;
- shifting the emphasis from grass-roots campaigning to reliance on the mass media and public relations;
- organizing a policy review which abandoned unpopular policies on public ownership, defence, and industrial relations;
- reducing the authority of Conference and its policy-making role by the creation of a Policy Forum, consisting of seven commissions;
- reducing the policy role of the NEC by establishing joint Policy Committees drawn evenly from members of the NEC and Shadow Cabinet;
- centralizing power in the party leader's office.

The purpose of these changes was to enable the party leadership to promote policies that would appeal to the electorate as a whole, particularly to the floating voters (Kavanagh 1995).

Conclusion

The 1992 election defeat was the Labour Party's fourth in succession, but it was also the most unexpected of the four. Earlier general-election reverses could be explained in terms of particularly adverse circumstances—the Winter of Discontent in 1979, the effects of the Falklands victory and Labour division in 1983, tax cuts and prosperity in 1987. The 1992 election was more difficult to explain away. The Conservative Government should have suffered because of the recession and the widespread mood that it was 'time for a change'. Moreover, the opinion polls and most of the media encouraged the expectation of a Labour victory. Immediately after the election, party leaders were convinced that it was their tax-and-spend proposals as well as Neil Kinnock's leadership which had prevented the party from winning. In fact, survey evidence disputes this interpretation (Heath, Jowell, and Curtice 1994). What did seem to be important was the party's image, particularly the electorate's perception that Labour lacked competence in managing the economy and was backward looking. Conservatives, aided by the tabloid press, were able to play on the voters' 'fear of Labour'. An effective Conservative poster campaign proclaimed 'YOU CAN'T TRUST LABOUR'. Peter Jenkins, writing in the *Independent*, succinctly stated: 'Labour lost because it was Labour.' This was shorthand for saying that too many voters still thought that the party had not changed sufficiently from the 1970s and 1980s. The modernization project would have to continue under Kinnock's successors and the party would have to accept even more of the Thatcherite settlement.

9 From Thatcher to Major

Much interest in the 1990s has centred on the extent to which John Major has furthered the Thatcher project or returned the party to progressive Conservatism. That Major's premiership and the record of his government were discussed in terms of their relationships to his predecessor is a mark of how much Mrs Thatcher seized the political imagination. It is difficult to think of any other government this century that has been judged in a similar way. It has been a source of irritation to Major, as his predecessor celebrated what he dismissed as a golden age that never was.

This chapter reviews the circumstances of Mrs Thatcher's sudden removal from office and shows how this affected the early stages of John Major's premiership. It then argues that since he replaced Thatcher in 1990 there has been much greater continuity in policy than discontinuity. Majorism is a large dose of Thatcherism, minus the abrasiveness and much of the hyperbole. Many of the lady's supporters, however, have refused to recognize this, in large part because of the salience of Europe or because they were not reconciled to her departure. The European issue has dominated the agenda of British government and divided the Conservative Party, as a consequence of changes in the party and changes in the European project itself.

A wide range of powers, over government and the party, gives a new Conservative Prime Minister great opportunities to make a fresh start. Such opportunities are, however, tempered by pressures for continuity, not least if he or she assumes office in the lifetime of a Parliament and inherits a party, policies, and Cabinet which can be changed only marginally in the short run. The new leader has rarely prepared for such an eventuality, for it is usually unexpected; the succession is not the result of a general election and does not confer a democratic mandate. Yet this is how most changes of government in Britain take place. Fourteen of this century's nineteen twentieth-century Prime Ministers, and five of the last eight (Eden in 1955,

Macmillan in 1957, Home in 1963, Callaghan in 1976, and Major in 1990), first came to office without a general election. It is often claimed that a Prime Minister who takes over in such circumstances aches to have his or her own endorsement from the electorate, and it was said of John Major before 1992.

Thatcher's Downfall

According to the textbooks, it is difficult, indeed well-nigh impossible, to get rid of a Prime Minister who is in good health and commands a party majority in the House of Commons. Between 1900 and 1989 there had been only three cases of prime ministerial *coups*, in the sense that a Prime Minister was clearly forced from office without a general election. They include Asquith in 1916, Lloyd George in 1922, and Neville Chamberlain in 1940. Each departure was brought about by a withdrawal of support among a significant number of the governing party's MPs. Mrs Thatcher's fall adds a fourth case. In post-war Britain, prime-ministerial resignations have fallen into one of three categories. The first is resignation on grounds of ill health—for example, Eden and Macmillan. The second follows a government's defeat in a general election, which usually terminates the Prime Minister's party leadership. Although Winston Churchill and Harold Wilson came back to Downing Street after earlier election defeats, Attlee, Home, Callaghan, and Edward Heath stood down or were forced out of the party leadership soon after ceasing to be Prime Minister. The final category is where the party uses its own leadership-election mechanism to force a change of leadership. To date, Mrs Thatcher has been the only such case.

Few Prime Ministers have been willing to step down, usually pleading that the time is 'unripe'. Churchill and Macmillan were obviously reluctant, even though at the end both were dogged by ill health, old age, visibly declining grip, and mounting disenchantment among the voters. Just as Churchill hung on, claiming that he wanted to attend an international summit and pointing to the defects of his heir apparent (Eden), so Mrs Thatcher claimed that she wished to see through the Gulf War and feared that there was no obvious successor—or not one that would not divide the party (1993: 755). In her memoirs she speculates that she would have stepped down two years into the Parliament after the next (1991 or 1992) general election and so provided time for younger people to prove themselves (1993: 755). During her premiership she had seen off many would-be successors, including those who, it was assumed, enjoyed her blessing. Like some of her predecessors, Mrs Thatcher appeared to believe in her own indispensability. Some of her staff in Downing Street encouraged this belief (cf. Lawson 1992: 467–8; Howe 1994: 691).

Only in recent years have the Labour and Conservative parties employed election procedures for replacing a leader who is Prime Minister, although Labour for long had such a procedure in place. By tradition, when the Conservative Party was in office and a vacancy occurred, the monarch consulted senior party figures and then invited a recommended figure to try and form a government. This happened in 1940, 1957, and 1963. In 1965, however, the party had moved to electing the party leader by Conservative MPs, but for twenty-four years this system was used only when the party was in opposition, in 1965 and 1975. In theory, MPs could vote out a party leader who was Prime Minister, but this was largely regarded as unthinkable. The decision of a little-known backbench Tory MP, Sir Anthony Meyer, to challenge Mrs Thatcher in 1989 created a precedent. Although Mrs Thatcher won that election easily, dismissing a Prime Minister was now thinkable. Labour has only once elected a Prime Minister and that was in 1976 when James Callaghan was elected after Harold Wilson resigned. No Labour Prime Minister has yet faced a leadership challenge.

The reasons which Sir Anthony Meyer gave for challenging Mrs Thatcher in 1989—her abrasive style of leadership, the poll tax, and an approach to Europe that was negative and divided the party— still largely applied a year later. The annual leadership election in November 1990 came at a bad time for Mrs Thatcher. It occurred soon after embarrassing by-election defeats and when the party was trailing Labour by 20 points in the opinion polls. The shock resignation of Sir Geoffrey Howe in October was followed by his dramatic resignation statement in the House of Commons which attacked her leadership, accused her of dividing the party and acting against Britain's interests in Europe, and invited Cabinet colleagues to consider their own positions. It was almost inevitable that she would face a challenge. This time a major figure, Michael Heseltine, announced his candidacy.

Sir Geoffrey was, apart from herself, the last remaining member of the original 1978 Cabinet. As Chancellor and Foreign Secretary, he had played a major role in the achievements of the 1980s. His resignation from Cabinet followed those of Heseltine and Lawson, both of whom had also complained of Mrs Thatcher's high-handed leadership. She (not Europe) appeared to be a cause of instability at the top of the party. Conservative MPs were also alarmed at the unpopularity of the poll tax. Compared with the household rating system, which it replaced, losers greatly outnumbered gainers, it lacked fairness, and surveys as well as doorstep canvassing confirmed that it was the greatest single cause of voters' disaffection with the party. Unless Mrs Thatcher's 'tax' could be repealed or substantially reformed, many Tory MPs were convinced that they would lose their seats. A large number, including perhaps a hundred or so who had gained no preferment, or had been dismissed from ministerial posts under Mrs Thatcher, or were due to retire anyway, had no obvious incentive to support her. A change of leader would present fresh opportunities for the careers and policy positions of a number of Conservative MPs. As noted in Chapter 6, less than a fifth of MPs could be termed Thatcherite—that is, out-and-out supporters of the leader. Finally, she was now faced by a credible candidate, one who had prepared for this moment since he had dramatically walked out of her Cabinet in 1985. Opinion polls reported over the weekend before the ballot that Heseltine would transform the party's electoral prospects. Under Thatcher the party trailed in the polls by a wide margin, under a hypothetical Prime Minister Heseltine the party led Labour. He could promise MPs 'Vote for me and you will be elected'.

Mrs Thatcher won the first ballot by 204 votes to 152 for Heseltine, but was four short of the requisite 15 per cent majority to win outright. Having failed to win a clear majority on the first ballot she was swayed by Cabinet colleagues who warned that she would lose on a second ballot. Colleagues argued that to protect her legacy

and prevent a Heseltine succession she should make way for somebody who would defeat the challenger. During the campaign she had
dismissed him as a corporatist, almost a socialist, a pro-European,
and one who would not carry on with her programme. The two obvious contenders were the Foreign Secretary, Douglas Hurd, and the
Chancellor, John Major. But they were her nominees and could enter
only if she stood down. Under considerable pressure from the
Cabinet, she did so and campaigned for Major, wanting 'to believe
that he (John Major) would safeguard my legacy' (1993: 860).

John Major gained 185 votes on the second ballot, comfortably
ahead of Heseltine (131) and Hurd (56) but two short of the requisite figure for outright victory. His opponents conceded and he succeeded as party leader and Prime Minister.

The leadership election provides several insights into the working of the Conservative Party today (cf. Alderman and Carter 1990;
M. Smith 1994*b*). In so far as the system is designed to reinforce
consensus in the party it worked. The case for having the 15 per cent
majority threshold, about which Mrs Thatcher's supporters subsequently complained, was to demonstrate that the leader enjoyed
widespread support in the party. A reasonable objection was that, if
an incumbent could not gain the support of more than 55 per cent
of MPs, including the large payroll vote, then it was time for a
change. That view has to be set against the claims of her supporters
that she was unseated as a result of a plot by ministers (Watkins
1991) or her own claims in her memoirs that she had been too trust-
ing and promoted people such as Chris Patten, Ken Clarke, and
Malcolm Rifkind who 'did not share my political values'. The exercise also demonstrated the continuing political importance of the
Cabinet. Mrs Thatcher's growing carelessness in Cabinet management was reflected not only in the resignation of key ministers but
also in the ill will accumulated over the years towards members of
her Number 10 staff, particularly the foreign-policy adviser, Charles
(later Sir) Powell, and her Press Secretary, Bernard (later Sir)
Ingham (Lawson 1992; Baker 1993: 320; Howe 1994: 473). As
Martin Smith (1996) observes, power at the top of British government is interdependent, requiring give and take between significant
Cabinet ministers.

The election also demonstrated the growing influence of back-bench MPs, particularly at a time when they were becoming more rebellious and career-minded (Riddell 1993). As incumbents, Mrs Thatcher in 1990 and Ted Heath in 1975 had attracted the over-whelming support of their Cabinet and Shadow Cabinet colleagues respectively on the first ballot of the leadership election, but were undone by the resentment of backbenchers. Just as Mrs Thatcher owed her first election as leader in 1975 to backbench dissatisfaction with Heath, so she was unseated by the same force in 1990. Both in 1975 and 1990 the desire to change the leader was probably a stronger force than positive support for the successful challenger. Michael Heseltine could reflect that, where Sir Anthony Meyer's candidacy in 1989 had been widely regarded as a stalking horse for himself, it was his own challenge in 1990 which created the oppor-tunity for John Major. He toppled Mrs Thatcher but failed to gain the ultimate prize for himself. Finally, the election system presents a growing difficulty for a Conservative leadership which wishes to win and exercise power. The holding of annual leadership elections among a more factionalized and more independent-minded group of Conservative MPs is now a significant potential limitation on the power of a Prime Minister. The fact that he or she may be so chal-lenged, even by a Cabinet colleague (as happened to Major in 1995), and the candidates then campaign on distinctive platforms and attract rival supporters and at a time when the Government is embarking on unpopular policies, is hardly helpful for prudent pol-icy-making or party unity (Douglas 1996).

The significance of the downfall of such a dominant figure as Mrs Thatcher gave rise to much analysis. Did it signify the end of Thatcherism; had MPs had enough of radical measures and voted for consolidation and a return to the political centre? Was it more a repudiation of her leadership style (clearly made an issue by Sir Geoffrey Howe and Michael Heseltine, as they called for the restora-tion of Cabinet government); was the vote for Major one for Thatcherism with a human face, as Kenneth Clarke said? Was it pri-marily a means to have something done about the poll tax and improve MPs' election prospects? Opinion polls were certainly important before the first ballot in boosting Michael Heseltine's claims that he was an electoral asset and those of John Major's before the second ballot. Did it debunk claims of prime-ministerial government, demonstrate the latent power of the Cabinet, and the necessity of the Prime Minister ultimately to be able to work with senior colleagues?

Majorism

There has been much inconclusive discussion of what Majorism is. The topic is in large part a tribute to the influence of Mrs Thatcher. A lasting effect of her long premiership may have been to colour popular perceptions of political leadership in Britain and the criteria which one applied to effective leaders. The media and voters have come to expect a premier who is visionary, decisive, authoritative, and able to personify the party. Mrs Thatcher was as much a product of these pressures as a cause of them (cf. Foley 1992). Any successor would be evaluated in comparison to Mrs Thatcher.

The circumstances of John Major's succession were particularly constraining. As the candidate, by default, of the outgoing leader and many of her supporters, his election was widely regarded as one for continuity. Major's leadership rivals, Douglas Hurd and Michael Heseltine, with their pro-European credentials and Heseltine's belief in an active economic role for government, clearly represented a different kind of Conservatism from Mrs Thatcher's, and he was the only candidate that the centre right could possibly identify with. Yet at the time few MPs were aware of John Major's views on many issues. He had written no books or pamphlets and given no set-piece lectures expounding his brand of Conservatism. He was also widely regarded as a unifier, in large part because of ignorance about his views on the salient issues. This last point was important. For many in the party, the first ballot and its outcome had been divisive, even traumatic, for many in the party. The Thatcherites felt betrayed by the circumstances of the leader's withdrawal, and a number of Conservative associations threatened to deselect MPs who had voted for Heseltine.

From the outset of his premiership John Major rejected the

comparison with his predecessor, in the sense of not wishing to be identified with an 'ism'. Being a Conservative was sufficient for him, and, after all, by 1990 nearly half of the Conservative MPs had wanted Mrs Thatcher to go. At one stage (1991) he expressly forbade his Downing Street staff to use the term Majorism. At times, commentators have tried to elevate the 'back-to-basics' campaign, Chris Patten's speeches about Christian Democracy's lessons for Conservatism, or the Citizen's Charter into a 'big idea'. None worked. As noted, one looks in vain for statements of John Major's political philosophy before he became leader in November 1990. But in this he was not unusual; much the same could be said about Attlee, Eden, Home, Callaghan, and Harold Wilson. He may also have calculated that to cultivate his own 'ism' ran the risk of echoing his predecessor, or, if he adopted a politically distinctive approach, might emphasize discontinuity and perhaps exacerbate divisions in the party. But nothing in his career suggested that he would be promoting a new agenda.

Major is interesting in part because of his social background. In the party of social 'toffs', he was the third leader in succession to be drawn from a modest social background and the ranks of the grammar schools, and the first since Winston Churchill not to have attended a university, let alone Oxford or Cambridge. He had personal experience of poverty, unemployment, and a lack of success at school. Yet his political career had been attended by a silver spoon. He entered parliament in 1979 as member for one of the safest Conservative seats in the country. After a spell in the Whip's office, he joined the Cabinet in 1987, the first of the 1979 intake to do so. He was then, for short periods, Foreign Secretary, replacing Sir Geoffrey Howe, and Chancellor of the Exchequer, replacing Nigel Lawson. With such a background he would almost certainly have emerged as party leader under the old system of informal consultation. Compared to Margaret Thatcher when she became leader in 1975, he was less of an outsider, had served in the Cabinet for as long as she had (3½ years), and had held more senior offices.

In climbing the greasy pole John Major enjoyed luck, although it is difficult to think of any political leader who rises without this ingredient. Harold Wilson and Tony Blair owed their promotions to the Labour Party leadership to the relatively early deaths of Hugh Gaitskell (aged 56) and John Smith (aged 55). When elected party leader in 1983, Neil Kinnock was fortunate that the standard-bearer of the left, Tony Benn, was out of Parliament, and that the new party rules gave 70 per cent of the vote in the electoral college to the extra-parliamentary party (the trade unions and the constituency parties). Thatcher owed much to the discredited Ted Heath's decision to carry on as leader after the second election defeat in 1974, rather than stepping aside to facilitate the prospects of a Heathite successor, and to Sir Keith Joseph's withdrawal from the leadership race.

It is difficult to construe the vote by Conservative MPs for Major in 1990 as one for ideological change. Although some Conservative MPs rejected the rolling agenda of Thatcherism, there was little party support for reversing policies, beyond the repeal of the poll tax. Most wanted a change of leader so that the party would gain victory at the next general election, a change of face with broad continuity of policy (Baker 1993: 431). John Major's personality and political style differed from his predecessor's. The story has often been told of how Major planned his political ascent with his fellow Conservative MP, Robert Atkins, in 1987. They agreed that the key was in not being too closely identified with any one wing of the political party. A biographer notes that, on many issues in Cabinet, Major was 'a floating voter. On any issue he always sought to narrow the focus of the discussion to a specific issue which could be assessed pragmatically' (Anderson 1991: 254). Not an ideologue, Major was regarded by some colleagues as slightly left of centre, by others as slightly right of centre (Anderson 1991: 254). A quintessential Majorism was his remark in early January 1996 on Conservative divisions over Europe: he complained of the polarization between those 'who are very very hostile to it and those who see nothing wrong with it. The truth, I believe, lies somewhere down the middle.'

Opinions differ on whether the Major record represents a continuation of Thatcherism or a return to progressive conservatism. Some of her supporters and his critics point to an alternative scenario, had Mrs Thatcher remained. On Europe, for example, she would not have accepted Maastricht, would have expressly vetoed British membership of a single European currency, in the first wave at least, and resisted all rulings of the Europe Court of Justice which infringed the Parliament's ability to make domestic laws for the UK. On health, there would be greater scope for privatization and in education greater incentives for schools to opt out of local-authority control and become grant maintained. The poll tax would have survived, for in her memoirs she claims that 'Its benefits had just started to become apparent where it was abandoned' (Thatcher 1993: 667). The hefty increase in taxes imposed in the 1993 and 1994 budgets were clearly the obverse of economic Thatcherism, but they followed from the recession that began when she was still Prime Minister.

Much of this is speculative: 'What I would have done, if I was still in office.' Some of the claims seem fantastic. The poll tax was a major factor in her downfall and many MPs plausibly regarded her departure as the essential precondition for getting rid of the hated tax. If the tax had been retained, one can imagine the chagrin of Conservative MPs in marginal seats who feared that it was a sure path to their electoral oblivion. On Europe and related matters her approach had already lost her five Cabinet Ministers (Heseltine, Brittan, Lawson, Ridley, and Howe) and a party split was beginning to loom. Had she still been in office and refused to sign the Maastricht Treaty in December 1991 and insisted on ruling out membership of a single currency, a split could not have been averted. As for the incursions on Britain's sovereignty by the Commission and the European Court, it was she who had signed up to the single market and its qualified majority voting provisions. The tax increases in 1992 and subsequent years followed from the recession and the regime of high interest rates from the failure of membership of the ERM which had been achieved under Mrs Thatcher. The record of eleven years hardly suggested a determination to privatize health ('safe in our hands') and schools, although her final party conference speech hinted at school vouchers. Mrs Thatcher's agenda, largely dictated from political exile, seems wilfully to ignore the problems of party management, particularly over Europe, and the pressures which led many colleagues to consider that she had outlived her usefulness as party leader.

Continuity stands out when we compare the big shifts in policy and rhetoric between the Conservative Governments of 1964 and

1970, or within the life of the Heath Government, say pre- and post-1972, on industrial relations, wage-bargaining, public spending, and state intervention in industry.

Major and Thatcher share the vision of a low tax economy. The flagship of privatization has been maintained. Indeed the Major Government brought two of the most difficult candidates, British Rail and British Coal, to the market and sold off the nuclear industry. Apart from Royal Mail, whose planned sale was abandoned in the face of Conservative backbench opposition, there are now virtually no more utilities to sell off.

Steps were also taken to remove the relics of corporatism. Shortly after the 1992 general election Norman Lamont wound up the NEDC, a survival from 1962, and wages councils were abolished. The actions were largely symbolic, because both bodies had been weakened in the preceding years. The last measure was taken under the 1993 Trade Union and Employment Rights Act, which consolidated the legislation of the 1980s curbing the trade unions' legal immunities. This also allowed users of public services to seek injunctions to prevent disruption of services by unlawful industrial action, and employers to be given seven days' notice of strike action. Again, continuity was the order of the day, rather than reversal or striking out in a new direction.

The creation of agencies in the civil service has continued apace, with agencies responsible for the delivery of services—for example, tax collection, the issue of driving licences, the payment of benefits. By the end of 1995 over three-quarters of civil servants were employed in agencies. The changes in Whitehall have meant that 'Permanent secretaries are becoming policy managers, rather than policy advisers' (M. Smith 1996: 164). The creation of quangos and agencies to oversee traditional local-government responsibilities has accelerated under John Major. But the above steps, together with privatization, the creation of agencies, and the growing power of the EU, amount to a redrawing of the role of the state (M. Smith 1996), or what Rhodes (1994) calls a 'hollowing-out' of the new British state.

The main impact of the Major Government has been on the public services, but even here the story is of continuity. It was not until the third term that the Thatcher Government tackled the social agenda. The wide-ranging Education Act (1988) and loans for students in higher education were introduced, the health-service and civil-service reforms had just started, and the Housing Act allowed council-house tenants to opt for private landlords. John Major's search for mechanisms other than privatization to give people more opportunity and choice resulted in early 1991 in the Citizen's Charter. Mrs Thatcher's notion of empowerment allowed little scope for providing means of redress of grievances. It concentrated on facilitating opt-outs—of schools and council tenants from local authorities—and some tax relief for private health care for the over-60s.

Having rejected large-scale privatization of health and education, the Major Government sought to import the best of private-sector management practice, as a means of improving the performance of these services. This includes performance pay, audit, competition, and more information about standards—a combination of managerialism and consumerism. League tables report each school's performances on the national curriculum tests, public examinations, and truancy. It has also tried to mobilize consumers to expect and demand a level of service comparable to that from, say, Marks & Spencer. They should be able to complain, insist on value for money, and ultimately be reimbursed or compensated for poor service. In health, the devices have been internal markets, hospital trusts, and fund-holding doctors; in schools, a national curriculum, testing, and the right for schools to control their own budgets. These were all set in train by 1990, but the Major Government has implemented them energetically.

The Charter has been John Major's initiative, and Britain's answer to the reinvention of the government movement in the USA (Osborne and Gaebler 1993). This promotes the idea of government as an entrepreneurial activity, one which prefers market over bureaucratic solutions, measures and publishes performances, and increases competition in service provision and consumer choice. The Charter is a philosophy of administration as well as an attempt to change the culture of the public services. It provides consumers with more information about their rights and the performances of services. Deliverers of services are set targets for improved performance, and faced with more competition, independent inspections, and better complaints procedures for consumers. There are sharper divisions now between consumers of services, on the one hand, and producers and providers, on the other. At the heart of the Charter is the notion of the citizen as an individual consumer of public services and of a new relationship between the client and the provider of the service. The election and accountability of government are missing from this equation, with services being contracted out to such bodies as grant-maintained schools and hospital trusts.

No New Agenda

The lack of a new agenda under Major is not unusual; neither his election as party leader in 1990 nor his general-election victory in 1992 was a turning point (Kavanagh 1994). There was no massive dissatisfaction with the status quo or availability of an electorally persuasive alternative prospectus. By 1990 much of the Thatcherite agenda had already been accepted by much of the Labour leadership, and this increased in the following years. It is, however, worth considering the secondary causes that constrained the emergence of new thinking after 1990. The first was the general sense of the need for consolidation after a decade of radical policy changes. Few ministers denied the need to digest the consequences of radical legislation and rushed measures, notably in local-government finance, the school curriculum, and criminal justice—witness the numerous revisions of policies in these areas. John Major did not see the Conservative Party, as some Thatcherites seemed to do, as the party of permanent cultural revolution, dedicated to continuously disturbing interests. He rated continuity, community, and stability more highly than his predecessor. His liking for the traditional and the familiar explains his reluctance to disturb institutions or pursue constitutional reform. At the same time, however, except for the poll tax, there has been no going back on the Thatcher legacy, even on Europe. Differences between Major and Thatcher are largely of personality and rhetoric, and more of style than substance. 'In policy area after policy area, Major has maintained the Thatcherite agenda' (Ludlam and Smith 1996: 279).

A second factor is that the Thatcher Governments may have tackled the easier, or more obvious targets. These included inflation, the powers of trade unions, making the public sector responsive to its users, the nationalized industries and high-spending local authorities. If the agenda in the 1980s was largely economic, in the 1990s it has been largely social. Such problems as soaring crime figures, family breakdown, a growing underclass, poor schooling, and run-down inner cities did not start in 1979, but it is an open question whether the policies of the 1980s and the soaring unemployment and growing economic inequality exacerbated them. The free market creates, indeed probably depends on, a sense of insecurity. The encouragement of individualism, private ownership, efficiency savings (often a euphemism for job cuts), and competition created casualties. Such problems are more complex to tackle than those of the 1980s and require multi-faceted and multi-agency solutions.

A third reason is that Thatcherism was defined to a significant degree by what it was against. It had a long list of enemies: inflation, the 'dependent society' and the undeserving poor, corporatism, high taxes, left-wing local authorities, the European Commission, trade unions, bureaucracy, and much of the public sector. Taming them called for a determined, even abrasive leadership. An apparent unwillingness to listen or to compromise was a virtue when dealing with Arthur Scargill, Michael Foot, Jacques Delors, and General Galtieri. It has been less clear what or who the dangers are in the late 1990s, given the reformed New Labour Party, weaker trade unions, run-down local government, and the collapse of the Soviet Union.

Since the 1992 election the government has also suffered from a quite staggering decline in its popularity. It is usual for modern British governments to suffer mid-term slumps in electorate popularity and then recover. This happened to each of the Thatcher Governments but did not prevent the party from recovering support by polling day. But no British government has suffered such a severe sudden and enduring electoral decline as the Conservative Party has since September 1992. Britain's forced exit from the ERM under pressure from financial markets transformed the situation from one in which the Labour and Conservative parties were virtually level pegging in the opinion polls to one in which the Conservatives quickly suffered a 20 per cent deficit. That figure only widened over the next four years. Other indicators of support, in local elections, by-elections, European elections, as well as opinion poll readings of satisfaction with the government and with the Prime Minister, have all reached record low levels. The fiasco of the ERM exit severely damaged the Conservative reputation for economic competence. The tax increases, following so soon after a general election fought on a tax-reducing platform, added to the voters' sense of betrayal and of the government's dishonesty. This mood must have struck deeply, because the Conservative electoral depression lasted for the Parliament and the party got little credit for the economic recovery which followed the exit from the ERM.

A good part of the criticism fastened on John Major's leadership, which, in contrast to Mrs Thatcher's, was seen as weak. His loyalty to his first Chancellor, Norman Lamont, who was discredited after the ERM exit, was widely seen as misplaced: Lamont's retention of the Treasury post until 27 May 1993 was a stark reminder of the events of 16 September 1992. Major pledged his support for troubled colleagues but was then often forced to let them go, as in the case of David Mellor. At times he talked tough but then backed down, as over his initial refusal to accept the change to qualified majority voting in Europe, which he then accepted. On Europe he seemed unable to call his Eurosceptics, such as Portillo or Howard, or pro-Europeans, like Clarke, to heel. Mrs Thatcher allegedly complained: 'He stands for nothing'.

A final limitation has been the circumstances of John Major's personal mandate—namely, the broken-backed election victory in April 1992. The margin of victory, 42 per cent to Labour's 34.4 per cent of the vote, was impressive not least because it was so unexpected. The government had entered the election against a background of the longest post-war economic recession and faced by a revived Labour Party. It also won against the final forecasts of opinion polls and the expectations of political commentators. In the weeks after the election there was much informed discussion about the Japanization of British politics, as Britain had a period of one-party rule (A. King 1993). Analysts who looked to the next election, which would almost certainly be fought on a better economic record and after a redistribution of seats which would favour the Conservative Party, warned of Labour's bleak prospects. If it could not unseat the Conservatives in the circumstances in 1992, then when could it? On the other hand, the government's overall majority of seats was only 21, even though it was 64 over Labour. As by-election losses depleted the number of Conservative MPs, and Europe as an issue dominated the parliamentary agenda and divided the party, so the government was increasingly at the mercy of rebels. Whereas majorities of 100 plus enjoyed by the Thatcher Governments in the 1983 and 1987 Parliaments had enabled the party managers to withstand rebellions, John Major had no such cushion.

European Divisions

Overshadowing every other Conservative problem in the 1990s has been Europe, now the principal fault-line in the party. Party divisions on the issue did not begin with John Major, for tensions helped to bring down Mrs Thatcher. Although the party had been strongly pro-European in the 1960s, 1970s, and 1980s, it had always contained a small core of MPs who were opposed to the project from the outset or were sceptical of greater integration. But at the defining moments, such as British applications for entry in 1961, 1967, and 1970 or the referendum on membership in 1975, a large majority of Conservative MPs were supportive. It was Labour which contained the bulk of the anti-European MPs. By the 1990s, however, the two parties had reversed their positions on Europe: Labour had become pro-European, while the Conservative Party contained most of the sceptics.

In the early years of her government, Mrs Thatcher's relations with the EC were dominated by battles to reduce the UK's net budget contribution to Community funds. Her efforts to reclaim some of 'our money' bore some fruit at Fontainebleu in 1984 but also made her and the UK unpopular in Brussels. Mrs Thatcher was a keen defender of British sovereignty and had little sympathy for what she regarded as the 'Euro-waffle' emanating from the Commission. In meetings with other heads of state she liked to play to her reputation as an iron lady and a prudent housewife. She was also more of an Atlanticist, not least when President Reagan was in the White House; the two leaders shared common views on many domestic politics and the need for a strong military Eastern Europe presence to deter the USSR. But her Cabinets, including two of her Foreign Secretaries, Howe and Hurd, were strongly pro-European. British ministers, including Mrs Thatcher, were at the forefront of the efforts to pass the Single European Act (SEA) in 1986, which provided for the completion of the internal market by 1992. But signing the act involved Mrs Thatcher in making two important concessions. The agreement stated that political union was the ultimate aim; creating a single market was not an end in itself, as Mrs Thatcher held, but part of an integrative project which would culminate in political unity. The act also extended the principle of qualified majority voting (QMV) to legislation relating to the SEA, so significantly reducing the role of the national veto. The UK entered the single market for economic benefits, in line with Thatcher's view of the EC as an economic union of free sovereign states. Other states, however, viewed the project differently.

For at least six years Mrs Thatcher had resisted pressures from much of the country's economic establishment, including the Treasury and the Foreign Office, for the UK to enter the ERM. Her fear was that entering a fixed exchange rate would limit the UK's control over its money supply and interest rates. She finally agreed to entry in October 1990, having been persuaded that the ERM membership would help to promote a stable exchange rate and curb inflation. But the regime of high interest rates required to keep the UK in the exchange-rate zone severely damaged the economy, harming exports, causing the bankruptcy of companies, and boosting unemployment.

Having lost so many senior Cabinet ministers over differences relating to Europe, it was appropriate that these tensions should set in train the chain of events which brought down Mrs Thatcher. Her combative speech in the House of Commons in October 1990 rejecting British participation in a single currency or any surrender of the sovereignty of Parliament, led to Sir Geoffrey Howe's resignation, and set in train the events that led to her downfall.

The burden of trying to keep the party together over Europe then passed to John Major. Where Mrs Thatcher had led the party from the Eurosceptic position, he tried to straddle the views of supporters and critics. For a time he seemed to have some success, and at the intergovernmental conference at Maastricht in December 1991 he was applauded within the party for his achievements. The treaty, however, contained provisions which were to cause great problems later on. Member states agreed under the treaty to work towards 'an ever closer union', and the competence of the EU was extended to foreign and defence policy, as well as to immigration, policing, and asylum matters. Although these issues would be decided on an intergovernmental basis (which meant that there was no role for the European Court and only a limited one for the Commission), it was also agreed that decisions would be by QMV. The member states (except for Denmark) agreed to work towards economic monetary union and a single currency. Britain negotiated an opt-out from the provisions of the social chapter, and another which left it to a future parliament to decide on British membership of a single currency.

Europe, however, was moving in a direction opposite to that in Britain. The Social Chapter (in spite of the British opt-out) and the rulings of the European Court usually worked against the thrust of the free-market, flexible-labour, and anti-regulatory policies of Thatcher and Major. Moreover, the pressures for monetary union and the integration of internal security, defence, and foreign policies provoked fears among many Conservatives that a European superstate was emerging and would limit Britain's sovereignty. When she declared in May 1992 that she would never have signed the Maastricht Treaty, Mrs Thatcher spoke for the growing number of Conservative nationalists who disliked the newly emerging Europe.

If Europe was changing, so was the Conservative Party. Research by Sheffield University academics showed that the new cohorts of MPs who entered the Commons in the late 1980s and the 1990s were more sceptical of Europe than those who had entered in the 1960s and 1970s—Ted Heath's generation (Ludlam 1996). A trouble was the gap between Cabinet ministers and backbenchers. John Major's Cabinets, like those of Margaret Thatcher, always contained pro-European majorities, including major figures such as

Hurd (until 1995), Heseltine, and Clarke. The Euro-rebels' defiance of Conservative whips was fuelled in part by the knowledge that some of their positions were supported by the Tory press, other Conservative backbenchers, and many activists. They were supported in particular in their demand for at least a referendum on a single currency, if not a dismissal of the idea, and a rejection of the Commission's right to initiate legislation. The changing mood among MPs was shown at the beginning of the 1992 Parliament when over 100 Conservative MPs signed a House of Commons motion calling for a fresh start in the EU. The differences between the Conservative élite and sub-élite, although both were moving in a sceptical direction, at a time when European integration was dominating the agenda, posed acute problems of party management.

More than any other issue in the 1992 Parliament, Europe dragged down the Conservative Party and sapped the authority of John Major as he tried to hold the balance between supporters and opponents of the European project. The first year and a half of the new Parliament was dominated by the ratification of the Maastricht Treaty. This began against the background of the disastrous exit from the ERM on 16 September. That event cost the government authority, electoral popularity, and its reputation for economic competence. The sceptics had their doubts about the goal of a single currency confirmed. Maastricht was a trial and a humiliation for the party managers, as they tried to buy off the rebels with threats, concessions, and innovations (Baker, Gamble, and Ludlam 1994). In November 1992, twenty-six Conservatives voted against the government, which, supported by the Liberal Democrats, survived by just three votes. In March 1993 the government lost a vote on a Labour amendment, as twenty-six Conservatives voted with the opposition. In May 1993 the Maastricht bill was carried on its third reading, but forty-one Conservatives voted against and five abstained. In July 1993 the government lost on a motion on the social chapter which had to be approved if the treaty was to be approved, but then managed to win a vote of confidence. In November 1994 eight Conservative rebels voted against a budget increase for the EU, and lost the party whip. The withdrawal of the whip from such a large number was unprecedented in the post-war period and wiped out the government's majority. The whip was then restored, without any pledges from the rebels about future conduct. Backbench rebellions against the Major Cabinet were largely on Maastricht and European votes, and dissenters were predominantly supporters of Thatcherism, or MPs who emphasized an authoritarian stand on law and order, national sovereignty, and free-market economics (Cowley 1996).

The bulk of the Conservative-supporting press also gave up on John Major. Editorial doubts about him had already been expressed before the 1992 election, although most of the anti-Labour papers returned to the cause by polling day. But sections of the press, particularly the papers owned by Murdoch and Black, grew increasingly hostile to the EU and to Major. In the leadership contest with John Redwood in June 1995, Major was supported by only one Conservative daily newspaper, the *Daily Express*.

Conservative disagreements over Europe were more complex than a reflection of simple left-versus-right or wet-versus-dry division. They were part of a historic tension in the party between supporters of Britain's national sovereignty and those who thought that Britain had to forge relationships with other countries. It was sovereignty versus interdependence; these cut across divisions over the role of the state and the market. An architect of Thatcherism like Geoffrey Howe favoured the single currency and greater integration, as did Kenneth Clarke, a major figure in the reforms of the public services and industrial relations. Baker, Gamble, and Ludlam (1993) have pointed out that the contemporary tensions have parallels to the great Conservative splits of 1846 (over the corn laws) and 1903 (over tariffs). Both were about Britain's place in the world economy and the role of the state at home. On both occasions the bulk of the leadership opted for interdependence and a positive role for the state, while many MPs wanted to give priority to national sovereignty and a limited state. Historically, the party leadership in the twentieth century followed the path of interdependence abroad, while promoting full employment and welfare to accommodate the demands of labour at home. By the 1960s Europe had taken the place of the Empire as a means by which Britain could play a role in the world stage. But in the 1990s the integrationist push in Europe, reflected in the extension of majority voting and monetary union, struck a sensitive nerve in the party.

In many respects the Conservative Party since 1990 has come to bear a greater Thatcherite imprint than it did when she was leader. It is firmly wedded to free-market economics and has become increasingly uneasy with the European project. John Major has tried to resist further integration by pointing to the opt-outs he negotiated, restating the importance of subsidiarity and advancing the case for a multi-speed Europe. The sceptics wish to rule out membership of a single currency for the lifetime of the next Parliament, whereas Major's Cabinet wishes to keep all options open, so that it can participate in the debate about the currency. The vision of the low tax, low public spending, deregulated economy, one which views Britain as an offshore Hong Kong, is very different from the European model. Indeed, it is one that is probably incompatible with full British membership of the EU (Gamble 1996: 32).

Groups such as 'No Turning Back' spoke for the Thatcherite agenda of Euroscepticism, tax cuts, and spending reductions, as well as more privatization of welfare. Their most prominent spokesman was John Redwood, who resigned from the Cabinet in June 1995 and challenged John Major for the leadership. Redwood called for the repatriation of some powers from Brussels to national parliaments and a statement ruling out British participation in a single European currency. He was Major's second Cabinet casualty (along with Norman Lamont) over Europe. In the resulting leadership election, Major won by 218 votes to 89, with 20 abstentions or spoilt ballots. The irony was that Major, who had been elected in 1990 with the votes of the right of the party, had conceded this constituency to John Redwood and now had to rely on the centre left. Eurosceptic MPs, with considerable press support, harried Major after his re-election and sought a clear statement from him that Britain would not enter a single European currency, if one was established. Such a promise would have split the Cabinet. Eurosceptics also embarrassed ministers by introducing bills in 1996 to curb the powers of the European Court of Justice and for a referendum on Britain's relations with the EU. The bills were defeated but showed that perhaps a third of Conservative backbench MPs were hostile to the direction that the European project was taking.

An additional difficulty for the Conservatives was that, for the first time in many years, they faced a credible Labour alternative. Under Tony Blair, Labour had moved into the centre right, thereby removing many Conservative targets. To be distinctive, the Conservative Party was forced to move into more right-wing territory and risk alienating voters. The party had also to combat the mood for change—understandable after eighteen years in office.

10 **New Labour**

Labour's 1992 election defeat proved to be a watershed in the party's history. Not since the 1820s had one party been in government or the principal opposition party out of office for so long. If Conservative dominance was apparent to some in 1987, it appeared even more so in 1992. In general elections since 1918 Labour had trailed the Conservatives by an average of 6 per cent of the vote. Over the four elections 1979–92 the deficit had grown to 10 per cent. Where should Labour turn? This chapter discusses the steps which Labour took to adapt itself even further.

Election Postmortems

There were three possible analyses and political responses to the defeat. One was the left's claim that the election defeat showed that Kinnock's move to the middle ground had failed. Rather than compete on ground chosen by the Conservatives, the party should offer a choice—of left-wing policies. Few in the party heeded this analysis. Labour's modernization and shift to the centre, following the policy review, had been perceived by the electorate and broadly approved. The trouble was that the gains in terms of votes had been small, in large part because the Conservatives, once Major had replaced Thatcher, were also seen to have moved to the centre (Heath, Jowell, and Curtice 1994). In addition, the party's image still suffered from its past, particularly doubts about its competence to manage the economy and popular perceptions of the last Labour Government's record and memories of divisions in the early 1980s.

A second analysis suggested that Labour had made up so much ground from 1987 that it only required 'one more heave' for victory, marginal changes to policy, and the replacement of Neil Kinnock as party leader; the party could then wait for the Conservatives to make a mess of things and for the swing of the electoral pendulum. The party had modernized sufficiently. To a large extent this *consolidationist* strategy represented the thinking of John Smith in his brief (1992–4) period of leadership.

A third response was to claim that the party had not changed enough, that it was still too much 'old Labour'. It must transform itself; the policies, the party structure, and the ethos must all be changed, to take account of shifts in society and values, and the impact of Thatcherism (Mandelson and Liddle 1996). The party had to adapt to a society which had become more bourgeois and individualistic. Social change would continue to work against Labour. Such, essentially, was the call of the modernizers. Some modernizers were pessimistic about the prospects of Labour gaining office on its own, and therefore claimed that proportional representation and a Lib.–Lab. pact, or at least greater cooperation, would be necessary to unseat the Conservatives. The main voting study of the 1992 election, *Labour's Last Chance?* (Heath, Jowell, and Curtice 1994), concluded that a hung Parliament was probably the party's best chance of averting a fifth successive Conservative victory.

Tony Blair

Tony Blair, Gordon Brown, and others close to Neil Kinnock were firmly in the camp of the modernizers. It was only when Tony Blair succeeded John Smith as leader, in July 1994, that the thrust of the modernization project was resumed. He campaigned for a 'new' Labour party and made no effort to present himself as a man of the left or who would try to balance the party factions. He built on the policy and organizational changes of Neil Kinnock, but his main achievement was to redefine the ethos of the party. Blair rose to the party leadership with little or no baggage (Rentoul 1995; Sopel 1995). He was not identified with the factions of the 1970s and early 1980s and did not have a background in the trade unions or the public sector. Indeed, he was educated at a public school and came from a household in which his father voted Conservative. He personified 'New Labour' in a way that Neil Kinnock never could. As Labour leader Blair resembled a *pathfinder*, to use the term coined by Philip

Williams (1982) to describe a leader who sought to move the party in a new direction. The leader, operating in a context of the division of powers and formal constraints, was often a bargaining, consensual figure, what Williams calls a *stabilizer*. Three pathfinders—Gaitskell, Kinnock, and Blair—all operated against the party's electoral decline and sensed that Labour needed to modernize or to redefine its message to take account of changing values and social and economic conditions.

An important indicator of Blair's determination to change the nature as well as the image of the party was the rewriting of the party constitution's Clause 4, the ark of the socialist covenant, as Harold Wilson once called it. In doing this he succeeded where Hugh Gaitskell and Neil Kinnock had failed. Instead of working towards the public ownership of the means of production, distribution, and exchange, the new clause claimed that the party would work for 'a dynamic economy . . . enterprise of the market . . . the rigour of competition . . . a just society—an open democracy'. Equally significant was how the change was accomplished. Blair appealed directly to the members, over the heads of the activists and the trade-union leaders. It was a stunning success, as the constituency parties which balloted their members voted 9 to 1 for the change, as did the trade unions, which also balloted their members. Resistance came by and large from unions which did not ballot members. Party democracy, by balloting individual members, was used to outflank the left. Nearly a third of the membership had joined over the previous year. Both the change and the manner of change intended to make clear that this was a new Labour Party.

Under John Smith the influence of the trade unions in the party had been further reduced. The 1993 party Conference had accepted a version of one member, one vote which, by eroding the block vote, weakened the unions' influence at Conference and in constituency party ballots to select parliamentary candidates. Individual political levy members of unions who declared themselves to be Labour supporters were allowed to vote. The trade-union share of the electoral college to elect the party leader and deputy was reduced from 40 per cent to a third, the same share as MPs and constituency parties. The Conference agreed to cut back the union share of the

Conference vote to 50 per cent when the party's individual membership reached the figure of 300,000. Blair persuaded the unions to switch sponsorship funds from MPs and candidates to a constituency party. The party reduced its traditional financial dependence on union affiliation fees as it raised large sums from wealthy individuals. In 1996 the party, against the wishes of most unions, revealed plans for binding arbitration to settle disputes involving public-sector workers. Blair also made clear that the unions could expect no special favours from a Labour government.

Above all, Blair was concerned to identify Labour with the aspirations of the majority of voters, which meant the middle class and prosperous working class. He had been impressed by surveys conducted after the 1992 election which showed that the party was no longer seen as providing opportunity and choice for ambitious working-class supporters. Between 1979 and 1992 the working class had declined from two-thirds to less than half of the electorate and trade-union membership from a half to a third of the workforce, and both trends were likely to continue. Psephologists calculated that by 1992 the party's *normal* or core vote was little more than one-third of the electorate, compared to over 40 per cent for the Conservatives.

The modernizers realized the necessity to reach beyond Labour's declining core vote to forge a new progressive coalition of voters. The split among non-Conservative voters between Labour and Alliance had helped Mrs Thatcher to power in the 1980s. Kinnock had already moved his party onto Liberal ground by accepting constitutional reform and in 1992 by broadening membership of his party's commission on electoral reform to include members from outside the Labour Party. By 1992 Labour had abandoned many of the policy positions which stood in the way of cooperation with the Liberal Democrats. Blair went further. In a lecture commemorating Labour's 1945 election victory, he paid tribute to the founders of the pre-1914 New Liberals (such as Hobson and Hobhouse) and the reforming achievements of Keynes, Beveridge, and Lloyd George. By 1995 the Liberal Democrats had formally abandoned the policy of equidistance between Conservative and Labour, assumed a pro-Labour stance, and were cooperating informally with Labour in Parliament. The strategy of broadening Labour's electoral support inevitably involved a dilution of the traditional emphasis on appeals to the working class and trade unions. Instead of public ownership, Blair emphasized community, social justice, and equal opportunities, the values of ethical socialism and of the pre-1914 New Liberalism (Freeden 1978; Marquand 1991). Such eclecticism disillusioned some in the party who suspected that Blair lacked feeling for identity with the party (Kettle 1996).

The Blair project was joined to a cult of leadership. This was both a legacy of Thatcher—Blair expressed admiration for her conviction style and sense of purpose—and a reaction against the public perception that Labour lacked strong leadership. Historically, the party has regularly been taunted by opponents to prove its 'fitness' to govern. In part, this was a consequence of the party usually being in opposition, undermining the leader, and the ignominious circumstances in which Labour governments had resigned in 1931 or lost office in 1951 and 1979. Demonstrating 'fitness' has often meant adopting policies which would reassure non-Labour interests, notably the City, industry, and the press. Kinnock and then Blair insisted on party discipline and support for the leadership. Under Blair, shadow ministers were sometimes presented with policy proposals over which they had little say. Dissenters, potential or actual, found themselves deprived of official party slots in the media. The Chief Whip, traditionally elected by the PLP, was appointed by the leader in 1995. The NEC, under the General Secretary Tom Sawyer, increasingly interpreted its role not as an alternative voice of the party as in the 1970s and early 1980s, but as a body which supported the Labour leadership. In 1997 changes were proposed which would emphasize and facilitate the NEC's role as a 'partner' to a Labour government rather than as an alternative source of powers and reduce the policy-making role of Conference.

In a replay of the successful campaign to rewrite Clause 4, Blair decided that the draft election manifesto *New Labour. New Life for Britain* would be voted on by the party members at the 1996 party Conference. As a meaningful exercise in democracy, the ballot was limited by being on a take it or leave it basis. It was a plebiscitarian style of leadership, in which Blair appealed directly to members, not through constituency management committees, union leaders, or union executive committees. Party critics tolerated Blair's assertive and personal style of leadership because it seemed to be electorally appealing and because he was regarded as the party's greatest electoral asset.

Party Modernization

The reform measures, which effectively centralized decision-making in the hands of the leader and those around him, and the embrace of public relations and market research for campaigning, were interconnected. In seeking votes the party moved to the metaphorical middle ground. The Labour Party, so often beset by disagreement over policy and campaign strategy, separation of powers among different party institutions, and the tendency to make decisions by an elaborate system of committees, was an unsatisfactory client for communications advisers. The changes were part of a larger agenda to marginalize the party's left wing and reassure middle-of-the-road voters and the financial and business sectors that Labour was a competent party of government, not a class-specific party or one that would run risks with the economy. The term socialism and the policy of public ownership were downgraded as electoral liabilities. The new buzzwords were fairness, stakeholding, community, training, and the 'enabling state'. Policies and communication strategies were drawn up with the aim of appealing to non-Labour voters, and the identities and concerns of target voters were studied through opinion polling and focus groups rather than the resolutions passed by party and trade-union conferences. Increased reliance was placed on the mass media and public-relations campaigns and the party played down links with the trade unions (Kavanagh 1995).

In its search for votes, Labour became more like a commercial firm in a competitive market, operating as an 'electoral professional organisation' (Panebianco 1988) or a 'catch-all' party. Robert McKenzie (1963) had controversially argued that the party's doctrine of intra-party democracy was incompatible with the British constitution. Cabinet ministers were accountable to Parliament, not to a party conference. He showed that in practice Labour ministers managed to wriggle free of being instructed by party activists and that the party's doctrine of intra-party democracy was a myth, a 'living lie'. The party reforms in the early 1980s were designed to make the myth a reality, but their effects were short lived. The interest in using modern methods of communications for campaigning purposes was another force for increasing the autonomy of the leadership from Conference and the NEC. Not surprisingly, the new methods and the redirection of policy were seen as interconnected and fiercely opposed by the party's left wing (Heffernan and Marquesee 1992).

Policy

The evolution of the Labour Party since 1979 has been remarkable, amounting to what Seyd (1993) calls 'The Great Transformation'. Little remains of the leftist triumphs of the early 1980s, particularly the promise of a more state-controlled economy, more powerful trade unions, and the activist-dominated party. The election as leader of Michael Foot and then Neil Kinnock, at the time of their election the party's most left-wing leaders in the post-war period, was followed by the election, by huge majorities, of John Smith and Tony Blair, both clearly of the right. The party operated under the impact of four successive election defeats, including one which was unexpected and two which were among the party's worst performances since its creation as a national party in 1918.

The pace of change continued after 1992. Party leaders were convinced that their spending promises, added to opposition lies, had cost them the 1992 election. They were determined to avoid any policy commitments which the Conservatives could cost and translate into tax increases. The Shadow Chancellor Gordon Brown insisted that he would rule out any increase in borrowing, provide a more independent role for the Bank of England, and bear down on inflation. In early 1997 he announced that in the lifetime of the next Parliament a Labour government would not increase the top rate of tax, and accepted Conservative plans for public spending for the next two years. The party made few explicit spending pledges; where it did, they were to be funded by switching spending from elsewhere (e.g. ending the assisted places scheme to fund lower class sizes in primary schools), or by earmarked taxes (e.g. a windfall tax on the privatized utilities to finance an attack on youth employment).

The tight control over policy-making and, ultimately, over spending was a clear contrast to the 1970s and 1980s. Then Labour's policy-making groups were under the authority of the NEC, dominated by interest groups, particularly those from public-sector unions, and policy specialists, and often proposed more public spending, with large increases, and with little concern for how the money would be raised. Such a process had been a gift for critics who attacked Labour as a tax-and-spend party.

Crucial to any plans to control public spending was how to curb the rising costs of social security, which was running at over 30 per cent of total public spending. The party floated ideas about workfare, and its welfare-to-work scheme made receipt of benefits conditional on seeking work or receiving training. The 1992 promises to upgrade child benefit and increase pensions by £5 and £8 respectively for single and married couples, and link future rises to movements in rises in prices or earnings, whichever was the higher, were abandoned. On education, the party would no longer abolish grammar schools but leave their future to be decided by ballots of parents, and would allow streaming in comprehensive schools. It would not abolish grant-maintained schools but allow opted-out schools to convert to 'foundation schools', although local authorities would be represented on a school's governing body and control admissions. On health Labour would abolish the internal market but preserve the split between providers and patients. There would be some sweeteners for the unions, including a statutory minimum wage signing up to the Social Chapter, and guaranteeing union recognition where a majority of workers wanted it. But there would be no special favours. The draft manifesto covering these proposals easily won NEC approval in July 1996 and was then approved by the membership in October. Even this step to 'lock in' the party membership to the programme echoed another theme of New Right politics in Britain and the USA—the idea of a contract between provider and consumer.

Since the 1992 general election, it is fair to claim that Labour's transformation represents a vindication of the now defunct Social

Democratic Party. The policy changes on Europe, defence, the role of the trade unions in the economy and the party, and public ownership, as well as the expulsion of the anti-democratic left from the party and the enfranchisement of all party members in the selection and reselection of candidates were among the policy goals of the Social Democrats in 1981. The existence of the Alliance party weakened Labour electorally by acting as a siphon for disillusioned Labour supporters and as a reminder of the party's 'extremism'.

Labour's policy changes amount to a reverse of Sir Keith Joseph's so-called 'ratchet effect'. As the Conservative Party moved from the middle ground to the right and won elections, so Labour gradually moved with it. The new Conservatism of Thatcher and Major helped to beget the new Labourism of Kinnock and Blair. Labour is a non-socialist party of the left. In many respects British politics in the late 1990s may be said to have arrived at a new consensus, one which is post-Thatcherite and post-socialist.

In retrospect, Labour's transformation can be seen to have moved through two phases. In the first, from 1979 to 1983, the party shifted to the left and adopted its most radical programme in over fifty years. The second phase started in 1985, when the party began a ten-year march to the centre right. The first was a repudiation of Thatcherism as well as the policy thrust of recent Labour governments; the second was a gradual acceptance of much of the Thatcher agenda. Some of the stimulus for the policy changes came from elsewhere (e.g. from Europe) and could be seen as a revival of part of the revisionism associated with Gaitskell and Crosland, notably the reform of Clause 4 and the concern to appeal to the prosperous working class. Some of the changes were responses to particular interests (e.g. the environment, gender issues, and constitutional reform) and owed little to Thatcher.

The Thatcherism of the 1980s has had a major political effect on the Labour Party in the 1990s. Labour now offers not so much an alternative to the policy status quo as a claim to manage it more fairly and efficiently. But Labour was not merely passive in the face of the Thatcher agenda. What was also crucial were the political and organizational choices made by Kinnock and Blair. Martin Smith's judgement applies as much to Blair as to Kinnock when he writes that 'The importance of Thatcherism is that it has allowed Neil Kinnock the space to transform the party more successfully than any other leader' (1992: 28). The shorthand term which the modernizers used to describe their transformation of the party was that it was a victory not of the right over the left but of 'new' over 'old' Labour. The latter was portrayed as favouring an amalgam of such policies as high taxation, high levels of spending and borrowing, according the trade unions a privileged position in the party and over economic policy, and preferring government planning over market forces. 'New' Labour accepted the case for substantially lower marginal rates of income taxes than pre-1979, low inflation, and levels of public spending and borrowing which would reassure financial markets. The role of the state should be to work with and not replace the market, and to help people achieve things for themselves (Mandelson and Liddle 1996). One critic has objected to this portrait.

The very vocabulary employed—'Old Labour', 'New Labour', 'modernizers' and 'traditionalists'—was an essential part of the modernizing project. These concepts were in effect stereotypes, that is simplified and value-loaded images designed to project a particular view of reality and like most stereotypes they were misleading, squeezing and distorting complex reality by neatly parcelling up people into crude categories which did little justice to the diversity of views within the Party. (Shaw, 1996: 217–18)

The adjectives 'new', 'modern', and 'young' littered Blair's speeches, and were regarded favourably by many voters. Shaw claims that modernization was centred around two concepts: a detachment from the party's traditional values and objectives, and an accommodation with established institutions and values. Reliance on Keynesian social democracy was replaced by a more market-oriented approach, and the objectives of full employment and greater equality by low inflation, competitive tax rates, and 'responsible' public spending. What was crucial was Labour's acceptance in the rethinking of the new macro-economic priorities. For all the efforts of centre-left think-tanks such as the Institute of Public Policy Research, *Demos*, or *Charter 88*, there was nothing comparable to the impact of the New Right and their advocacy of markets, deregulation, monetarism, and contracting out think-tanks in the 1970s. Work on such topics as constitutional reform, green taxes, using support from the welfare state as a springboard to independence, hypothecated taxes, and proportional representation have helped to broaden debate from the 1980s and had some influence on Labour thinking and rhetoric. The same might be said of the communitarian ideas of Amitai Etzioni or the stakeholding proposals of Will Hutton (1995), in which firms are urged to consider the impact of their decisions on workers, suppliers, and communities as well as shareholders. One sympathetic commentator has complained that, across the spectrum of political debate, except possibly for constitutional reform [traditionally a Liberal theme], 'it is hard to find one area where Labour is setting the agenda' (Elliott 1997).

But there were also other external factors making for the convergence. They included:

- Labour's comprehensive election defeats, particularly those in 1983 and 1987.
- The agenda of other West European Socialist parties, particularly their interest in constitutional change, the environment, women's rights, the EU's Social Chapter, and a socially responsive market economy. Labour's lengthy exclusion from office and the determination with which the Thatcher Governments used their parliamentary majorities to force through controversial policies stimulated the party's interest in constitutional safeguards against the abuse of power by government. Similarly, the party's adoption of a Policy Forum to consider policy was borrowed from the practice of Socialist parties in West Europe. Many of these policies owed little to Thatcherism, or indeed 'old' Labour.
- Demographic change, as Labour's traditional core vote in manufacturing industry, the working class, and council estates declined. Deindustrialization, shrinkage of the working-class and trade-union members, and the changing composition of the workforce were occurring in other Western states and creating problems for centre-left parties. Britain was becoming more bourgeois, home-owning, and suburban, while Labour represented the areas and groups which were declining economically and in population. The social changes did not necessarily mean that the party was doomed to lose votes, but they did require the party to rethink its strategy in the light of social and economic changes.

- Evidence about public opinion and values. Research for the party, backed up by the experiences of party members and candidates on the doorstep, suggested that the Conservatives had captured the themes of choice, ownership, low taxes, and law and order. According to one survey, Labour target voters were becoming more individualist, instrumental ('what's in it for me?'), and ambitious to get on economically and socially. Proposals for redistribution cost the party votes and were a fatal electoral handicap in a 'two-thirds, one-third' society (Radice 1992: 17). After the 1979 defeat, Labour defied Downsian expectations of moving to the centre ground, newly defined by the Conservatives. After the 1987 and 1992 reverses we have seen that it acted in accord with the analysis.
- The global political economy, or the relatively free movement of capital, labour, and goods across borders, which has weakened national governments. The growing interdependence of economies made socialism or even full employment by Keynesianism in one country virtually unattainable. The failure of the Mitterrand socialist government in France in the early 1980s was a warning. Its economically interventionist, pro-employment policies were reversed, as priority was accorded to the battle against inflation and the need to reassure the financial markets. Similar rethinking on the left was evident in other West European states (Gillespie and Paterson 1993). In an era of flexible exchange rates, Britain had to take account of the competition from pro-market, business friendly, low tax regimes found elsewhere.
- Changed circumstances. Abandonment of the closed shop, for example, was a consequence of signing up to the EU's Social Chapter. By 1987 Britain was too integrated in the EU to make withdrawal a credible policy; the high financial costs of compensating shareholders in the privatized utilities ruled out the possibility of large-scale renationalization.
- Pressures from particular constituencies—e.g. trade unions for the minimum wage and the Social Chapter, Scottish Labour for devolution, and supporters of Lib.–Lab. cooperation for electoral and constitutional reform.

Consensus Again?

(The following section draws on Kavanagh 1994: 14–16)

Since 1992 British politics has been passing through one of its eras of 'good feelings', in which many policy goals and views are broadly shared across the political spectrum (Kavanagh 1994). In other words, after the polarization of the early 1980s, we have returned to convergence, although the policies differ from those of the post-war years. Such a claim can only be made with confidence after a spell of Labour government—to see whether its actions on tax, spending, and markets match its present rhetoric. For the present it appears that Clause 4 socialism and redistribution have been removed from the agenda, and Labour has accepted much of the Thatcherite programme. A result of pay increases and the cuts in income tax, which disproportionately helped the well-off, was a sharp increase in inequality in post-tax incomes in the 1980s. Labour's macroeconomic stance suggests that little will be done to reverse this.

The common ground includes the following:

- A narrowing of choice in macro-economic policy. Britain's membership of the ERM between October 1989 and September 1992 largely determined macro-economic policy; decisions on public spending, interest rates, and borrowing had to be made with membership in mind. Even out of the ERM, however, economic policies have to take account of the likely reactions of financial markets. In a global economy national governments can pay a heavy price for pursuing policies regarded as 'imprudent'. A telling indicator of the convergence was Labour's decision, on the eve of the 1997 general election, to accept Conservative tax and public spending totals for the following two years.
- A greater reliance on markets for wealth creation and, to a lesser extent, allocation of welfare. The leaderships in both parties still remain tentative in pushing the idea of markets further on welfare because of perceived public resistance, and Labour prefers more management of markets. But all main parties now clearly accept the market as more effective in promoting greater choice. Private ownership of the utilities is now common ground,

although there are differences about the rigour of the regulatory regime, for the utilities.

- A need for public services to be more responsive to consumers. There is a shared concern with promoting the rights of consumers of services, emphasizing the importance of delivering satisfactory services, and establishing more equal relations between consumers and producers. A century ago Lord Harcourt said 'We are all socialists now.' Today it would be more accurate to say that 'We are all consumers'. The new outlook is consistent with Labour's weakening of its links with the trade unions. Its ties with well-organized public-sector trade unions made it appear as the party of the producers.

- An emphasis on cost-containment and value for money in the public sector. The strategies of new public management are here to stay, given the voters' demand for better public services, alongside a resistance to pay more income tax and constraints on increased public spending.

- A rethinking of the range of services and benefits provided by the state (e.g. via more selectivity and opting out) and of new ways to finance them. Given the commitment of the two main parties to regard the present levels of public spending as a ceiling, the search for alternatives will become more pressing. The reforming right will support the extension of user charges (e.g. tuition fees in higher education or encouragement for private provision for pensions and other benefits) as a means of reducing the role of the state and the scope of public spending. If 'New Labour' remains determined to break with its tax-and-spend image, it also will have to re-examine the present range of the state's spending responsibilities.

- A concern at how some of the social and economic policies of the 1980s have weakened the sense of community. It is not surprising that the left makes this charge, and proclaims the need for strong communities, not least to enable individuals to thrive. It figures prominently in Blair's speeches. But the right has also complained that the economic changes ignored the 'civic virtues' of solidarity, self-sacrifice, and service for others, and weakened the social fabric (Green 1993; see also Gray 1993).

- Caution about British membership of a single European currency. Both Labour and Conservatives have agreed to hold a referendum on the issue, once the Cabinet has made a decision and legislation to enter has passed through Parliament.
- A turning-away from top-down provision in universal services; greater flexibility and competition, as in schools and higher education, is the order of the day. In some ways, this is less a European than a North American model of government (partly because of federalism, partly because of a more modest state role as provider of welfare, and partly because of the lower social and political status of the federal bureaucracy).

One policy paradigm suggests that we have arrived at an *end* state, what Fukuyama calls *The End of History*. Reinventing government also belongs to the school that says liberal capitalism has won, socialism is dead, and ideological conflict has declined. Government is seen as a business; departments and agencies have missions, government institutions should be decentralized, play the role of an enabler more than a provider, and be judged by results and customer satisfaction.

An alternative paradigm is that public policy shifts *cyclically* between a focus on private concerns and a focus on public issues. The present is but another stage in a long-running story. The idea of cyclical change in the public mood has been an extremely powerful one, more so than the idea that history moves in one direction. Economists study the alternations of economic booms and depressions, political scientists the electoral swing of the pendulum between left and right, and philosophers the interaction of thesis and antithesis. As disillusion builds up with, for example, the pursuit of private interests, so the electorate responds more favourably to leadership calls to correct the imbalance which has involved neglect of the public concerns (Hirschman 1982). The 1990s have seen some reaction to the privatizing cycle of the 1980s. But it is more of a correction than a repudiation. The Thatcher administrations moved the centre of political gravity firmly to the right. John Major was not a Thatcherite, but he has largely accepted what he inherited. Much the same seems to be true of New Labour.

11 Postscript: The 1997 Election

The 1997 general election brought the long period of Conservative ascendancy to a spectacular end. The election result broke many records. It saw:

- the largest two-party swing in the twentieth century, with over 10 per cent shifting from Conservative to Labour.
- the century's biggest parliamentary majority for one party. Labour's majority of 179 exceeded that for 1945 (146) and the Liberal majority of 130 in 1906.
- the lowest number (165) of Conservative MPs in the century and largest ever number (419) of Labour MPs.

Some politicians and commentators were quick to see the outcome of the 1997 general election as a political turning-point. It brought eighteen years of Conservative rule to an end and was comparable to the elections of 1945 or 1906. All three elections ended a long run of Conservative governments and the party suffered landslide defeats. The Conservative Party had been in office for seventeen of the twenty years prior to 1906, sixteen years prior to 1945, and eighteen years prior to 1997. In each case the party had lost its sense of cohesion and appeared to lack a clear vision for the future. In 1906 and 1997 there were widespread complaints of weak leadership, by A. J. Balfour and by John Major respectively. Prior to all three elections, there was evidence of a decline among the grass roots and in organizational vitality. In the wake of the 1997 election, for example, it was revealed that Conservative membership in the constituencies had fallen by half over the previous five years and now stood at an all-time low of 400,000. Finally, in 1906 and 1997, the Conservative Party was spectacularly divided, as some candidates ran on what were personal manifestos—in 1906 over tariff reform, and in 1997 over British membership of a single European currency.

The Conservative Party was ending the twentieth century as it began, divided and in a clear minority. Yet in between, the party's electoral dominance was such that it has been fairly called the Conservative Century. Within four years of the 1906 humiliation the party was back on level terms with the Liberals and within six years of the 1945 rout it was back in government. Earlier landslide defeats were short-term in their effects.

A realigning election involves a significant shift in the balance of the party system. In 1922 Labour broke through as a major force when it replaced the Liberals as the second party. The term also applies when a traditional minority party displaces a former majority party for a number of elections, as the Democrats did in the United States in 1932. It is often associated with the emergence of new issues, or the entry of new groups of voters to the electoral register, as in 1922 and 1932. If the new party balance is durable, we can say that there has been a realignment of the party system.

Was 1997 a realigning election, in the sense of Labour moving from being the clear minority party to a long-term majority one? The appropriate answer is that it is too soon to say; the trends would be expected to last for at least one further general election before one could return an affirmative response. Labour's vote share of 44 per cent is comparable with that gained by the Conservatives when they won general elections under Thatcher and Major, and is on a par with the share gained by Harold Wilson in 1964. The landslide is clear in terms of seats (a Labour majority of 179), although some part of this was due to the disproportional effects of the electoral system and to tactical voting, and in terms of the gap in vote shares between Labour and Conservative. 1997 may be a first step in a realignment in which Labour becomes a new majority. Equally, insofar as the party attracted support across social groups and profited as much from dissatisfaction with the Conservatives as positive endorsement of its own policies, it may only be a short-term change.

More important and enduring were the shifts in the agenda in 1906 and 1945. At first sight 1997 has some similarities with those elections, notably in the election of a new government backed by a large majority in the House of Commons facing a divided and discredited opposition. But in contrast to the earlier elections 1997 was not preceded by a significant change in the climate of opinion or the promise of a radical shift in the policy agenda by the winning party. Sympathetic think-tanks like Demos and the Institute for Public Policy Research canvassed the case for constitutional reform, stakeholding, new patterns of work, and lifelong learning, but the corpus of ideas was designed more to correct than to overturn the Thatcherite policies.

Interpretations of the election varied (Butler and Kavanagh 1997). One, from the Conservative right wing, is that the party was not Thatcherite enough—that it abandoned the true path both by imposing tax rises in 1993 and 1994 and by not explicitly repudiating British membership of a single currency. There are grounds for questioning this explanation. Why should so many former Conservative voters have shifted to Labour, which is, if anything, a more pro-European party and one identified as equally likely to increase taxes? Why did Eurosceptic Conservatives do no better in the election than other Conservatives? Tax cuts have to be sustainable, not least in the light of a government's borrowing requirement and its need for the approval of the financial markets. Public spending and direct taxation as shares of GDP in Britain in 1997 were already well below the EU average. There were no more major state-owned assets to privatize and there was no good case for making yet more trade union reforms. The party leadership could have taken a clearer Eurosceptic line, but only at the cost of exacerbating party divisions, and it could cut taxes only at the cost of creating turbulence in the markets.

A second interpretation is that the election was an endorsement of Labour and the new agenda. According to surveys, the party led on virtually all image and policy questions. More important than policy issues, however, were valence issues, i.e. values or goals that were widely shared. Compared to the Conservatives, Labour was seen as more united, more competent, better for all classes, stronger in its leadership, and more forward looking. It even overtook the Conservatives on questions of economic competence and trust with regard to taxation. In other words, it stole many of the Conservatives' traditional strong themes. The leadership claimed that the election was a vote of approval for New Labour, a party of the centre which had given up its commitments to redistribution, more public spending, public ownership, and a special relationship with the trade unions.

A third and more prosaic explanation, not incompatible with the previous one, is that most voters simply felt that it was time for a change. Such a mood was reinforced by the ill discipline, disunity, and sleazy behaviour of some Conservative politicians, and by the government's broken tax promises. For all the talk of the economic recovery, there had actually been only a modest increase in living standards over the five years of the Parliament. Labour cleverly exploited the mood for change and its slogan 'Enough is Enough' warned wavering voters against returning the Conservatives for a fifth term. An ICM recall poll after the election found that half of the 1992 Conservatives who defected to Labour claimed to have done so because they thought it was time for a change. Disillusion with the Conservatives and the attractions of New Labour were the major forces making for change.

Labour, having lost four elections because of the voters' alleged fear of the party, now offered reassurance across virtually all areas. On law and order, industrial relations, privatization, health, education, and welfare it offered only minor differences from the Conservative Party. On the question of relations with the European Union, Labour accepted the Social Chapter but on the single currency it adopted the same stance as the government—to negotiate and decide to hold a referendum before entry. It also accepted the public spending totals of the outgoing Conservative government for the next two years and the rates of income tax for the five years of the Parliament. Labour's campaign posters reminded voters of the party's pragmatic pledges: 'Labour will cut class sizes', 'Labour will not increase income tax', and 'Labour will punish offenders'. There were clear differences on the constitution, but on the broad substance of programmes there was little difference between the parties.

The election was primarily about a change of face and not of programmes; an example of political ins and outs. New Labour was so safe that it could be endorsed by business, the City (the stock market reached new heights, in spite of the certainty of a Labour government), and much of the press. It was as if Labour had become the party of the cultural and economic establishment. The greatest paradox is that the 1997 election produced the biggest electoral change in votes and seats in the twentieth century but was accompanied by such a modest shift about the role of government and the balance between public and private sector and between tax and public spending.

In several respects the agenda in 1997 has grown out of the Thatcherite policies of the 1980s. This is particularly so in respect of the following:

Economic liberalism
This includes the acceptance of privatization, an inflation target of 2.5 per cent, curbing government borrowing, insisting on tough convergence conditions for a single European currency, and freeing the Bank of England to control interest rates.

Flexible markets
The trade union reforms of the 1980s remain in place. The likelihood is that a minimum wage, if introduced, will be at a relatively low level and, although the Social Chapter is to be accepted, Labour ministers have insisted that there will be no more legislation for the next two years. In the European Union, Prime Minister Blair has presented the case for the Anglo-Saxon model of a flexible labour market against the 'social market' model of his European Socialist colleagues.

Social conservatism
This is reflected in proposals that offenders make reparations for damage done to property and persons, that incompetent teachers be rooted out, tougher criteria be imposed for receiving long-term sickness and unemployment benefits, and that measures be taken to reduce the social security (or 'dependency') budget.

In a recent unpublished paper, Richard Heffernan (1997) has pointed to the 'uncanny resemblance' between Labour's economic priorities and the 1979 Conservative election manifesto. The latter promised to: control inflation as a first priority; curb public expenditure; reduce public borrowing; oppose punitive taxation; restore incentives to business and enterprise; and regulate trade unions. New Labour in 1997 shared these economic prorities. In other words, the 1997 election was more about policy continuity than discontinuity as Labour came to accept many of the policy changes of the 1980s.

In the late 1990s the Labour Party has succeeded in making itself something of a catch-all party. It increased its support impressively in all parts of the country and among virtually all groups. In the 1997 election it actually outscored the Conservatives among home owners (41 per cent to 35 per cent) and C1 or lower-middle-class voters (47 per cent to 26 per cent—a swing of 20 per cent). The only groups among which it trailed the Conservatives were the over-65s and the ABs, or upper-middle-class, and the only regions the South-East and the South-West. In a remarkable reversal of the two parties' electoral profiles in the 1980s, the Conservatives increasingly look like a party that is confined to one part of England and has the support of few sections of British society.

The British party system has undergone changes since 1945. Between 1945 and 1970 Conservatives and Labour operated in a system of evenly balanced two-party competition, as the parties' aggregate shares of electoral support and number of years spent in office were virtually identical. Since 1974 there has been a decline in electoral support for the two-party system and the competitiveness of the two parties. Both of these last features were a consequence of Labour's decline. 1997 provides a partial confirmation of the post-1974 system in that it confirms the reduced electoral support for the two parties; Labour and Conservative together garnered only 75 per cent of the total vote, compared to 90 per cent between 1945 and 1970. But Labour's huge lead in seats and votes over the Conservative Party precludes any talk of a restoration of balanced competition between the two main parties.

Changes in the party system do not necessarily mirror changes in the political agenda. The defeat of the post-war Labour government in 1951 and the run of Conservative governments over the next thirteen years accompanied broad continuity in policy. Broad continuity does not, however, mean similarity. The passage of time, combined with policy learning, changing circumstances, and the different values of the parties and priorities of key politicians, produces shifts, but these occur within a given set of parameters. The Conservative

Party in the 1950s was forced to come to terms with the work of the 1945 Labour government, not least because it considered that this was necessary to win elections. Tony Blair similarly thought that the Labour Party had virtually to reinvent itself and come to terms with the social, economic, and political changes in Britain as well as the policy achievements of Thatcher, if it was to remain an electorally viable political party. The Blair rhetoric of newness and change had as much to do with making a contrast with the old Labour Party as with the Conservative Party.

Further Reading

A more comprehensive guide to the relevant literature is available in the references at the end of the book. This brief essay refers to materials which the author found particularly useful.

Chapter 1

Much of the relevant literature is reviewed in the chapter. A brilliant guide and critique to the literature is available in Marsh (1995). Gamble (1994) on the broader picture, Letwin (1992) on ideas, Young (1990) on biography, and P. Jenkins (1987) on context, are all useful. On the specific issue of how agendas change, Chapter 1 of Kavanagh (1990) is relevant. An original and hard-hitting perspective is provided by S. Jenkins (1995).

Chapter 2

A good starting-point is Addison (1994). There is a review of what is now a large literature in Anthony Seldon (1994). On the economy, Middlemas (1979, 1990) is essential. On personalities, see Vaizey (1983) and Dell (1996). On ideas, see Marquand and Seldon (1996).

Chapter 3

Still useful are Skidelsky (1977), Rose and Peters (1978), Bacon and Eltis (1976), and A. King (1975).

Chapter 4

Useful overviews are provided in Ramsden (1995) and Seldon and Ball (1994). Bulpitt (1986) provides a provocative interpretation of Thatcherism in relationship to the Conservative Party. On Heath, see Ball and Seldon

(1996). For the relevant period there is much useful material in Ludlam and Smith (1996).

Chapter 5

For early arguments, see Joseph (1975) and Bosanquet (1983). On the IEA and other groups, see Cockett (1994), and, on ideas, Harrison (1994) and Marquand and Seldon (1996). Particularly useful on think-tanks is a special issue of *Contemporary British History* (1996).

Chapter 6

Kavanagh and Seldon (1989), Riddell (1989), Moon (1994), Marsh and Rhodes (1992), S. Jenkins (1995), and Gilmour (1992) provide a variety of interpretations. The authorized version is available in Thatcher (1993), which can be set beside the memoirs of her former Cabinet ministers.

Chapter 7

A brilliant examination of the role of political ideas and politics is Hood (1994). Marquand and Seldon (1996) is also useful. An impressive set of case studies is provided by Jordan and Ashford (1993). The special issue of *Contemporary British History* (1996) is essential reading, particularly the excellent overview by Denham and Garnett.

Chapter 8

Useful guides are Seyd (1987), Shaw (1996), and Minkin (1980). Neil Kinnock has given his own views in *Contemporary Record* (1994), and this issue contains other relevant articles. A good overview is Shaw (1996).

Chapter 9

On Thatcher's downfall see her own memoirs and those of former Cabinet colleagues. Detailed accounts are available in Anderson (1991) and Watkins

(1991). On Major, see Kavanagh and Seldon (1994), Hogg and Hill (1995), and Ludlam and Smith (1996). The latter has excellent material on Thatcher and Major. On Europe, see any of the numerous articles by Baker and his colleagues listed in the References.

Chapter 10

On 1992 election outcomes see Heath, Jowell, and Curtice (1994). This accurately conveys the electoral challenge facing Labour after the election. On modernization, see Shaw (1996) for a perceptive and hard-hitting account. On the convergence of policies, see Kavanagh (1994), Giddens (1994), Hay (1995), and Hutton (1995).

References

Addison, P. (1994), *The Road to 1945* (2nd edn., London: Pimlico; first pub. 1975).

Adonis, A. M., and Hames, T. (1994) (eds.), *A Conservative Revolution?* (Manchester: Manchester University Press).

Agar, H. (1943), *A Time for Greatness* (London: Macmillan).

Alderman, G., and Carter, N. (1990), 'A Very Tory Coup: The Ousting of Mrs Thatcher', *Parliamentary Affairs*, 44.

Alt, J. (1979), *The Politics of Economic Decline* (Cambridge: Cambridge University Press).

Anderson, B. (1991), *John Major: The Making of a Prime Minister* (London: Fourth Estate).

ASI (1986): Adam Smith Institute, *The Omega File* (London: ASI).

Bacon, R., and Eltis, W. (1976), *Britain's Economic Problems: Too Few Producers* (London: Macmillan).

Baker, D., Gamble, A., and Ludlam, S. (1993), '1846, 1906, 1996? Conservative Splits and European Integration', *Political Quarterly*, 64.

———— ———— ———— (1994), 'The Parliamentary Siege of Maastricht, 1993', *Parliamentary Affairs*, 47.

Baker, K. (1993), *The Turbulent Years: My Life in Politics* (London: Faber & Faber).

Ball, S., and Seldon, A. (1996) (eds.), *The Heath Government, 1970–1974: Reappraisal* (London: Longmans).

Banting, M. (1979), *Poverty and Politics and Policy* (London: Macmillan).

Barnett, C. (1986), *The Audit of War* (London: Macmillan).

Barnett, J. (1982), *Inside the Treasury* (London: Andre Deutsch).

Baston, L. (1996), 'The Social Market Foundation', *Contemporary British History*, 10.

Beer, S. (1965), *Modern British Politics* (London: Faber).

—— (1982), *Britain Against Itself* (London: Faber).

Beloff, M. (1984), *Wars and Welfare: Britain, 1914–1945* (London: Edward Elgar).

Beveridge, W. (1942), *Social Insurance and Allied Services* (Cmnd. 6404; London: HMSO).

Blair, A. (1996), *New Britain: My Vision of a Young Country* (London: Fourth Estate).

Blake, R. (1985), *The Conservative Party from Disraeli to Thatcher* (London: Fontana).

Blondel, J. (1992), *Voters, Parties and Leaders* (Harmondsworth: Penguin).

Bosanquet, N. (1983), *After the New Right* (London: Heinemann).

—— and Townsend, P. (1980) (eds.), *Labour and Equality* (London: Heinemann).

Boyson, R. (1975), *The Crisis in Education* (London: Woburn).

Brittan, S. (1971), *The Treasury under the Tories: Steering the Economy* (Harmondsworth: Penguin).

—— (1975), 'The Economic Contradictions of Democracy', *British Journal of Political Science*, 50.

—— and Lilley, P. (1977), *The Delusion of Incomes Policy* (London: Temple Smith).

Bulpitt, J. (1986), 'The Thatcher Statecraft', *Political Studies*, 36.

—— (1996), 'The European Question', in Marquand and Seldon (1996), 214–56.

Burton, J. (1993), 'Taxation Policy and the New Right', in Jordan and Ashford (1993), 102–19.

Butler, A. (1994), 'The End of the Post-War Consensus: Reflections on the Scholarly Uses of Political Rhetoric', *Political Quarterly*, 64.

Butler, D., and Stokes, D. (1974), *Political Change in Britain* (2nd edn., London: Macmillan; first pub. 1969).

—— Adonis, A., and Travers, T. (1995), *Failure in British Government* (London: Fontana).

—— and Kavanagh, D. (1997), *The British General Election of 1997* (London: Macmillan).

Butler, R. (1971), *The Art of the Possible* (London: Hamish Hamilton).

Callaghan, J. (1987), *Time and Chance* (London: Collins).

Campbell, J. (1993), *Edward Heath* (London: Cape).

Cockett, R. (1994), *Thinking the Unthinkable: Think-Tanks and the Economic Counter-Revolution 1931–1983* (London: HarperCollins).

Coleman, J. (1966), *Equality and Educational Opportunity* (Washington: Government Printing Office).

Cornford, J. (1990), 'Performing Fleas: Reflections from a Think Tank', *Policy Studies*, 11.

Cosgrave, P. (1985), *Thatcher: The First Term* (London: Bodley Head).

Cowley, P. (1996), 'Philip Norton's Conservative Party', British Politics Group, *Newsletter* (Fall).

Cowling, M. (1976), *Conservative Essays* (London: Cassell).

——(1989), 'The Sources of the New Right', *Encounter* (November).

Cox, B., and Dyson, A. (1969) (eds.), *Fight for Education—Black Papers* (London: The Critical Quarterly Society).

Crewe, I. (1984), 'The Electorate: Partisan Dealignment Ten Years On', *West European Politics*, 7.

—— (1989), 'Values: The Crusade that Failed', in Kavanagh and Seldon (1989), 239–50.

—— (1991), 'Margaret Thatcher: As the British Saw Her', *The Public Perspective* (January/February).

—— (1994), 'Electoral Behaviour', in Kavanagh and Seldon (1994), 99–121.

—— and King, A. (1995), *SDP: The Birth, Life and Death of the Social Democratic Party* (Oxford: Oxford University Press).

—— Norris, P., and Waller, R. (1992), 'The 1992 General Election', in P. Norris, I. Crewe, D. Denver, and D. Broughton (eds.), *British Elections and Parties Year Book* (Harvester: Wheatsheaf), pp. xv–xxxvi.

Crick, M., and van Kleveran, A. (1991), 'Poll Tax: Mrs Thatcher's Greatest Blunder', *Contemporary Record*, 5.

Crosland, A. (1956), *The Future of Socialism* (London: Cape).

—— (1975), *Socialism Now* (London: Cape).

Dell, E. (1991), *A Hard Pounding* (Oxford: Clarendon Press).

—— (1996), *The Chancellors* (London: HarperCollins).

Denham, A., and Garnett, M. (1996), 'The Nature and Impact of Think Tanks in Contemporary Britain', *Contemporary British History*, 10.

Dicey, A. V. (1905), *Law and Opinion in Nineteenth-Century England* (London: Macmillan).

DoE (1986): Department of the Environment, *Paying for Local Government* (Cmnd. 9714).

Dolowitz, E., *et al.* (1996), 'Thatcherism and the 3 "Rs": Radicalism, Realism and Rhetoric in the Third Term of the Thatcher Government', *Parliamentary Affairs*, 49.

Donnison, D. (1982), *The Politics of Poverty* (Oxford: Martin Robertson).

Donoughue, B. (1987), *Prime Minister* (London: Cape).

Douglas, J. (1989), 'Review article: The Changing Tide—Some Recent Studies of Thatcherism', *British Journal of Political Service*, 19.

—— (1994), Book review, *Journal of Public Policy*, 14.

—— (1996), 'Conservative Party Leadership', British Politics Group, *Newsletter* (Winter).

Downs, A. (1957), *An Economic Theory of Democracy* (New York: Harper & Row).

Edgell, S., and Duke, V. (1991), *A Measure of Thatcherism: A Sociology of Britain* (London: HarperCollins).

Elliot, L. (1997), 'In Place of Fear of Ethical Socialism', *Guardian*, 13 January, p. 18.

Eltis, W. (1993), *Classical Economics, Public Expenditure and Growth* (London: Edward Elgar).

Enthoven, A. (1985), 'Revolution in the Management of the NHS' (Nuffield Provincial Hospital Trust, Occasional Paper No. 5).

Faith in the Inner City (1985), the Report of the Archbishop of Canterbury's Commission on Urban Priority Areas (London: Church House Publishing).

Finer, S. (1972), 'The Transmission of Benthamite Ideas', in Sutherland (1972), 11–32.

Flora, P., and Heidenheimer, A. (1984) (eds.), *The Development of Welfare States in Europe and the United States* (New Brunswick, NJ: Transactions).

Foley, M. (1992), *The Rise of the British Presidency* (Manchester: Manchester University Press).

Forsyth, M. (1985), *The Case for a Poll Tax* (London: Conservative Political Centre).

Foster, C., and Perlmann, M. (1980), *Local Government Finance in a Unitary State* (London: Allen & Unwin).

Freeden, M. (1978), *The New Liberalism* (Oxford: Clarendon Press).

Friedman, M. (1962), *Capitalism and Freedom* (Chicago: Chicago University Press).

—— (1970), *The Counter-Revolution in Monetary Theory* (London: IEA).

—— (1975), *Unemployment versus Inflation* (London: IEA).

—— and Friedman, R. (1980), *Free to Choose* (Harmondsworth: Penguin).

—— and Schwartz, A. (1969), *A Monetary History of the United States 1867–1960* (Princeton: Princeton University Press).

Fukuyama, F. (1992), *The End of History* (London: Hamish Hamilton).

Gamble, A. (1994), *The Free Economy and Strong State* (2nd edn., London: Macmillan' first pub. 1988).

—— (1996), 'An Ideological Party', in Ludlam, S. and Smith, N. (eds.) (1996), 19–36.

Giddens, A. (1994), *Beyond Left and Right* (Cambridge: Cambridge University Press).

Gillespie, R., and Paterson, W. (1993), *Rethinking Social Democracy in Western Europe* (London: Cass).

Gilmour, I. (1978), *Inside Right* (London: Quartet).

—— (1983), *Britain Can Work* (Oxford: Martin Robertson).

—— (1992), *Dancing with Dogma: Britain under Thatcherism* (London: Simon and Schuster).

—— (1994), 'The Thatcher Memoirs', *Twentieth-Century British History*, 5.

Gourevitch, P. (1989), 'Keynesian Politics: The Political Sources of Economic Policy Changes', in Hall (1989), 87–106.

Gray, J. (1993), *Beyond the New Right* (London: Routledge).

Green, D. (1987), *The New Right* (Brighton: Wheatsheaf).

—— (1993), *Reinventing Civil Society* (London: IEA).

Greenleaf, W. (1983), *The British Political Tradition* (London: Methuen).

Guardian (1996), 'Anglican Clergy Lean to Lib-Dems' (14 Feb.).

Guttsman, W. (1963), *The British Political Élite* (London: Heinemann).

Gyford, J. (1985), *The Politics of Local Socialism* (London: Allen & Unwin).

Hadjimatheou, G., and Skouras, A. (1979), 'Britain's Economic Problem: The Growth of the Non-Market Sector', *Economic Journal*, 89.

Hall, P. (1989), *The Political Power of Economic Ideas* (Princeton: Princeton University Press).

Hall, S. (1988), *The Hard Road to Renewal: Thatcherism and the Crisis of the Left* (London: Verso).

—— and Jacques, M. (1983) (eds.), *The Politics of Thatcherism* (Lawrence & Wishart).

Halsey, A., and Trow, M. (1971), *The British Academics* (London: Faber).

Hames, T., and Feasey, R. (1994), 'Anglo-American Think Tanks under Reagan and Thatcher', in Adonis and Hames (1994), 215–37.

Harrison, J. (1994), 'Mrs Thatcher and the Intellectuals', *Twentieth-Century British History*, 5.

Hay, C. (1994), 'Labour's Thatcherite Revisionism: Playing the Politics of Catch-up', *Political Studies*, 42.

—— (1995), 'Past and Present, Present Tense: Majorism, Post-Thatcherism, and the Politics of Crisis Management', paper presented at Politics Studies Association Conference, University of York.

Hayek, F. von (1944), *The Road to Serfdom* (London: Routledge).

—— (1949), 'Intellectuals and Socialism', *University of Chicago Law Review*, 16.

—— (1960), *The Constitution of Liberty* (London: Routledge & Kegan Paul).

—— (1961), *Agenda for a Free Society* (London: IEA).

—— (1972), *A Tiger by the Tail* (London: IEA).

—— (1973, 1976, 1979), *Law, Legislation and Liberty* (3 vols.; London: Routledge & Kegan Paul).

—— (1975), *Full Employment at any Price* (London: IEA).

—— (1976), *Denationalization of Money* (London: IEA).

—— (1980), *1980s Unemployment and the Unions* (London: IEA).

Headey, B. (1974), *British Cabinet Ministers* (London: Allen & Unwin).

Healey, D. (1989), *The Time of My Life* (London: Michael Joseph).

Heath, H., Jowell, R., and Curtice, J. (1994) (eds.), *Labour's Last Chance?* (Aldershot: Dartmouth).

Heclo, H. (1984), 'Towards a New Welfare State', in Flora and Heidenheimer (1984), 383–406.

Heffernan, R. (1996), 'Blue Print for a Revolution? The Politics of the Adam Smith Institute', *Contemporary British History*, 10.

—— (1997), 'Ideology and Political Consensus: Some Thoughts on Political Change in the UK' (Unpublished paper presented to Political Studies Association, University of Ulster, April).

—— and Marquesee, M. (1992), *Defeat from the Jaws of Victory: Inside Neil Kinnock's Labour Party* (London: Verso).

Hennessey, P., and Seldon, A. (1987) (eds.), *Ruling Performance* (Oxford: Blackwell).

Hibbs, D. (1978), 'On the Political Economy of Long Trends in Strike Activity', *British Journal of Political Science*, 8.

Hills, J. (1991) (ed.), *The State of Welfare: The Welfare State in Britain since 1974* (Oxford: Clarendon Press).

Hirschman, A. (1982), *Shifting Involvements, Private Interests and Public Action* (Oxford: Martin Robertson).

Holmes, M. (1985), *The Thatcher Government 1979–1983* (London: Wheatsheaf).

Hogg, S., and Hill, J. (1995), *Too Close to Call: Power and Politics—John Major in No. 10* (London: Little Brown).

Hogg, Q. (1947), *The Case for Conservatism* (West Drayton: Penguin).

Hood, C. (1994), *Explaining Economic Policy Reversals* (London: Open University Press).

Hoover, K., and Plant, R. (1988), *Conservative Capitalism in Britain and the United States: A Critical Appraisal* (London: Routledge).

Howe, G. (1994), *Conflict of Loyalty* (London: Macmillan).

Hutton, W. (1995), *The State We're In* (London: Jonathan Cape).

Hurd, D. (1979), *An End to Promises* (London: Collins).

Ingham, B. (1991), *Kill the Messenger* (London: HarperCollins).

Jackson, D. (1975) (ed.), *Do Trade Unions Cause Inflation?* (Cambridge: Cambridge University Press).

Jackson, P. (1985) (ed.), *Implementing Government Initiatives: The Thatcher Administration 1979–1983* (London: Royal Institute of Public Administration).

Jeffrys, K. (1987), 'British Politics and Social Policy during the Second World War', *Historical Journal*, 30.

Jencks, C. (1973), *Inequality* (London: Allen Lane).

Jenkins, P. (1987), *Mrs Thatcher's Revolution* (London: Jonathan Cape).

Jenkins, S. (1995), *Accountable to None* (London: Hamish Hamilton).

Jessop, B. *et al.* (1988), *Thatcherism: A Tale of Two Nations* (Oxford: Polity).

Jones, K. (1989), *Right Turn: The Conservative Revolution in Education* (London: Hutchinson).

Jordan, G., and Ashford, N. (1993) (eds.), *Public Policy and the Nature of the New Right* (London: Pinter).

Joseph, K. (1975), *Reversing the Trend* (London: Barry Rose).

—— (1987), 'Interview with Antony Seldon', *Contemporary Record*, 1.

Kavanagh, D. (1982) (ed.), *The Politics of the Labour Party* (London: Allen & Unwin).

—— (1987), 'The Heath Government', in Hennessey and Seldon (1987), 216–40.

—— (1990), *Thatcherism and British Politics: The End of Consensus* (Oxford: Oxford University Press; first pub. 1987).

—— (1992*a*), 'The Post-War Consensus', *Twentieth-Century British History*, 3.

—— (1992*b*) (ed.), *Electoral Politics* (Oxford: Oxford University Press).

—— (1994), 'A Major Agenda', in Kavanagh and Seldon (1994), 3–17.

—— (1995), *Election Campaigning: The New Marketing of Politics* (Oxford: Blackwell).

—— (1996), '1970–74', in Ball and Seldon (1996), 351–70.

—— and Peele, G. (eds.), *Comparative Government and Politics* (London: Heinemann).

—— and Seldon, A. (1989) (eds.), *The Thatcher Effect* (Oxford: Oxford University Press).

—— —— (1994) (eds.), *The Major Effect* (London: Macmillan).

Keegan, W. (1984), *Mrs Thatcher's Economic Experiment* (London: Penguin).

Kettle, M. (1996), 'He Regards the Party he Leads as a Failure', *Guardian*, 18 September.

King, A. (1975), 'Overload. Problems of Governing in the 1970s', *Political Studies*, 23.

—— (1985) (ed.), *The British Prime Minister* (2nd edn.; London: Macmillan; first pub. 1969).

—— (1992), 'Political Change in Britain', in Kavanagh (1992*b*), 25–50.

—— (1993) (ed.), *Britain at the Polls 1992* (London: AEI).

King, D. (1987), *The New Right* (London: Macmillan).

Kingdon, J. (1984), *Agendas: Alternatives in Public Policies* (Boston: Little Brown).

Kinnock, N. (1994), 'Reforming the Labour Party', *Contemporary British History*, 8.

Klein, R. (1983), *The Politics of the National Health Service* (London: Fontana).

Knight, C. (1990), *The Making of Tory Education Policy in Post-War Britain 1950–1986* (Brighton: Falmer Press).

Krieger, J. (1986), *Reagan, Thatcher and the Politics of Decline* (Cambridge: Polity Press).

Kristol, I. (1978), *Two Cheers for Capitalism* (New York: Basic Books).

Lawson, N. (1980), *The New Conservatism* (London: Centre for Policy Studies).

——(1992), *The View From No. 11: Memoirs of a Tory Radical* (London: Bantam Press).

Le Grand, J., and Goodin, B. (1987), *Not Only the Poor: The Middle Classes in the Welfare State* (London: Allen & Unwin).

Letwin, S. (1992), *The Anatomy of Thatcherism* (London: Fontana).

Lipset, M. (1964), 'The Modernization of Contemporary European Politics', in M. Lipset, *Revolution and Counter Revolution* (London: Heinemann).

Lowe, R. (1990), 'The Second World War Consensus and the Foundation of the Welfare State', *Twentieth-Century British History*, 1.

——(1993), *The Welfare State in Britain since 1945* (London: Macmillan).

Ludlam, S. (1996), 'The Spectre Haunting Conservatism: Europe and the Back Bench Rebellion, in Ludlam and Smith (1996), 98–102.

—— and Smith, M. (1996) (eds.), *Contemporary Conservatism* (London: Macmillan).

McBriar, A. (1962), *Fabian Socialism in English Politics 1884–1914* (Cambridge: Cambridge University Press).

Macrae, N. (1984), 'Health Care International', *The Economist*, 28 April, pp. 23–39.

MacInness, J. (1987), *Thatcherism at Work: Industrial Relations and Economic Change* (Milton Keynes: Open University Press).

McKenzie, R. (1963), *British Political Parties* (London: Heinemann).

Mandelson, P., and Liddle, R. (1996), *The Blair Revolution: Can Labour Deliver?* (London: Faber).

Marquand, D. (1988), *The Unprincipled Society* (London: Cape).

—— (1991), *The Progressive Dilemma* (London: Heinemann).

—— and Seldon, A. (1996) (eds.), *The Ideas that Shaped Post-War Britain* (London: Fontana).

Marsh, D. (1995), 'Explaining Thatcherite Policy: Beyond Uni-Dimensional Explanations', *Political Studies*, 43.

—— and Rhodes, R. (1992) (eds.), *Implementing Thatcherite Policies: Audit of an Era* (Brighton: Open University Press).

Martin, D. (1989), 'The Churches: Pink Bishops and the Lady', in Kavanagh and Seldon (1989), 330–42.

Mason, D. (1985), *Revising the Rating System* (London: Adam Smith Institute).

Matthews, R. (1968), 'Why has Britain had Full Employment since the War', *Economic Journal*, 78.

Middlemas, K. (1979), *Politics in Industrial Society* (London: Deutsch).

——(1990), *Power, Competitiveness and the State*, ii (London: Macmillan).

Midwinter, A. (1993), 'Reaganomics, Thatcherism and Public Finance', in Jordan and Ashford (1993), 81–101.

Mill, J. S. (1845), 'The Claims of Labour', *Edinburgh Review* (Apr.).

Minkin, L. (1980), *The Labour Party Conference* (Manchester: Manchester University Press).

—— (1991), *The Contentious Alliance: The Trade Unions and the Labour Party* (Edinburgh: Edinburgh University Press).

Mitchell, A. (1983), *Four Years in the Death of the Labour Party* (London: Methuen).

Moggridge, D. (1976), *Keynes* (London: Fontana).

Moon, J. (1993), *Innovative Leadership in Democracy: Policy Change under Thatcher* (Aldershot: Dartmouth).

—— (1994), 'Evaluating Thatcher', *Politics*, 14.

Muller, C. (1996), 'The IEA: Undermining the Post-War Consensus', *Contemporary British History*, 10.

Murray, C. (1984), *Losing Ground: American Social Policy 1950–1980* (New York: Basic Books).

Norton, P. (1978), *Conservative Dissidents* (London: Temple Smith).

—— (1990), 'The Lady's Not for Turning: But What About the Rest?', *Parliamentary Affairs*, 43.

O'Connor, J. (1973), *The Fiscal Crisis of the Capital State* (New York: St James' Press).

Olson, M. (1982), *The Rise and Decline of Nations* (New Haven: Yale University Press).

Osborne, R., and Gaebler, T. (1993), *Reinventing Government* (London: Penguin).

Panebianco, A. (1988), *Political Parties: Organization and Power* (Cambridge: Cambridge University Press).

Peacock, A., and Wiseman, J. (1961), *The Growth of Public Expenditure in the United Kingdom* (Princeton: Princeton University Press).

Peele, G. (1984), *Revival and Reaction* (Oxford: Oxford University Press).

Penniman, H. (1981) (ed.), *Britain at the Polls, 1979* (London: AEI).

Phillips, A. (1958), 'The Relationship between Unemployment and the Role of Money Wages in the UK, 1861–1957', *Economic Journal*, 6.

Pierson, C. (1996), 'Social Policy', in Marquand and Seldon (1996), 139–64.

Pimlott, B. (1988), 'The Myth of Consensus', in L. Smith (1988), 129–41.

Pinto-Duschinsky, S. (1981), 'Manifesto Speeches and the Doctrine of the Mandate', in Penniman (1981), 383–406.

Pryke, R. (1981), *The Nationalized Industries* (Oxford: Martin Robertson).

Raab, C. (1993), 'Education and the Impact of the New Right', in Jordan and Ashford (1993), 230–50.

Radice, G. (1992), *Southern Discomfort* (London: Fabian Society).

Ramsden, J. (1995), *The Age of Churchill and Eden 1940–1957* (London: Longmans).

—— (1996), 'The Influence of Ideas on the Modern Conservative Party', *Contemporary British History*, 10.

Ranelagh, J. (1992), *Thatcher's People* (London: Fontana).

Rentoul, J. (1989), *Me and Mine* (London: Allen & Unwin).

—— (1995), *Tony Blair* (London: Little Brown).

Rhodes, R. (1992), 'Local Government Finance', in Marsh and Rhodes (1992), 50–64.

—— (1994), 'The Hollowing Out of the State: The Changing Nature of the Public Service in Britain', *Political Quarterly*, 65.

Ricketts, M., and Shoesmith, E. (1990), *British Economic Opinion* (London: IEA).

Riddell, P. (1989), *The Thatcher Decade* (Oxford: Martin Robertson).

—— (1993), *Honest Opportunism: The Rise of the Career Politician* (London: Hamish Hamilton).

Robertson, D. (1976), *A Theory of Party Competition* (London: Wiley).

—— (1984), 'Adversary Politics, Public Opinion and Electoral Cleavages', in Kavanagh and Peele (1984), 214–41.

Rose, R. (1969*a*) (ed.), *Policy Making in Britain* (London: Macmillan).

—— (1969*b*), 'The Variability of Party Government', *Political Studies*, 17.

—— (1976), 'Disciplined Research and Undisciplined Problems', *International Social Science Journal*, 28.

—— (1984), *Do Parties Make a Difference?* (2nd edn., London: Macmillan; first pub. 1982).

—— (1985), *Public Employment in Western States* (Cambridge: Cambridge University Press).

—— and Davies, P. (1995), *Inheritance in Public Policy: Change Without Choice in Britain* (New Haven: Yale University Press).

—— and Peters, G. (1978), *Can Government Go Bankrupt?* (Boston: Basic Books).

Schoen, D. (1977), *Enoch Powell and the Powellites* (London: Macmillan).

Schumpeter, J. (1942), *Capitalism, Socialism and Democracy* (London: Allen & Unwin).

Scruton, R. (1980), *The Meaning of Conservatism* (Harmondsworth: Penguin).

Seldon, Anthony (1981), *Churchill's Indian Summer* (London: Hodder & Stoughton).

—— (1994), 'Consensus: A Debate Too Far', *Parliamentary Affairs*, 47.

—— (1996*a*), *How Tory Governments Fall* (London: Fontana).

—— (1996*b*), 'Ideas Are Not Enough', in Marquand and Seldon (1996), 257–89.

—— and Ball, S. (1994) (eds.), *The Conservative Century: The Conservative Party since 1900* (Oxford: Oxford University Press).

Seldon, Arthur (1981), *The Emerging Consensus* (London: IEA).

—— (1986), *The Riddle of the Voucher* (London: IEA).

Seyd, P. (1987), *The Rise and Fall of the Labour Left* (London: Macmillan).

—— (1993), 'Labour: The Great Transformation', in A. King (1993), 70–100.

Shaw, E. (1996), *The Labour Party since 1945* (Oxford: Blackwell).

Shepherd, R. (1996), *Enoch Powell* (London: Hutchinson).

Sherman, A. (1983), *Interview BBC Radio 3*, 21 October 1983.

Shonfield, A. (1965), *Modern Capitalism* (Oxford: Oxford University Press).

Skidelsky, R. (1977) (ed.), *The End of the Keynesian Era* (London: Macmillan).

—— (1983), *John Maynard Keynes*, i. *Hope Betrayed, 1883–1920* (London: Macmillan).

—— (1992), *John Maynard Keynes*, ii. *The Economist as Saviour, 1920–1937* (London: Macmillan).

Smith, L. (1988) (ed.), *Making of Britain: Echoes of Greatness* (London: Macmillan).

Smith, M. (1992), 'A Return to Revisionism? The Labour Party's Policy Review', in Smith and Spear (1992), 13–28.

—— (1994*a*), 'Understanding the Politics of Catch-Up: The Modernization of the Labour Party', *Political Studies*, 42.

—— (1994*b*), 'The Core Executive and the Resignation of Mrs Thatcher', *Public Administration*, 72.

—— (1996), 'Reforming the State', in Ludlam and Smith (1996), 143–63.

—— and Spear, J. (1992) (eds.), *The Changing Labour Party* (London: Routledge).

Smith, P. (1967), *Disraelian Conservatism and Social Reform* (London: Routledge & Kegan Paul).

Smith, T. (1979), *Politics of the Corporate Economy* (Oxford: Martin Robertson).

Sopel, J. (1995), *Tony Blair: The Modernizer* (London: Bantam Press).

Stewart, M. (1977), *The Jekyll and Hyde Years* (London: Dent).

Sutherland, G. (1972) (ed.), *Studies in the Growth of Nineteenth-Century British Government* (London: Allen & Unwin).

Swann, D. (1993), 'Privatization, Deregulation and The New Right', in Jordan and Ashford (1993), 120–43.

Tant, M. (1993), *British Government: The Triumph of Elitism* (Aldershot: Dartmouth).

Titmuss, R. (1950), *Problems of Social Policy* (London: HMSO).

Thatcher, M. (1977), *Let the Children Grow Tall* (London: Centre for Policy Studies).

—— (1993), *Downing Street Years* (London: HarperCollins).

—— (1995), *The Path to Power* (London: HarperCollins).

Tunstall, J. (1970), *The Westminster Lobby Correspondence* (London: Routledge & Kegan Paul).

Tyrell, R. (1977) (ed.), *The Future that Doesn't Work* (New York: Doubleday).

Vaizey, J. (1983), *In Breach of Promise* (London: Weidenfeld & Nicolson).

Waldegrave, W. (1994), *The Little Platoons* (London: Social Market Foundation).

Walters, A. (1981), *The Economic Adviser's Role: Scope and Limitations* (London: Centre for Policy Studies).

—— (1985), *Britain's Economic Renaissance: Margaret Thatcher's Reforms 1979–1984* (Oxford: Oxford University Press).

Watkins, A. (1991), *A Conservative Coup* (London: Duckworth).

Webster, C. (1990), 'Conflict in Consensus: Explaining the British Health Service', *Twentieth-Century British History*, 1.

Welsh, D. (1993), 'The New Right as Ideology', in Jordan and Ashford (1993), 46–58.

Whiteley, P., and Gordon, I. (1980), 'Labour Delegates', *New Statesman* (11 Jan.).

—— Seyd, P., and Richardson, J. (1994), *True Blues: The Politics of Conservative Party Membership* (Oxford: Clarendon Press).

Wilensky, H. (1976), *The New Corporatism: Centralization and the Welfare State* (Political Sociology Series, London: Sage).

Wilkinson, F., and Turner, J. (1975), 'The Wage–Tax Spiral and Labour Militancy', in Jackson (1975), 63–110.

Williams, P. (1982), 'Changing Styles of Labour Leadership', in Kavanagh (1982), 50–68.

Williamson, P. (1993), 'Good for your Health: The New Right's Ideas and Health Reform', in Jordan and Ashford (1993), 193–212.

Willson, F. (1969), 'Policy-Making and Policy-Makers', in Rose (1969), 355–69.

Wood, J. (1965) (ed.), *A Nation Not Afraid: The Thinking of Enoch Powell* (London: Batsford).

—— (1970), *Powell and the 1970 Election* (Right Way Books; Kingswood, Surrey: Elliot).

Young, H. (1984), 'On First Opening the Pages of Hayek's *Road to Serfdom*', *Guardian* (8 Oct.).

—— (1989), *One of Us* (London: Macmillan).

—— and Sloman, A. (1986), *The Thatcher Phenomenon* (London: BBC).

Index